Conspiracy in the French Revolution

MANCHESTER
1824

Manchester University Press

Conspiracy in the French Revolution

Edited by Peter R. Campbell, Thomas E. Kaiser and Marisa Linton

Manchester University Press
Manchester and New York
distributed exclusively in the USA by Palgrave

Published by Manchester University Press
Oxford Road, Manchester M13 9NR, UK
and Room 400, 175 Fifth Avenue, New York, NY 10010, USA
www.manchesteruniversitypress.co.uk

Distributed exclusively in the USA by
Palgrave, 175 Fifth Avenue, New York,
NY 10010, USA

Distributed exclusively in Canada by
UBC Press, University of British Columbia, 2029 West Mall,
Vancouver, BC, Canada V6T 1Z2

British Library Cataloguing-in-Publication Data
A catalogue record for this book is available from the
British Library

Library of Congress Cataloging-in-Publication Data applied for

ISBN 978 0 7190 7402 8 *hardback*

First published 2007

16 15 14 13 12 11 10 09 08 07   10 9 8 7 6 5 4 3 2 1

Typeset
by Florence Production Ltd, Stoodleigh, Devon
Printed in Great Britain
by The Cromwell Press Ltd, Trowbridge

For the children of our two families:
Sophie; and Harry, Elena, and Sophia.

Contents

Notes on the contributors

Dr David Andress is Reader in Modern European History at the University of Portsmouth (UK). He has published numerous articles on the political culture of the French Revolution, particularly focusing on attitudes to the activities of the common people. He has also written more broadly on the course of the Revolution, and is currently developing research into the connections between the culture of sentimentalism and melodrama and the social and political assumptions that underlay revolutionary political discourse. His recent books include *Massacre at the Champ de Mars* (Woodbridge: Royal Historical Society, 2000), *The French Revolution and the People* (London, 2004), and *The Terror; Civil War in the French Revolution* (London: Little Brown, 2005).

Dr Simon Burrows lectures on Modern European History at the University of Leeds (UK), and was formerly a lecturer in the History Department at the University of Waikato in New Zealand. His main research interests concern French *émigré* writers during the period 1760–1815, together with their political, publishing, and espionage activities. He is author of *French Exile Journalism and European Politics, 1792–1814* (Woodbridge: Royal Historical Society, 2002) and coeditor with Hannah Barker of *Press, Politics and the Public Sphere in Europe and North America, 1760–1820* (Cambridge: Cambridge University Press, 2002), and has published numerous journal articles and chapters in books. His latest work, *Blackmail, Scandal and the French Revolution: London's French Libellistes, 1760–1790* was published by Manchester University Press in 2006.

Dr Peter Campbell is Senior Lecturer in History at Sussex University (UK). He works on the political culture of France from Louis XIV to the Revolution. He has published four books on the ancien régime and several articles: *The Ancien Régime in France* (Oxford: Blackwell, 1988); *Louis XIV 1661–1715* (Harlow: Longman, 1993), and *Power and Politics in Old Regime France, 1720–1745* (London and New

York: Routledge, 1996), currently being translated into French, and edited *The Origins of the French Revolution* (Basingstoke: Palgrave, 2005). He is working on patriotism in eighteenth-century France and the relationship between ideology and politics in the 1780s. His next book is on *Crisis and Revolution: France in the 1780s.*

Dr John Hardman was formerly Lecturer in History at the University of Edinburgh and until recently Senior Research Fellow at the University of Sussex. His most recent books include *Louis XVI* (New Haven and London: Yale, 1993), *French Politics, 1774–1789* (Harlow: Longman, 1995), and *Robespierre* (Harlow: Longman, 1999), and with Munro Price, *Louis XVI and the Comte de Vergennes: Correspondence, 1774–1787* (Oxford: Voltaire Foundation, 1998). He is presently completing a major study on *The Assemblée des Notables of 1787.*

Dr Thomas E. Kaiser is Professor of History at the University of Arkansas at Little Rock (USA). He is coauthor of *Europe, 1648–1815: From the Old Regime to the Age of Revolution* (Oxford: Oxford University Press, 2003), and has also published nearly twenty articles on the politics and political culture of eighteenth-century France in such scholarly journals as *Journal of Modern History, French Historical Studies, French History, Eighteenth-Century Studies*, and *Studies on Voltaire and the Eighteenth Century.* His early work dealt with the public image of the French monarchy in the early eighteenth century as reflected in public finance, public opinion, royalist propaganda, and royalist historiography. His later work has focused on the impact of royal mistresses and queens, especially Madame de Pompadour and Marie-Antoinette, on the politics and diplomacy of the French monarchy. Currently he is working on a book entitled *Devious Ally: Marie-Antoinette and Austrophobia in Eighteenth-Century France.*

Dr Marisa Linton is a Senior Lecturer in History at Kingston University (UK). She has written a book on *The Politics of Virtue in Enlightenment France* (Basingstoke: Palgrave, 2001), and has also published a number of articles on the French Revolution and on the political culture of eighteenth-century France, including: 'Robespierre's political principles' (in W. Doyle and C. Haydon, eds, *Robespierre* (Cambridge: Cambridge University Press, 1999)), 'Ideas of the future in the French Revolution' (in M. Crook, W. Doyle, and A. Forrest, eds, *Enlightenment and Revolution* (Aldershot: Ashgate, 2004)), and ' "The Tartuffes of patriotism": fears of conspiracy in the political language of revolutionary government, France 1793–1794' (in B. Coward and J. Swan, eds, *Conspiracies and Conspiracy Theory in Early Modern Europe*

(Aldershot: Ashgate, 2004)). She is currently working on a full-length study of conspiracy, faction, and friendship in the politics of the Jacobins.

Dr Laura Mason is Associate Professor of History at the University of Georgia (USA). She is the author of *Singing the French Revolution: Popular Culture and Revolutionary Politics, 1787–1799* (Ithaca and London: Cornell University Press, 1996); and the coeditor of *The French Revolution: A Document Collection* (New York: Houghton-Mifflin, 1998). She is the author of numerous articles on the French Revolution, including, 'The "Bosom of Proof": Criminal Justice and the Renewal of Oral Culture during the French Revolution,' *Journal of Modern History* 76(1) (March 2004). She is currently writing a book about the trial of the Equals and the political culture of the Directory.

Dr Barry M. Shapiro is Professor of History at Allegheny College, Meadville PA (USA). He is the author of *Revolutionary Justice in Paris* (Cambridge: Cambridge University Press, 1993) and of several articles on psychohistory, revolutionary justice, and early revolutionary politics, including most notably 'Self-Sacrifice, Self-Interest, or Self-Defense? The Constituent Assembly and the "Self-Denying Ordinance" of May 1791' (*French Historical Studies*, Fall 2002). He is currently working on a book-length project examining the psychological ramifications of the early revolutionary confrontation between the deputies of the Constituent Assembly and the monarchy.

Dr Jill Maciak Walshaw is a Postdoctoral Fellow at the Université de Montréal (Canada). She recently completed a dissertation at the University of York (UK) on the communication of political news and ideas in rural France during the eighteenth century. Her research on the seditious speech trials in rural areas and on rural politics during the Revolution has appeared in *French History* and in *The European Review of History*. She is currently working on a book that expands upon her doctoral research to compare rural political culture in south-western and central France in the early modern period.

Acknowledgements

We wish to acknowledge the support of the History Research Unit and the Faculty of Arts and Social Sciences at Kingston University, particularly the unfailing support of Peter Beck, and of the National Center for the Humanities for providing a research fellowship funded by the Florence Gould Foundation to one of the editors. We would also like to thank the Arts and Humanities Research Council for their invaluable financial contribution for the research for Chapter 6, and the British Academy and the Leverhulme Trust for funding research for Chapter 1. We are grateful to the editors at Manchester University Press, particularly Alison Welsby and Emma Brennan, for their enthusiasm for the project. We are indebted to the anonymous readers at Manchester for their encouragement and very helpful comments to the project – their humour, patience and sturdy professionalism made the business of being an editor as pleasurable as it can ever be. Last, but certainly not least, we would like to thank our families for their patience and gentle reminders that historians live in the present no less than they study the past.

Peter Campbell, Thomas Kaiser and Marisa Linton

Introduction: conspiracy in the French Revolution – issues and debates

Thomas E. Kaiser, Marisa Linton, and Peter R. Campbell

When Edmund Burke in 1790 called the French Revolution 'the most astonishing that has hitherto happened in the world,'[1] he was hardly alone in his opinion. As the most ambitious effort yet undertaken to recreate a society from the ground up, the French Revolution was intended to regenerate the nation by means of a new politics founded upon liberty, virtue, and patriotism. In place of the 'corrupt' politics of the discredited ancien régime, the Revolutionaries sought to fashion a new transparent political system wherein citizens could voice their opinions by means of an elected legislature, political clubs, and a free press. Whereas under the ancien régime a vague, contradictory set of governing laws had allegedly allowed corrupt ministers, mistresses, and factions to exploit state power behind closed doors for their own selfish ends, the Revolutionaries enacted a new constitution with an explicit delineation of public powers and private rights to ensure that state officials – subject to public scrutiny – ran the government exclusively for the common good.

As it turned out, however, this bold experiment in transparent government was attended from its start by preoccupations with conspiracy so deep and widespread that within four years it helped generate and inform the Terror, a coordinated effort to repress by means of fear just that sort of conspiratorial behavior the new politics was supposed to have eliminated. Conspiracies against the new order appeared to spring not only from among those like the many 'aristocrats' who had opposed the Revolution from the start, but also from among erstwhile 'patriots' who had been its most vocal supporters and ardent champions. Indeed, as the Revolution proceeded, conspiracy accusations were leveled against virtually all the major political personalities of the age, from the king and the queen to the very radicals – Hébert, Danton, and Robespierre – who had employed the Terror to crush counter-Revolutionary conspiracy. As the wars of the Revolution expanded the zone of conflict beyond France's borders, conspiracies seemed to be hatching across Europe.

Why did the Revolutionaries become so preoccupied with conspiracy that their politics changed profoundly as a result? Strangely enough, until recently historians provided few coherent answers, notwithstanding the study of certain individual conspiratorial episodes such as Georges Lefebvre's celebrated analysis of the agrarian 'great fear' of 1789.[2] One reason for this neglect of such a critical Revolutionary phenomenon may have been that the majority of twentieth-century historians of the Revolution were to a greater or lesser extent partisans of that great event. To take seriously the myriad of charges leveled by the Revolutionaries against one another might have played into the hands of the still vocal minority of counterrevolutionary historians, who had been denouncing the Revolution as a godless conspiracy since 1789. 'Conspiratorial' seemed like such an ugly word to apply to the dynamics of the first French experiment in liberal democracy; far better to view it as the worthy Enlightenment put into practice. A second reason that conspiracy may not have attracted the attention it deserved was that the reigning 'social interpretation' of the Revolution played down the importance of political culture. Within this paradigm, the Revolution was explained as a clash of bourgeois and noble classes that in turn was driven by the emergence of capitalism. Viewed as transparent expressions of class interest, politics in general, and ideology in particular held relatively little interest, because they seemed to explain so little about the origins and course of the Revolution. It was thus easy to overlook and neglect the fact that so much political thought and mobilization during that decade took 'conspiratorial' forms.

Conspiracy did begin to attract scholarly attention by the 1960s, although its first locus was the American rather than French Revolution. Richard Hofstadter published a book of essays entitled *The Paranoid Style in American Politics* in 1965 that captured the tone of these early efforts.[3] Under the influence of psycho-history and the association of ideology with Fascism and Communism, historians represented belief in conspiracy as a symptom of psychosis, even if Hofstadter stopped short of calling conspiracy believers 'certifiable lunatics.'[4] The problem with this line of argument soon became apparent to perspicacious historians such as Gordon Wood. If the American Revolutionaries were to be judged 'mentally disturbed' merely because – as Bernard Bailyn and Wood himself brilliantly demonstrated[5] – they believed an English conspiracy had sought to crush American liberty in the 1770s, they had a lot of company, for belief in conspiracy was ubiquitous in the early modern period. Could all these believers in conspiracy have been truly delusional? In a thoughtful reconsideration of the problem, Wood concluded in 1982 that this form of thinking was neither 'pathological' nor uniquely American.[6] But he continued to condescend to believers in conspiracy by historicizing their manner of conceptualizing politics, which he claimed had become obsolete by the nineteenth century. The dawn of social science, Wood argued, made conspiracy belief in the modern age appear 'increasingly primitive and quaint' and 'out of place.'[7] John Roberts made a similar argument when addressing the question of secret societies in this period.[8] His highly skeptical and rationalistic view was that the belief in the effective action of secret societies was the product of an age, an unhistorical explanation, one that is the consequence of a mind set that cannot cope with the complexities of causation in a large society. The fact that so many eighteenth-century founders of social science – e.g. Turgot and Condorcet – had believed in politics by conspiracy, as had, to a considerable extent, the later 'heirs of Machiavelli' – Pareto, Mosca, Michels[9] – and other 'social scientists' such as C. Wright Mills, apparently gave Wood and Roberts little pause when advancing this argument.

In the context of French history, matters began to change when – for reasons that cannot be reviewed here – the 'social interpretation' collapsed in the 1970s and the Revolution was re-interpreted as a broad-based struggle against royal 'despotism' rather than as a bourgeois attack upon 'feudal' aristocracy.[10] In the wake of this transformation, politics and political ideology once again reemerged as a critical area of analysis. Drawing upon the work of the right-wing historian Augustin Cochin, François Furet put a new face on the old argument for a 'conspiratorial' origin and motor for the Revolution in his revisionist attack on the 'social interpretation'.[11] In 1789, he argued, the revolutionaries had seized absolute sovereignty from the king in order to create a reign of Rousseau-inspired democracy. But convinced from the outset that their impossible dream was vulnerable to conspiracies engineered by counter-Revolutionaries at home and abroad, they cast their vision of democracy in the mold of the Terror. In other words, the dominating ideology of the Revolution, which Furet condemned as contrary to the 'real' social interests of the nation, was inherently counterconspiratorial and, being relatively unresponsive to the rise and fall of 'real' threats, by its very nature required victims to slay. In Furet's view, the Terror of 1793–94 was not – as some historians had alleged – a product of 'circumstances,' such as the war beginning in April 1792, which Furet also attributed to the wiles of Revolutionary ideology. Rather, for Furet the Terror emerged ineluctably from the premises of Revolutionary rhetoric already operational in 1789.

Far more sympathetic to the Revolution and far more sensitive to context than Furet, Lynn Hunt also made conspiracy a key element in her pioneering analysis of the Revolution's political culture.[12] In this work, she demonstrated how fears of conspiracy, real and imagined, led revolutionaries into an endless search for 'transparency,' that is, the elimination of all guises that counterrevolutionary conspirators might use to undermine the Revolution. It was this imperative, she argued, that lay behind the Jacobins' demand for repeated demonstrations of patriotic virtue on the part of every citizen.

Although their insights were original and highly suggestive, neither Furet nor Hunt dealt with revolutionary conspiracy at length or in detail. But having focused fresh attention on the issue, their intriguing findings encouraged other historians to advance on their work by tracking more precisely in time and space the rise and fall of conspiratorial activity and fears. Among them was an editor of this volume, Thomas Kaiser, who has traced the course of conspiracy fears regarding Marie-Antoinette as an alleged Austrian agent.[13] Another was Timothy Tackett,[14] who challenged the notion that pre-Revolutionary high politics were driven by conspiracy fears. He contended that apart from a few brief spikes of what he called 'conspiracy obsession' – such as occurred on the eve of the Bastille's storming on 14 July 1789 – the early Revolution, too, was relatively free from preoccupation with conspiracy, at least among political elites. Even the peasantry during the 'Great Fear' of 1789, he found, was not nearly so much given to belief in aristocratic conspiracy as Georges Lefebvre and other historians had alleged. If they feared anything at that moment, Tackett argued, peasants feared the collapse of order. For Tackett, the turning point came in June 1791, when the royal family tried and failed to escape control by the Assembly and its factions by fleeing Paris and relocating near the French border.[15] Now condemned as a perjurer for having violated his oath to support the new régime, the king, upon whom revolutionary leaders had hitherto counted to provide the keystone of the new régime, could no longer be trusted. Indeed, according to Tackett, trust generally appears to have disappeared by the summer of 1791, leaving the French state in the grip of multiple factions struggling for power amidst growing fear and mutual recrimination. This atmosphere provided the perfect setting for the escalation of conspiracies and conspiracy fears that eventually climaxed in the Reign of Terror.

The important work of Furet, Hunt, and Tackett has raised a number of critical questions to which the contributors to this book have given further consideration: How widespread were conspiracies and conspiracy fears before the Revolution and who held them? How much did their incidence and nature change during the Revolution? To what extent did conspiracy fears reflect the reality of conspiratorial activity? Who were accused of fomenting conspiracy and why? How much variation was there among the conspiracy fears entertained by different social groups? What impact did conspiracy and conspiracy fears have on the course and legacy of the Revolution? The editors solicited contributions that would provide chapters focusing on all the key moments of conspiratorial thinking, such that the book offers a comprehensive and accessible overview of the subject. Contributors were encouraged to address these questions, but the editors imposed no explanatory framework a priori, and each contributor has drawn his/her conclusions independently. The editors' working premise was that conspiracy merited analysis from different angles, in different contexts, and in different periods from the late ancien régime to the Directory. This approach drew inspiration from the collection of essays edited by Barry Coward and Julian Swann, which demonstrated that the practice and belief in conspiracy were a feature of virtually every political culture of the early modern period.[16]

To eighteenth-century observers, the banality of conspiratorial thought and action was not a pleasant fact of political life, but it could hardly be denied. As Duport de Tertre noted in his ten-volume *Histoire des conjurations, conspirations et révolutions célèbres, tant anciennes que modernes* (1754–1760) all governments faced the threat of malcontents willing 'to commit every sort of excess, be it to free themselves of a yoke that crushes them, to improve or reestablish their fortune, or to rise to a rank to which the modesty of their birth prevents them from aspiring.'[17] Although certain political cultures were undoubtedly more given to conspiracy and conspiracy fears than others, even relatively 'open' societies like that of late Stuart England were not immune from conspiratorial forms of politics.[18] There, as Mark Knights has persuasively shown, free-wheeling party conflict and a thriving political print culture – far from calming 'irrational' fears of conspiracy – paradoxically fueled belief in government by plots.[19]

Each chapter in the present volume on the French Revolution offers a new investigation of the evidence and new conclusions. As Peter Campbell demonstrates in Chapter 1, French politics at this time revolved around the interplay of semi-formalized associations – court clientage networks, noble entourages, political factions, and religious bodies – that closely resembled 'conspiracies' as contemporaries conceived of them. In light of the cynical view of human nature propounded by so many moralists and political analysts of the age from Machiavelli and Pascal to Mandeville and Helvétius, it did not take an unhinged mind to suppose that these organizations were plotting some form of criminal mischief, especially if one belonged to a competing group. Whether one believed that a 'plot' was 'real' and constituted a nefarious conspiracy depended a great deal on one's view of its goals and methods. Of course, many conspiracy accusations turned out to be wrong or highly exaggerated – just like many 'social scientific' projections. But contemporaries did not construe belief in the existence and potential influence of conspiracies as a sign of psychosis, and neither should we. After all, it is not a priori delusional or passé to think that some events occur because some people are covertly working together to make them happen.

That some modern historians have thought otherwise, Campbell suggests, may be attributed to their overestimation of the reach of the early modern state. To be sure, the development of armies, militias, and legal institutions did enable princes to police their subjects more effectively than in previous eras, thereby reducing the frequency and destabilizing effects of conspiracies in the form of armed noble revolts. Nevertheless, contemporaries had good reason to believe in the covert manipulation of power by groups seeking to impose their own political agendas. For if the early modern state had increasingly more effective forces at its disposal to impose order and thereby repress conspiracies, those same instruments were susceptible to backstairs manipulation by agents located within the power structure – be they royal mistresses, foreign spies, or suspect religious orders – who could harness the growing power of the state for their own subversive ends.

In that light, it is perfectly plausible that – and Campbell shows just why – eighteenth-century French political culture before and after 1789 provided fertile grounds for belief in conspiratorial activity. Among the popular urban and agrarian classes, conspiracy helped explain a number of puzzling phenomena that had life-and-death implications for most people, such as the fluctuation of grain prices and the incidence of taxes. Far from enjoying immunity to the phenomenon by their superior education or exposure to the Enlightenment, the French elite, too, subscribed to belief in conspiracy. This was hardly surprising in an absolute régime dominated by a single royal court, the primordial public space wherein power was concentrated and negotiated and wherein organized factions lobbying for a cause or interest enjoyed no legally-protected status unless authorized by the king. When ministers and their protégés came and went – which happened with great frequency during the reigns of Louis XV and Louis XVI – there was often talk of a 'cabal,' if not a 'conspiracy' launched on their behalf or against them. And when major court figures died prematurely or when two members of the same faction died in quick succession, rumours frequently spread that they had been poisoned. Thus it was that in the early eighteenth century much elite suspicion surrounded the regent duc d'Orléans, whose enemies accused him of trying to usurp the place of his charge, the young Louis XV. Likewise, the religiously dissident Jansenists repeatedly peddled the notion that their enemies, the Jesuits, were conspiring to impose 'despotism' on France by covertly manipulating the monarchy. So successful was the Jansenists' campaign that the Jesuits were exiled from France in 1762.

It was within this context that the Revolutionaries came to political consciousness. Already inclined by their political education and the events of the pre-Revolution of 1787–1789 to think of politics in conspiratorial terms, the Revolutionaries construed their 'victory' over the forces of reaction on 14 July 1789 as a precarious one that had nearly failed. As Simon Burrows demonstrates, the departure of the *émigré* princes in the wake of the Bastille's storming was but the prelude to a series of counter-Revolutionary plots over the succeeding decade, for which enough proof exists to conclude that a good many – if not all – of these plots had some foundation in reality. That counter-Revolutionaries often resorted to conspiracy must obviously be in part explained 'objectively,' i.e., by the nature of the opportunities they had to overturn the Revolution. But as Burrows suggests in Chapter 7, their conspiracies were also motivated by their sincere belief that the Revolution constituted a series of plots directed against them, which they hoped to preempt via their own conspiratorial activities.

Did counter-revolutionary conspiracy begin at the top? John Hardman has in Chapter 3 taken another look at the murky case for Louis XVI's alleged participation in a conspiratorial plot by examining three major revolutionary episodes. Again the results are paradoxical. Hardman argues that given his situation and political convictions, the king could hardly have acted other than as he did, that is to say, by deploying the stealth and deception characteristic of conspiracies. But Hardman contends that if Louis XVI's behavior was conspiratorial, it was no more, and probably less so than that of the National Assembly, the Feuillants, the Girondins, and the Jacobins, all of whom suspected him of covertly undermining the Revolution. As in the case of the *émigrés*, both the king and his adversaries felt driven and entitled to engage in conspiratorial-like behavior by the fear that such activity was being plotted by their adversaries, and there is ample evidence to support many of these beliefs.

The impact of such thinking, Barry Shapiro argues in Chapter 2, was apparent as early as the autumn of 1789, when the National Assembly prevented Mirabeau from assuming a ministerial position. There may have been good 'objective' reasons to throw obstacles in Mirabeau's path, but Shapiro proposes that something else, something more elusive was also at work here. He points to an unconscious fear of executive power aroused by the 14 July crisis, when the king, to whom the French people continued to feel a strong filial attachment, appeared to have abandoned his people, indeed, to have acquiesced in their extermination. If the French deputies were traumatized by Louis XVI's alleged complicity in a conspiracy against the nation as Shapiro maintains, it suggests that 'conspiracy obsession' among the elite after July did not decline as much as Tackett contends, or at most, was so superficially repressed that this 'obsession' could easily be reactivated each time the Assembly debated the limits of executive power. It can thus be affirmed that the Revolutionaries' belief in conspiracy, although certainly given to distortion, did spring from perceptions of clear, present, and altogether real dangers.

But did it also arise from the very nature of the Revolutionary project, as Furet alleged? Discussions by Jill Walshaw and David Andress give us reasons to think so, reasons that go well beyond the ideological ones proposed by Furet. As Walshaw points out in Chapter 5, the gradual entry of previously excluded groups, e.g. the peasants, into the sphere of national politics had the unintended effect of creating new opportunities for and theaters of political malfeasance, even when these groups were acting on their traditional fears of a 'famine plot' directed against them. As a result, peasants who had been beneath suspicion of committing acts of *lèse-majesté* during the ancien régime were frequently accused of committing acts of *lèse-nation* under the new order. In the eyes of Revolutionary authorities, peasants were worthy enough to merit some degree of citizenship, but they also appeared vulnerable to the seductions of elite counter-Revolutionary plotters and thus required, particularly given their large numbers, increasing surveillance, interrogation, and prosecution. National pride and an unwillingness to admit that the 'good' peasantry had freely rejected the Revolution, Walshaw concludes, reenforced the Revolutionary will to attribute peasant malfeasance to the wiles of counterrevolutionary conspirators, even if such was not actually the case. Only in the nineteenth century, when the peasants had sufficiently turned into Frenchmen, did elite political culture begin to pay them the dubious honor of acknowledging their capacity to conspire on their own initiative.

Similarly, Andress argues in Chapter 4 that in the cities conspiracy played a critical role not only in the political thinking of the underclasses, but also in how revolutionary authorities responded to the threats of disorder from below. A great deal of this belief and action was a residue from the ancien régime. Like the peasantry, the urban underclasses did not abandon traditional fears of conspiracies directed against them at the outbreak of the Revolution; nor did the coming of a new democratic ethos incline Revolution authorities to put much faith in the people's ability to resist entrapment by counter-Revolutionaries or criminals. But, Andress shows, just when new organs of popular opinion, such as the radical clubs and Parisian sections, provided fresh means for publicly ventilating popular conspiracy fears, the splintering and constant shifting of organized power at the top created a growing cast of new enemies to indict for having conspired to inflict upon the people the old scourges of starvation and violence. Unlike Tackett, Andress does not consider Varennes a decisive turning point. But he does concur that the September Massacres of 1792 were a product of popular and elite fears of conspiracy that had been intensifying since 1791.

This widening and deepening spiral of suspicion helped produce the Jacobin-dominated Terror, that phase of the Revolution which is generally regarded as the most deeply informed by conspiracy fears and activity. As Marisa Linton shows in Chapter 6, if the Jacobins were obsessed by conspiracies directed against them, they had grounds to be fearful. However much the lens of their education may have distorted their perceptions in innumerable cases, they did face great and perfectly credible threats to their shaky régime stemming from undeniably real conspiracies. To be sure, some Jacobins inwardly doubted some of the more exaggerated conspiratorial claims of the Terror, unlike Robespierre, whose fearsome reputation was enhanced by the supposition that he believed everything he said. But at least until the Terror distanced itself from the urban popular movement in the spring of 1794, the government felt obliged to take seriously and act in response to the conspiracy fears of the *sans-culottes*, as it did, for example, when prosecuting Marie-Antoinette instead of exiling her as part of a diplomatic hostage exchange. In Linton's account, the fear that the Jacobins visited upon France through the Terror appears as a projection of their own escalating fears of the bloody repression that declared counterrevolutionaries might inflict and of the sinister conspiracies allegedly plotted by their fellow 'patriots.' The paradox uncovered by Linton is that the more violent the Terror became, the less politically secure the Jacobins felt and had reason to feel. Even when the military situation improved in the spring and summer of 1794, there appeared to be no exit from the vicious cycle of mutual recrimination. Indeed, conspiracies seemed to be sprouting at every level of government and in all sectors of society: inflation reignited fears of famine plots among peasants and urban workers; a counter-Revolutionary revolt in the Vendée fanned belief in a conspiracy of refractory priests; factional disputes within the Committee of Public Safety produced fears of a coup d'état; and the protracted war with Europe engendered belief in a Foreign Plot to be executed by dissident 'moderate' and 'ultra' elements of the Jacobin establishment. In the end, it is difficult to determine whether the Terror collapsed chiefly because its enemies undermined it or because of its own internal contradictions.

How did conspiracy look after the Jacobin debacle? Gracchus Babeuf, the notorious organizer of the 'Conspiracy of Equals' against the Directory, provided one reconsideration. As Laura Mason shows in Chapter 8, Babeuf was a radical not merely in that he advocated a primitive form of 'communism,' but also in that he inverted the dominant discourse of the Revolution by contending that conspiracy could be a noble enterprise if undertaken for the right purposes. Far from viewing conspiracy as antithetical to the republican tradition, Babeuf – drawing upon Machiavelli and Mably – impugned the Directory for having tried to repress just the sort of benign conspiratorial activity responsible for the Revolution's great leaps forward since 14 July 1789. The long-term contribution of Babeuf and his colleague Buonarroti, Mason concludes, was to provide a bridge between the French Revolution and nineteenth-century conspiracies intended to complete the French Revolution's unfinished agenda.

Mason's analysis sets up very nicely the critical conundrum faced by French Revolutionaries that Thomas Kaiser examines in Chapter 9 which concludes this volume. How could the Revolutionaries denounce conspiracy as the tool of despotism and at the same time engage in activities so closely resembling conspiracies that counterrevolutionaries might credibly brand them as such? Were most revolutionaries willing to embrace Babeuf's idea that conspiracy might, in fact, be the vehicle for progress rather than its most deadly enemy? Kaiser's answer is that while most Revolutionaries did not formally embrace Babeuf's view of the Revolution as a sort of conspiracy, neither could they abandon it altogether. Notwithstanding calls for slowing the pace of mutual accusation that accelerated between 1789 and the Terror, Revolutionary governments seemed unable to resist the urge to unmask and prosecute alleged conspirators, including many erstwhile 'patriots,' with the result that conspiracy appeared nearly inseparable from the Revolution itself right into the reign of Napoleon Bonaparte. The implications of this development for the legacy of the Revolution were profound. Not only did the Revolution leave behind it a deeply divided French constituency, but in addition the uncertainties about the future that had always attended the Revolutionary project were passed down in the next century to its major partisans. The Revolution would have to be fought again many times before it became safely institutionalized as the accepted political foundation of the French Republic.

Despite the importance of the theme of conspiracy in the recent historiography of the Revolution, this is the first in-depth book on the subject. The sum of its chapters is greater than that of the parts in that our research supports wider conclusions of significance for our understanding of the Revolution – both in terms of the contemporary mentality and modern historiography. We firmly agree with Hunt, Furet, and Tackett regarding the importance of conspiracy for an understanding of revolutionary politics, but our conclusions have given rise to a different framework of explanation for its emergence, development and impact. Whereas Furet viewed belief in conspiracy as a product of Rousseauistic ideology that filled the political vacuum left by the collapse of the ancien régime, we argue that it emerged out of the ordinary processes and practices of factional contestation associated with the court and of popular perceptions of elite politics as a plot directed against the interests of the lower orders. Unlike Tackett, we maintain that conspiracy was integral to every phase of the Revolution, although we agree that belief in conspiracy escalated in the run-up to and during the Terror, culminating in what Tackett aptly calls 'conspiracy obsession.' However fantastical in some respects, conspiracy claims did have some basis in reality, for there were very real plots to undermine the Revolution. At the same time, counterrevolutionary plots were inevitably perceived through the lens of Revolutionary ideology, which made them appear as products of a corruption that threatened to fuel the restoration of despotism. As fears of conspiracy intensified, all citizens, but especially those who stood out for their ambition and/or wealth, became vulnerable to the accusation that they were party to plots against the new order. The difficulty in identifying conspirators only fueled fear and anxiety, and it partly explains the constant reference to masks and duplicity said to be concealing the nefarious activities of those who best spoke the language of virtue and patriotism, the enemy within. Even Robespierre, the greatest master of Revolutionary discourse and the so-called Incorruptible, was eventually felled by the charge that he had participated in nefarious plots against the Revolution. Given the provenance of such accusations, it made perfect sense that in the wake of 9 Thermidor he – of all people – would be accused of having secretly plotted to marry the daughter of the decapitated king and queen.

In our view, the fear of conspiracy underlay the call for persistent demonstrations of patriotic virtue under the Terror, which were intended to allay suspicion of covert dealing with the dark forces of the counter-Revolution. But because patriotism itself had become a conspiratorial mask, professions of *civisme* carried increasingly less weight, and in the end everyone remained a potential conspirator. Many indeed were the seductions of power, ambition, wealth, and distinction allegedly proffered by Pitt and the Austrian princes, who appeared to have endless resources at their disposal. Their point of leverage was clearly the corruptibility of the human soul, a vulnerability that had been repeatedly underlined in republican polemics and Christian discourse, especially of the Jansenist variety, and had long been associated with the royal court, a public space allegedly devoid of virtue and patriotism. This was the original enemy within.[20] After repeated betrayals – both real and imagined – the Republic appeared increasingly more, not less, vulnerable to hijacking by the running dogs of despotism, a vision that emerges clearly from Camille Desmoulins' *Histoire des Brissotins*, which depicts Brissot as the successor to Lafayette and the duc d'Orléans as the leader of the counterrevolution. In the Jacobin perspective, the *longue durée* of the Revolution was punctuated by a series of interlinked conspiracies, culminating in the 'foreign plot,' which subsumed all the other conspiracies against the Republic. Little wonder, then, that the securing of liberty seemed an ever receding goal.

The nineteenth century would hardly put an end either to the organization of conspiracies or to a belief in their far-reaching powers. Some among the radical left – taking their cue from Babeuf and Buonarotti – saw in benign conspiracy the only hope for a successful renewal of the Revolution and the fulfillment of its uncompleted agenda. The right, never certain – and for good reason – that the Restoration had removed once and for all the threat of revolution, hunted down 'Jacobins' all over Europe after 1815 in the belief that Masons, Protestants, Jansenists and/or latter-day Voltaires were plotting their conspiratorial revenge. In the view of the right, the Revolution had merely been Act I of a horrific drama that threatened to continue if eternal vigilance over the activities of suspicious types were not maintained.

It is thus clear that the Revolution's heritage consisted not merely of celebrated myths of "enlightenment" and "reason," but also of fears and suspicions of covert malfeasance which, however overlooked by textbook writers, are no less part of our modern political culture. Although the total number of published works has, of course, vastly increased in the last two centuries, it is still significant in our view that in the catalogues of the British Library and the Bibliothèque nationale works published during the Revolution with the words *complot*, *conjuration*, *conspiration*, or *intrigue* in their title account for only a tiny proportion of the total number of such titles. The overwhelming majority – well over 90 percent – were published in the nineteenth and twentieth centuries. In them, we discover alleged plots by capitalists, Jews, the duchesse de Berry, freemasons, Nazis, communists, and spies, making one wonder which historical era has been the most obsessed with conspiratorial modes of historical explanation. In that context the preoccupation with conspiracy during the French Revolution should be less surprising to us, for when we study those who executed conspiracies and/or believed in them, we are really examining ourselves.

Notes

1 E. Burke, *Reflections on the Revolution in France*, ed. Thomas H. D. Mahoney (Indianapolis and New York, 1955), p. 11.

2 G. Lefebvre, *La Grande Peur de 1789* (Paris, 1932); another example is A. Lestapis, *La Conspiration de Batz (1793–1794)* (Paris, 1969).

3 R. Hofstadter, *The Paranoid Style in American Politics and Other Essays* (New York, 1965).

4 G. S. Wood, 'Conspiracy and the Paranoid Style: Causality and Deceit in the Eighteenth Century,' *The William and Mary Quarterly*, 3rd Series 19 (1982), p. 404.

5 B. Bailyn, *The Ideological Origins of the American Revolution* (Cambridge MA, 1967); G. S. Wood, *The Creation of the American Republic, 1776–1787* (Chapel Hill, 1969).

6 Wood, 'Conspiracy,' p. 429.

7 Ibid., p. 441.

8 J. Roberts, *The Mythology of Secret Societies* (London, 1972).

9 The phrase is taken from H. Stuart Hughes, *Consciousness and Society: The Re-Orientation of European Social Thought, 1890–1930* (New York, 1958), chap. 7.

10 For a recent historiographical analysis, See P. R. Campbell, ed., *The Origins of the French Revolution* (Houndmills and New York, 2006), introduction.

11 F. Furet, *Penser la Révolution française* (Paris, 1978).

12 L. Hunt, *Politics, Culture, and Class in the French Revolution* (Berkeley, Los Angeles, and London, 1994). See also J. Starobinski, *Jean-Jacques Rousseau: La Transparence et l'obstacle* (Paris, 1971).

13 T. E. Kaiser, 'Who's Afraid of Marie-Antoinette? Diplomacy, Austrophobia, and the Queen,' *French History* 14 (2000), pp. 241–271; Kaiser, 'From the Austrian Committee to the Foreign Plot: Marie-Antoinette, Austrophobia, and the Terror,' *French Historical Studies* 26 (2003), pp. 579–617.

14 T. Tackett, 'Conspiracy Obsession in a Time of Revolution: French Elites and the Origins of the Terror, 1789–1792,' *American Historical Review* 105 (2000), pp. 691–713; 'Collective Panics in the Early French Revolution, 1789–1791: A Comparative Perspective,' *French History* 17 (2003), pp. 149–171.

15 T. Tackett, *When the King Took Flight* (Cambridge, MA, 2003).

16 B. Coward and J. Swann, *Conspiracies and Conspiracy Theory in Early Modern Europe: From the Waldensians to the French Revolution* (Hampshire and Burlington, 2004).

17 François-Joachim Duport de Tertre, *Histoire des conjurations, conspirations et révolutions célèbres, tant anciennes que modernes*, 10 vols (Paris, 1754–60), 1, pp. 1–2.

18 Some of these variations are discussed in J. Van Horn Melton, *The Rise of the Public in Enlightenment Europe* (Cambridge, UK, 2001), pp. 70–75.

19 M. Knights, 'Faults on Both Sides: The Conspiracies of Party Politics under the Later Stuarts,' in Coward and Swann, *Conspiracies*, pp. 153–172.

20 On the long history of religious discourses of conspiracy, see the major study
    by D. Van Kley, *The Religious Origins of the French Revolution: From Calvin
    to the Civil Constitution, 1560–1791* (New Haven, 1996). This book details
    numerous and repeated aspects of conspiratorial thinking by both Jesuits
    and Jansenists in the seventeenth and eighteenth centuries.

1

Perceptions of conspiracy on the eve of the French Revolution

Peter R. Campbell

In this chapter, after showing that the concept of conspiracy had a range of elements and meanings during the ancien régime, three main points will be made. First, that despite the decline in major noble conspiracies since the mid-seventeenth century, the idea of conspiracy in some form was still widespread in France before the Revolution. Second, against recent assertions to the contrary, that according to contemporary definitions of conspiracy, ancien régime politics comprised many elements that could plausibly be called conspiracy, by people before the Revolution – and all the more so looking back during the Revolution. A historical analysis of the characteristics of politics reveals this clearly (though it does raise the question of how we define 'politics' in the regime, for which a modern definition would be inappropriate).[1] The third point is about their conception of politics: it will be argued that ancien régime politics was objectively (that is, on the basis of historical evidence), in its unofficial structures, more or less 'conspiratorial'. Importantly, it is clear that although the king's subjects rarely dared to use the word about the politics of their own government – after all with censorship it would have been dangerous to label normal practice 'conspiracy' – they were fully aware that several of the key elements were present. Frenchmen were but a short step from changing their terminology and understanding, and the shift to revolutionary politics would enable them to do that.

To substantiate these views, it will be interesting to consider how the future revolutionaries acquired their vision of politics on the eve of revolution. We shall therefore briefly explore their political education, and their reading matter – much of which did indeed stress intrigue and plotting as a way of politics. While considering a range of sources that influenced them, we shall stress the importance of one major but neglected source of their conceptions of political conduct: historical memoirs.

Finally, a brief consideration of the influence of the perception of politics under the ancien régime on the conspiracy obsession during the Revolution will help to situate the following chapters.

Definitions: plots and intrigues

What practices, then, were thought before the Revolution to be involved in a conspiracy, and were there many before 1789? The eighteenth-century area of meaning is wide, covering intrigue, covert actions, attempts to achieve political ends secretly by collaborating, caballing, or working together. Significantly, by 1789 a conspiracy involves moral corruption. Here we can perhaps identify a legacy of the heretical elements associated with the earlier idea of doing Satan's work – but let us not make too much of this because much more important in the eighteenth century was the legacy of a revived Greek and Roman history and the influence of the new secular morality of the age. Historical models of conspiracy might be Sallust's account of the Catiline conspiracy, and the assassination of Caesar.[2] More recent history also fed into their perceptions: the Fronde had become a byword for intrigue and conspiracy, especially as revealed in the memoirs of the cardinal de Retz, and the assassination of the King of Portugal was widely commented upon.

The key words in French are: *cabale, complot, conspiration, conjuration, intrigue, brigue,* and their verbs. These words are used in ways which range from the matter-of-fact to the condemnatory. The *Encyclopédie* does not have an entry for *complot,* but briefly defines a *conjuration* as a 'plot by ill-intentioned persons against the prince or the state,' and then has a lengthy dissertation on magic. *Conspiration* is 'a union of several persons with the aim of doing harm to someone or to something. One says a *conjuration* of several individuals, and a *conspiration* in the case of all the orders of a state; the *conjuration* of Catiline . . . a *conjuration* against the state; a *conspiration* against a courtier.' *Intrigue* is defined as 'the improper conduct of people who are seeking to arrive, or advance themselves, or obtain posts, graces, or honors by a cabal or stratagem. It is the recourse of weak and corrupt souls, just as fencing is the trade of the coward.' Eleven and a half columns follow on plot in drama.

The edition of Richelet's *Dictionnaire portatif de la langue française* revised by de Wailly in 1775 describes a cabal as 'an *intrigue, conjuration, société* [association] in which people act together for common or private interests: it can have an innocuous meaning, as in amusing ourselves in our little cabal'; to cabal means 'to win over a group of people who will support us, and to try to succeed in a plan by means of secret actions, by subtle means.' *Complot* has a negative connotation, being a dark and wicked scheme to do harm to someone, to make him fall [from favor] or ruin him. A *conjuration* is 'a party of people united against the interests of the state, of a sovereign, etc.' *Conjurer* retains this sense of acting against the state, but also means to conspire against an individual. For Richelet, *conspirer* has much the same sense as *conjurer*, except that it can be used of either a good or a bad intention.[3]

The definitions are largely in agreement, but have in common an area of meaning that goes beyond doing harm to a state or sovereign and incorporates normal practice. Littré (1865) saw a similarity in meaning between *cabale* and *complot*, in that they expressed the association of several to attain an object, but discerned a distinction in that a *complot* was directed to a subversive political end and aimed to change by force something in the government, whereas a *cabal* was not. It is notable that most of these definitions contain the idea of doing harm, and this could be a matter of opinion, in that it supposes the plotters or intriguers were morally corrupt. They are doing more than ambitiously furthering their own interests: the words for that were *intrigue*, *cabal*. The words *brigue* and *intrigue* are often employed together in the same phrase as near synonyms.

There is thus a wide and somewhat imprecise area of meaning involved, which should put historians on their guard. Clearly, it can be said that writers under the ancien régime could either exercise a degree of choice in characterizing practices as legitimate factional behavior, or condemn it as conspiratorial or plotting. Indeed, painstaking research by Jean-Claude Waquet has stressed the blurring of definitions by the authors of dictionaries.[4] He writes: 'Their use, moreover, does not suggest any regularity: what is conspiracy with one becomes cabal for another, plot for a third, when it is not intrigue or monopoly. Thus each event does not appear in the texts [of dictionaries] under the name given to it in history books today, but bears in the course of these writings as many as six or seven different appelations' that reflect the political intentions of the author.[5]

The idea of conspiracy and plot had a legal use and many people were prosecuted for criminal conspiracy. If we peruse the *arrêts du parlement*, we can see that there were indeed many condemnations for plotting criminal acts, and many of these were linked to some of the famous criminal gangs. But when we consider politics, recognizing conspiracy is more problematic: a given historian's assessment can depend upon the meaning of *conspiration*, *conjuration*, and *complot* chosen. Bercé is surely right to argue that there is a decline of conspiratorial activity in the eighteenth century – if by that he means attempts to change the government or system of the state.[6] This would certainly be true in the sense that the monarchy as an institution seemed well established and more secure by then, and there were no challenges to the legitimacy of the Bourbons. And yet, there certainly were constant maneuverings as different Bourbon branches positioned themselves for the possibility of a succession that might be disputed. Timothy Tackett thought that conspiracy beliefs in the later ancien régime were 'the exception,' 'remarkably rare,' that 'there was a relative absence of conspiracy fears in French political culture.'[7] I would argue in contrast to both Bercé and Tackett that – at least in those senses of the words implying conspiring for positions of power, plotting for places in the system, and intriguing to undermine individuals and policies– we should recognize that the type of explanation associated with 'conspiracy' was still a central feature of political life.

Moreover, there were certainly widespread assumptions of plotting and conspiracy. Let us consider quickly some events or cases in which a form of conspiracy was thought to be involved. On the government side was the idea shared by the elite that popular revolts involved the conspiracy of the local authorities against royal authority. The lower orders were thought incapable of leadership and organization, and thus revolt must have involved conspiracy by those entrusted with enforcing order. This idea persisted up to 1789, as evidenced in the Flour War, the Réveillon riots, and the Great Fear.[8]

From the other end of the social scale, the 'famine plot' persuasion persisted right up to and into the Revolution.[9] The poor were convinced that the market in grain was being manipulated by capitalists and hoarders in order to make vast profits from the creation or exacerbation of dearth which would drive prices higher. Although the reality of such actions on a grand scale cannot be substantiated, debate in the 1760s and 1770s on freeing the grain trade may have filtered down through the edicts. Certainly, the popular belief did reflect what happened year in year out on a smaller scale, in that those who could afford it inevitably made profits from their relative wealth by selling their surplus grain toward the spring when prices were higher because the peasants had been obliged to sell just after the harvest to pay their rents and taxes. Prices would usually double over the year and those with sufficient stocks would always profit from their 'hoard'.

Turning to 'politics' in court society, one can cite the religious plots and the dynastic feuds of the sixteenth century; the Day of Dupes and Cinq Mars under Richelieu; the fear of Protestant, Jansenist, and Jesuit plots in the seventeenth and even eighteenth centuries; the intrigues and conspiracies of Retz or Condé during the Frondes – we might stress (*pace* Bercé and Tackett) the continuation of conspiratorial practices up to the eve of the Revolution. A far from exhaustive list drawn from the eighteenth century would include the Cellamare conspiracy of 1718, which was a genuine plot. Soon after this the Regent Philippe d'Orléans was unfairly said to be thinking of poisoning young Louis XV (as he had already been suspected of poisoning Louis XIV's heirs in1711), in which case he stood to inherit the throne. In 1725 the Pâris brothers and the duc de Bourbon imprisoned the Belle-Isle brothers for some murky financial dealings involving a murder. The abbé Montgon's memoirs give an account of the intrigues of the grands and Philippe V to secure the French throne in the event of the premature death of Louis XV without an heir before 1728 when the Dauphin was born.[10] From the 1720s to the 1760s the *parti janséniste* was behaving in a very organized – some might say conspiratorial – way in publicizing, organizing, and coordinating protest at the religious policy of the Crown, which they saw as essentially Jesuit-inspired (and this gave them the opportunity to refer to the old beliefs in Jesuit plots). The year 1750 saw the popular conviction that Louis XV was having children abducted.[11] The Damiens affair of 1757 gave rise to a very determined search by the authorities for the 'other' presumed conspirators, and reminds us that whole aspects of the judicial system were predicated on the assumption of conspiracy.[12] For a long time during the ancien régime the Jesuits were believed to have been conspiring to mislead the king, attack their enemies, and further the cause of despotism. On the other hand, the supposed Jansenist plot of Bourgfontaine, invented by a Jesuit lawyer in 1655, remained a persistent enough theme of conspiracy for a volume to have been published in 1787 entitled *The Reality of the Bourg-Fontaine Project, Demonstrated by its very Deeds*.[13] Moreover, the expulsion of the Jesuits stemming from the trial of 1762 was believed to have been a plot by the *philosophes*, although many saw it as Jansenist inspired – which in fact it was, as Dale Van Kley has shown.[14] Certainly the Jansenist lawyer Le Paige's collection of correspondence shows that the Jansenist magistrates and lawyers were actually 'breathing together' to denounce the Jesuit order.

Also in the 1760s, the Brittany affair witnessed the assumption that the *procureur général* of the Rennes parlement, La Chalotais, was conspiring against royal authority. It led of course to another perceived plot, that of the *parti dévot* and anti-Madame du Barry faction, to defend the governor of Brittany the duc d'Aiguillon against the Jansenist-led Paris parlement which became involved in the defense of the Breton magistrates.[15] Even historians' very different attempts to summarize it show how murky the waters were! The pamphlet literature following the Maupeou coup sees the idea of conspiracy drawing upon the old idea (namely, attacks on Richelieu and Mazarin) of the evil minister conspiring against the citizenry or political system for personal reasons, using underhand court maneuvers. In an important development, this was now labelled *unpatriotic*, and his opponents have become 'citizens' and 'patriots'.

The period from 1774 to 1789 was not without its accusations of plots and conspiracy. Turgot felt the Flour War of 1775 to have been partly inspired by covert opposition to his reforms, as indeed it may have been. There was of course the idea that Marie Antoinette was a stooge for the House of Habsburg, and here there was great continuity with the revolutionary accusations.[16] Then the Diamond Necklace affair of 1785 might be said to have explored notions of conspiracy in public rumor and speculation. It linked the interests of the state with criminal plotting in suggestive ways.[17] Soon after, the notion that the 'ancient constitution' of France was under renewed threat from the conspiracy of despotism against liberty became one of the great themes of the pre-revolution – and there are continuities with the specter of the Jesuit plots of Jansenist paranoia earlier in the century. The pre-revolution in Brittany in 1788–89, with its vehement split in the Estates between the nobility and the Third Estate, represented a powerful model for the deputies in the Estates General, fueling their fear of a counterrevolutionary coup in June and July 1789. After all, the Breton nobility's hostility to the Third Estate had led to violent attacks by noble lackeys on students and members of the Third Estate in Rennes. In the Estates General, the idea was current in the chambers of both the Nobility and the Third Estate that plots were afoot, especially at court and by extension within the d'Epresmesnil faction in the chamber of the Nobility, to subvert the possibility of national regeneration or, in July after the Revolution, to bring about counterrevolution. This spilled over into the audience in the *palais royal* and the cafés of Paris and Versailles – or perhaps these beliefs were a reflection of the suspicions of the Parisian *nouvellistes*.

It is also notable how in both the seventeenth and eighteenth centuries, fears of conspiracy held by the king and his most trusted ministers dictated some of the characteristic political practices of the ancien régime.[18] Disgraced courtiers and ministers were habitually exiled to places from which they could not easily journey to Paris or Versailles. In order to break their network of contacts it was forbidden to visit them without special permission and at the known risk of disfavor. The fear of popular violence and political plotting had certainly led to development of the extensive system of spies in Paris and the focus in the police reports is chiefly on faction and potential subversion.

Notwithstanding all the evidence of activities that could be broadly defined as conspiratorial, we might still ask were there actually conspiracies in the manner of those of the sixteenth and seventeenth centuries? It is true that words associated with conspiracy are much in evidence, *cabal* and *intrigue* especially. Accusations of corruption are commonly leveled at courtiers and financiers. On some occasions the case might be made, perhaps against the duchesse du Maine and the murky negotiations between Philip V and certain grands for a return to France should Louis XV die. Bercé is probably right to say that out and out, clear and unequivocal, acts of conspiracy against powers in the state were rare in the eighteenth century. Although the evidence remains equivocal, at the start of the Seven Years War the prince de Conti may nevertheless have attempted to conspire with Huguenots and the English against Louis XV.[19] Tellingly the Huguenots were not interested. In 1787–79 the activities of the Orleanists perhaps lend credence to a *frondeur* interpretation. We must conclude that that although some genuine plots did exist during the century, what was certainly more important was the general and widespread belief in the later eighteenth century that all court politics was by its very nature corrupt and full of intrigues, plots and conspiracies. This helped provide the curious twist that the greatest conspiracy was by the government controlled by corrupt nobles and ministers and directed against the people.

A conspiratorial style of politics?

So, was the practice of ancien régime politics effectively conspiratorial? There is not a simple answer to this question: such an assessment of 'politics' depends of course on how one sees the state. If it was by this period essentially an administrative monarchy, having been modernized by Louis XIV in particular (as Bercé and many others appear to still believe), then politics was more about administration and policy than about other issues – and patronage and clientage would have become relatively unimportant and thus conspiracy hardly possible. Now, even one so committed to combating this old orthodoxy as the present writer would have to admit that the state had evolved in terms of administrative structures and practices. But even if the state is seen as having been partly administrative, its governance still took place within, one must stress, a court society, and the court was the center of patronage and plotting. So to treat seriously of conspiracy, one has to accept recent research on the informal structures of politics, and for some this may require a conceptual shift and a reintegration of the court into the overall perspective.

Recently historians have tended to accept the case for the centrality of the court to the social and political system. In a sense, the social system *was* the political system. The court centered upon the king's household. The focal point of politics was the king, and the king resided at court – more precisely, the court was in attendance on the king. A courtier was therefore a noble honored with some task in the royal domestic service: gentleman of the bedchamber, master of the hunt, lady-in-waiting, valet, or simple page. The administration itself developed from household offices, and the key administrators were also courtiers. The court had a long history but Louis XIV had expanded it, rendered it sedentary and refined it as a sociopolitical instrument. Over two centuries the court had developed from a relatively circumscribed household of retainers, friends, and clients until it had become a large, unwieldy but sophisticated instrument. On one level, that most noticed by contemporaries, the court now existed to exalt the monarch and concentrate the gaze of observers. An elaborate system of etiquette and hierarchy enmeshed the aristocrats who surrounded the king, making opposition difficult but encouraging quarrels among the courtiers. Life at court became a byword for deceit, intrigue, and manners refined to the point of absurdity. Everybody watched everybody else for the smallest indication of ambition, intrigue, or advancement in royal favor. The courtier thus concealed his true character and motives behind a mask. The memoirs of the duc de Saint-Simon and the duc de Luynes offer well-known and privileged insights into these aspects as they operated on a daily basis well into the eighteenth century.

The masking of feelings was one characteristic of the courtier. La Bruyère expressed this very clearly:

> A man who knows the court is master of his every gesture, of his eyes and his face; he is deep, opaque; he dissimulates bad offices, smiles at his enemies, controls his moods, disguises his passions, denies his heart, speaks, acts against his sentiments . . . to lift the mask for a single moment at court, is to renounce the court.[20]

To be a courtier was thus a full time occupation and one for which it was constantly necessary to wear a mask. The coded language of the court was more than nuanced: every word, every phrase, posture, gesture, and expression was significant. To let the mask slip for a moment was to reveal oneself, and this would enable more subtle minds to add to their knowledge and subsequently to triumph over one. Knowledge was indeed power. Complete discretion was essential for success and every mood was adopted in public in the full knowledge of its possible interpretations. Courtiers had to juggle the need for civility – another defining charac-teristic – with discretion. This masking of feelings and ambitions means that observers learned to scrutinize faces with skill in order to detect signs of anger or pique that might enable them to deduce the result of an interview or a council meeting. Only long experience and hindsight would show contemporaries if they were right, but they had to act before such confirmation was available.

It is abundantly clear that this world was also of immense political importance. The court was the only central institution for the whole state. Patronage and clientage were fundamental precepts of society and the networks came together at court where the king was the ultimate provider of graces. The village or urban notables had connections with the local bishop, or with seigneurial agents or a seigneur himself.[21] These men in turn had their patrons and networks of friends, and formed a tightly knit if often divided local elite.[22] Every local or provincial elite had links with great provincial landowners, leading magistrates, or royal governors, all with close connections or places at court.[23] Grand aristocrats with easy access to the king and his ministers would intervene to secure favors for their clients or would act as brokers to reduce opposition and promote covert compromises over royal policy. It was unbecoming to royal majesty to be seen to negotiate, but the reality of politics was that almost everything was a compromise. (This was of course anathema to many revolutionaries for whom all politics was a matter of principle.) As may be seen from its religious, *parlementaire*, and financial policies, the royal government therefore relied upon its centralization of patronage to ensure that the administrative machinery continued to operate. Sometimes it was a question of informal networks parallel to the formal administrative structures, sometimes the patronage system was at the core of the bureaucracy itself. The court provided the inducements and it provided the means for this system to function on the whole fairly successfully.

Demonstrably, every minister was a courtier and had to operate as such, even if his bureaux were based in Paris instead of at Versailles. "Ministers have of necessity become courtiers, and, if they are not, they are quickly disgraced ... Thus they have to participate in all the wishes of the courtiers."[24]

Patronage, soon to be seen by the revolutionaries as corruption, was actually essential to good and effective government under the ancien régime. Within this system, because social rank and privilege were linked, to the extent that social privilege itself conferred a measure of political authority, the high nobility remained essential to the functioning of the sociopolitical régime. It had never been cut out of government under Louis XIV nor did its importance diminish significantly during the greater part of the eighteenth century. Its role was important because political power can be said to have operated as much through the social system as through the administration, and must not be identified too closely with the bureaucracy *qua* bureaucracy. The administrative or courtly offices held by individuals were acquired by them through a process that was as much a reflection of their existing positions of influence as because of the administrative power inherent in the office.

If personal relations were an important part of the social and political system, faction – that anathema to the revolutionaries – was the inevitable by-product. There was bound to be competition to influence the king and his ministers in favor of family, friends, and clients. Life was expensive at Versailles and the great families needed royal largesse and profitable financial investments in order to maintain themselves in the proper fashion. In 1790, the famous *Livre rouge*, published to expose this system during the Revolution, mentioned only two million livres in pensions, but there is evidence that the true figure was nearer thirty million. So pensions, lucrative sinecures, and contracts were hotly competed for by cabals of the most important families.[25]

Courtiers and power brokers also had networks of clients to whose demands they had to accede by acquiring favors. But factional competition was not just for places, it was also over policies – with serious consequences for the monarchy. The priorities of King and of courtier were often very different, the king having to concentrate upon the formation and execution of state policy (although this had a strongly familial dimension), while courtiers often were involved in policy as a means to social advancement or the preservation of acquired positions. Courtiers were more concerned to advance their interests than they were to encourage sound policies. Thus, when a minister began to pursue unpopular measures of economy or centralization his supporters at court would abandon him. 'Economy' meant fewer opportunities for profit, and centralization meant pressure from clients in the provinces anxious to retain local power. By contributing to a reformer's dismissal, courtiers hoped to remain on the winning side and consequently secure greater influence for themselves – as with the falling away of Bourbon's support in 1726, or Calonne's in 1787. Reforming ministers were sure to run up against powerful vested interests, especially if, like the duc de Bourbon in 1725 and Loménie de Brienne in 1787–88, they reduced the household expenses. The great reformer Turgot fell foul of this mentality in 1776 and so did Necker in 1781. As Elias so rightly pointed out, all the king could hope to do was balance the factions in order to divide and rule. The court was an arena in which intense competition took place. A king or a first minister had to keep fully abreast of the factional interplay, intervening constantly to preserve the necessary equilibrium. One of the main problems during the Revolution was how to do politics without getting involved in patronage and clientage. These practices were redolent of faction and the very antithesis of the role of virtuous citizens.

Indeed, corruption and conspiracy (to pervert the cause of justice, say, or to get power for a member of a faction) were under the old regime an essential part of doing politics. Whether it was actually labeled 'conspiracy' was a question of degree and prudence. But this question of degree is significant too. Under the ancien régime there were few political prosecutions for conspiracy, but plenty of actions against corruption, as in the *chambres de justice*, pamphlet attacks on financiers, even the dismissal of a minister was associated with this (Le Peletier Desforts in 1730) and it was a major theme of the attack on Calonne. It appears to have been accepted that many different and (after 1789) incompatible interests could be served at once: king, state, faction, family. Under the Revolution we have the predominance of the idea that the Revolution represented a kind of meta-system of virtue and patriotism within a transparent political system. This takes away the idea of relative degrees of difference and acceptability, making the serving of multiple interests illegitimate, by replacing them with absolute moral imperatives for conduct. Thus it came about that any form of corruption at all could be said to undermine the new system.

The governance of the ancien régime state thus saw considerable confusion between the emerging doctrine of public and private – a confusion the revolutionaries wished to combat (but could never wholly do). During the ancien régime, commentators might have made a distinction between *intrigue, complot, cabal, brigue de cour*, and *conspiration* and *conjuration*. But these words refer to practices that the revolutionaries would assimilate to the notion of *conspiration* and *conjuration*, so that from the perspective of the Revolution, all the normal political practices of the court system of politics became illegitimate and liable to fall into the category of 'conspiratorial'. How did they arrive at this position?

Perceptions of politics

When answering this question, we must remember that although as historians we might identify elements of politics as conspiratorial, we have access to a range of documents most contemporaries could never have seen. The isolation of the king from political conversation with his courtiers was almost complete, so there was no public access to the arcanae of the king's business. The baron de Besenval reflected that it was impos-sible for a courtier to engage in any meaningful conversation with a king.

> One certainly cannot talk politics to them, nor about the news of the day that refers to it. that would be to show a lack of respect for them, by the impossibility of their replying. To dwell on the administration or to discuss it, would in the same way put them in the position of having to keep silent, while to fall into the error of attacking those responsible for it, to run them down, would be to make enemies for no good reason.[26]

Religion too was out of the question. Moreover, most of the king's subjects only had a very limited experience of courtly politics, from the outside, through contacts or business they had done involving, as did so much, the court. The great majority of future Third Estate deputies – and the general public of all three estates – had no direct experience of state politics at all, so we must recognize that they acquired a vicarious experience from books and conversation. Let us therefore briefly consider how some of them might have arrived at similar conclusions to some recent historians that ancien régime politics was very nearly conspiratorial. The main evidence available to historians but unavailable to them was administrative records, diplomatic reports, and correspondence in depth, and private papers of those nobles involved in politics. Such correspondences were rarely if at all published before the Revolution. Apart from some sets of ecclesiastical correspondence and documents, the only volumes of French political correspondence to be published before 1789 were those of Madame de Pompadour and Madame de Maintenon.

So, what access to politics did they have then? This is not the place to write a history of reading and discussion in the later ancien régime, so let us briefly evoke the ways in which an education in interpreting politics might have been acquired. First, there was their lower-level experience: those who believed in the 'famine plot' felt they knew the realities of everyday life in the marketplace, but had no idea of politics, and this unsubtle mentality was characteristic of the revolutionary crowds. But members of the revolutionary assemblies were educated men, and if they were not nobles or clerics they were predominantly lawyers or officeholders, and they usually had experience of local political life: in town councils, local estates, the judicial system – as Timothy Tackett has recently stressed.[27] Life and ambitions must have taught them how important (and often unfair) the patronage system was, how the rich and well-connected won their cases more often than not, how progress within the royal administration was dependent upon the intervention of courtiers. The educated derived their ideas of politics largely from three kinds of sources: the classics, general texts that sought to prescribe better political systems in the abstract, and the numerous publications that purveyed a vicarious political experience. These last might be historical or topical, and many were illegal.

As is well known, the revolutionaries were deeply influenced by the classics: it was a fundamental part of their education in rhetoric, and provided many of the examples they cited in speeches and works on politics. On history and politics they were familiar with their Cicero, Tacitus, Sallust, Livy, and Plutarch.[28] They were taught to love republican virtues which were contrasted to the decadence of the Empire, to praise the three Horatii, Junius Brutus, Mucius Scaevola, and Cincinnatus; with Cicero they praised the death of Caesar as a blow for liberty, and all were familiar with the Catiline conspiracy as recounted by Sallust and Cicero.

As has often been noted, the *philosophes* dealt more with general principles than with specific plans for reform, and were wary of entering the political fray in France with explicit condemnations of the way everyday politics worked. Of course, the rise of an understanding of comparative political systems in this period – fueled by the *philosophes*, travel literature, and the examples of England, Holland, America, and Geneva – clearly showed that the desirable qualities did not square with the 'practice'. The marquis d'Argenson was a thought-provoking self-styled republican critic of the régime.[29] Voltaire was a believer in enlightened reform by the existing régime in France (at least until Maupeou's failure to carry through meaningful changes disillusioned him). Mably's anti-noble theme of a monarchy in alliance with the Third Estate against an ambitious and factious nobility, however, found an enthusiastic audience. Montesquieu was thought especially useful for his vision of the balancing of powers which the ministry's reform plans seemed determined to avoid; Rousseau for an idea of virtue that was divorced from social status. Such very basic ideas helped some observers of the politics of 1787–89 in particular to conceive of politics as a plot by unvirtuous courtiers and ministers against liberty.

The Enlightenment of course saw the publication not only of numerous works of political philosophy, but of books on political economy as well. Such works not only enjoyed a limited educated readership, for printings were usually limited to a few hundred or rarely 1,000 copies of such texts, but also were not necessarily understood. Although there were discussions of economic theory in some circles, most educated readers were more interested in fiscality and finances. From the middle of the Seven Years War there was considerable growth in such publications, as France debated its failure compared to circumstances in Britain. The physiocratic works of Gournay and Quesnay were well known, and the main precepts of physiocracy were also explained in the preambles to legislation on the grain trade.[30] Works on fiscality were indeed sold much more widely than those on political economy. Jean-Claude Perrot cites 11 editions of Vauban's *Dixme royale*, 18 editions of Mirabeau's *Théorie de l'impôt*, maybe 40 editions of *L'Ami des hommes*, and a wide distribution in various forms of the ideas in the *Tableau économique*. All these were often theoretical and thus, during the régime itself, rather utopian or at least aspirational, even if the more popular ones were written in an accessible style. Nevertheless, the lack of agreement between the economists was rather discouraging for the general reader.

On the other hand, the works of the finance minister Jacques Necker, his *Compte rendu* of 1781 and *De l'Administration des finances de la France* in 1784, were extraordinarily popular, the first selling 40,000 copies almost immediately, and the second having numerous editions and perhaps 80,000 copies. The reason was that these works by a minister described how French government actually worked, opening wide a window on the secret world of state politics. As we shall see, Necker's *De l'Administration des finances* influenced the future terrorist Billaud-Varenne a great deal. Necker writes in his chapter 32 on the changes of principles and persons in financial administration:

> What would be better, no doubt, would be to choose this minister neither according to his rank, nor his dress, nor according to any conventionally agreed sign; but according to the qualities of his heart and his mind: a difficult enterprise it is true, and above all for princes, before whom truth is ceaselessly hidden and disguised. From childhood grown used to keeping those who surround them at a great distance from their person, or to allow them near only at times destined for pleasures, the impressions that they receive about men depend most often upon the insinuations made by a small number of courtiers whom they allow into their inner circle; but how could one expect an impartial view from those who are preoccupied with ideas of fortune and ambition? The first rule of these ardent passions is to love or hate, according to interest.
>
> The art of intrigue has indeed today so much progressed that by its subtle refinements it escapes the most attentive of watchers: it acts by the most incredible detours, it uses all means, both the most subtle approach, the most audacious lies, and the appearance of good faith, and even the mask of austerity. It studies the actions of the princes themselves, so as to discover all that may serve their projects, and to more cleverly nuance their intrigues [*combinaisons*].[31]

It was one thing to have general assertions and innuendo about corruption, but to actually have a revered ex-minister confirming this explicitly was another matter.

Modern history was a major and increasingly popular category of publications,[32] with readers familiar with European History, and history meant the deeds of kings and ministers, civil wars, changes of régime. Intrigue and faction tended to be considered in terms of the fomenting of civil disturbances or political disorder, and not as an element of political management. In this historical awareness the Wars of Religion, Henri IV, Richelieu and the Frondes, and Louis XIV figured prominently. These periods could also be understood through a new and vital source for their understanding, and the one I want to stress here as relatively neglected by historians of literate culture: historical memoirs.

Particularly in the eighteenth century, noble memoirs became easily available through publication and no doubt through the reading rooms of academies and *sociétés de lettres* later in the century, giving certainly a very wide access to them. Through these memoirs, a certain idea of politics was built up. These texts must have been avidly read, as most went through multiple editions, although writers often cite old editions rather than the latest one. As some representative examples show, it was very much an eighteenth-century phenomenon. Under Louis XIV there were scattered publications, such as the *Oeconomies politiques* or memoirs of the duc de Sully in 1638, 1640, 1652, and 1663, with abridged editions a century later in 1745, 1766, and 1768;[33] Richelieu's *Journal* of 1630 and 1631 bore witness to an early fascination with the defeat of a conspiracy on the Day of Dupes (five editions in 1648, 1649, and 1664), and Antoine Aubery's *Memoirs for the History of the Cardinal de Richelieu* (two editions, 1660, 1667) profited from this early fascination; Richelieu's *Political Testament* first printed in 1688 went through more than ten editions up to 1764, with a big debate on their authenticity in 1750. The story of his politics had become available in part in other, earlier publications, of course. Courtilz de Sandras's *Memoirs of the comte de Rochefort* saw five editions from 1687 to 1742, and Sandras wrote numerous other apocryphal memoirs.

The vogue developed in earnest after the death of Louis XIV, when in 1717 the memoirs of that archconspirator the cardinal de Retz were published (10 editions 1717–77). The Fronde fascinated everyone, and Retz could be supplemented by Mademoiselle de Montpensier, the daughter of Gaston d'Orléans, the first edition of whose memoirs was confiscated by the Regent in 1717. They became available in three editions of 1729, 1746, and 1776. The memoirs of Marie d'Orléans-Longueville, the duchesse de Nemours, were available in 1709, 1718, and 1738; those of the abbé de Choisy in three editions from 1727 to 1747. A popular read on the scandalous regency was the memoirs of the chevalier de Poissens.[34] The real nitty-gritty of politics was further and more seriously exposed in the marquis de Torcy's memoirs which had two editions at the start of the Seven Years War, 1756–57 and 1757, with English and Dutch translations; and the abbé Millot's *Mémoires politiques et militaires pour servir à l'histoire de Louis XIV et de Louis XV*, done from and reproducing the Noailles's private archives, went through four editions in 1777 alone. C. P. Duclos, *Memoirs to serve towards the history of morals*, was popular with three editions during the period 1751–77, and one more in 1791. Saint-Simon on the other hand, although he was writing in the 1740s, and perhaps inspired by so many publications, was not made available, and then only in part, until that crucial year of 1788, by the abbé

Soulavie. He was used quite heavily, however, by Duclos for his *Secret memoirs of the Regency*, which dealt with factions and the Cellamare conspiracy in detail. Indeed the 1780s saw the successful publication of a complete 72-volume edition of a collection of French memoirs – a huge publishing and marketing achievement at that time.[35] It is clear that these sources were good sellers and widely read, and that must have been because, in a regime that forbade the discussion of contemporary politics, they provided a form of understanding. They are essentially tales of the careers and ascension of noble families involved in intrigue on a daily basis, recounting political strife – be it frondeur or religious – and deeds of arms.

During early years of the Revolution there were several important publications by Jean-Louis Giraud Soulavie, geographer, naturalist, and former secretary to the maréchal de Richelieu. From 1790 to 1792 he put together apocryphal memoirs or biographies of d'Aiguillon, Madame de Pompadour, Maurepas, and Massillon. His popular life of the scandal-prone rake the maréchal de Richelieu, in the form of memoirs, was rivaled by another version by Laborde. Both were based on documents but neither of them was written by Richelieu himself. Although most of the documents Soulavie used were genuine, he certainly embroidered the truth and gave the texts a telling antimonarchical slant by revealing a courtly world of intrigue and corruption that was influencing government and feminizing power.

To a large extent noble memoirs, written by participants for the most part, revealed the strategies and values of courtiers as they struggled for power, and opened a window onto maxims of state and statecraft. The world they portrayed was seen from the point of view of the higher nobility, and there would be much material at which bourgeois out-siders, if they had access to *sociétés des lettres* and reading rooms, could be scandalized, especially as the new virtuous morality of the eighteenth century took hold. They portray patronage, intrigue, duplicity, con-spiracy in detail – exactly what the Revolution was to be against indeed. They would have reinforced the moral stance against intrigue and courtly ways.

Indeed, memoirs containing 'the whole truth' were in such demand that borrowing their format was a popular way of composing scurrilous pamphlets at the time of Maupeou. Together with correspondence, so little of which was actually published before 1790, but whose form also found favor with novelists and pamphleteers, memoirs became one of the classic templates of libelous and titillating publications. It is surely no accident that authors of scandalous chronicles chose the memoir format for their works. The mock memoirs or correspondences were perhaps yet more powerful in creating a certain image of politics. The many volumes of Maupeouiana, especially the *Journal historique* and the *Correspondance secrète et familière de M. de Maupeou*, the (*Anecdotes* or)*Memoirs of Madame du Barry* (all by Pidansat de Mairobert and the salon of Madame Doublet), Mouffle d'Angerville's *Private Life of Louis XV* (1781 and 1788), and Bouffonidor's *Fastes de Louis XV* (three printings in 1782), exposed the everyday tale of power and riches misused, of the courtly intrigues behind the despotic attack on French liberties by a monarchy in which regal power had been debased through the immoral dependency of the king upon his mistresses.[36]

The tale of intrigue and corruption at the heart of the state was carried up to date by Pidansat's *L' Observateur anglois* (10 vols 1777–84) and Petit de Bachaumont's *Memoirs secrets*, which were *nouvelles à la main* published in 36 volumes in the 1780s. They tell of the comings and goings of courtiers, review the theatrical and artistic works of the day, repeat the witticisms and the 'on-dits' of the court, and provide a plausible and, to their readers, apparently well-informed analysis of developments in policy. 'It is thought that Linguet is persecuting d'Aiguillon before the courts to discredit him to prevent a return to the ministry, where he might become another Maurepas, and that he is put up to this by powerful hidden interests,' wrote the *Mémoires secrets*.[37] In fact, their access to the real details of politics was extremely limited, and they were often quite wrong in their analysis. Affairs of state and royal council meetings being part of the mysteries of state, their participants were not indiscreet, so analysis tended to be highly speculative. In a sad irony for the regime, had politics been more open, the misconstruction of it might not have been so damaging. Robert Darnton classes all these among the best-sellers of the major underground book dealers in the twenty years before the Revolution.[38]

Pamphlets tended to convey the same message, perhaps inadvertently, as they often originated from the court. The self-centered intriguers who were responsible for them were quite prepared to use the basest slanders and accusations of corruption (not all of which was untrue of course) against their enemies, apparently oblivious to the wider effects of such reading matter on a fascinated but scandalized public:

> One would hardly be believed today if one reproduced the libelles that were in circulation at that time, and above all if one named their authors . . . We have referred to the effect produced by a bad farce entitled The plenary Court, and a worse one in which the king, portrayed drunk was allowing the queen to steal the keys to his strong box, who gave them to her lover a prelate. All these infamies were believed or applauded in what was then called *good company*, whose wickedness had reached the point of having

credence given to the clandestine memoirs of Madame de Lamotte; it was
even whispered that the Queen could not deny the truth in them. So how
could it be surprising that what had gone the rounds in Paris and Versailles
should be believed in the street and the shops.[39]

This was true of so many *libelles*, whether accusing the 'Austrian
committee', Calonne, or Necker, or whether generated by members of the
royal family or the Orleanist machine (which included a publishing
enterprise located in the Palais Royal) against Marie Antoinette. Augeard,
a well-connected financier, admitted writing anti-ministerial pamphlets
during the Maupeou era when 'ministerial despotism' was a key theme.[40]
Whereas memoirs, eulogies, and classical lives tended to stress the virtues
of the individuals and the vices of conspirators, in a kind of inversion
pamphlets would usually suggest the individual responsibility of unvirtuous courtiers, financiers, or ministers. All these genres imply a notion
of historical causation based upon individuals. Things happened because
individuals or groups made them happen.

Newspapers in the 1780s had little deep analysis of politics of the
day, though the *Gazette de Leyde* and the *Courier de l'Europe* kept
people generally informed, even printing long extracts from the judicial
mémoires.[41] With these widely read lawyers' briefs, the two definitions of
conspiracy come together: the legal definition of conspiracy to commit
a crime, and the political definition of plotting, intrigue, and faction. In
several cases discussed by Sarah Maza – those of Véron-Morangiès,
Madame de Saint-Vincent versus the maréchal de Richelieu, and the
Diamond Necklace affair – courtiers and nobles were seen to be conspiring
to commit fraud. As the factional resonances were so clear to observers,
the judicial memoirs would have been particularly telling in their
exposition of corruption and misdeeds among the elite, who seemed
singularly lacking in virtue. Many of these texts give their readers an
insight into corruption in high places, be it sexual or political, and this was
an age when the sex and politics were seen to be inextricably linked. As
is well known, Beaumarchais's judicial memoirs against Goezman played
a part in discrediting the Maupeou parlement, creating a sense that politics
and justice were corrupt. Mercier even wanted real drama to portray the
kind of scenes played out in the courtroom.[42]

Thus it was that the rise of the educated classes, the spread of reading
habits, the emergence of a more discursive public sphere, all created a
market for the sorts of publications that portrayed politics in this
intriguing, plotting, and conspiratorial way. But how did political
outsiders put all this together to arrive at their version of the reality
of politics? Clearly we can only reconstruct a plausible scenario, but
there are some telling examples. While it would be foolish to argue that

everyone in the pre-Revolutionary period felt politics was essentially conspiracy, almost everyone thought them corrupt. The interpretation of everyday politics was based upon access to courtiers, gossip, the noting of visits, and the arrival of liveried couriers, the scrutiny of expressions, the pseudo-science of physiognomy, the consideration of who were the clients or patrons of individuals, with known interests – all brought together to deduce strategies and interpret conduct. Their interpretations imply a number of assumptions about courtiers (who dissemble) and financiers (who are corrupt), individual responsibility, and a certain view of human nature. Thus we find in the works of Retz, Pidansat de Mairobert, Saint-Simon, d'Argenson, and Barbier – the latter two unknown to the eighteenth century but revealing examples of the way they thought – a sort of courtly science of interpretation.

But why did even the normal practices become increasingly unacceptable in the last decades of the ancien régime, such that even the usual personal elements of political conduct could soon be associated with conspiracy? One factor that stands above all others is the rise of a new morality. From about 1750 classical republican ideology with its heroes and villains came much more into fashion. The two key concepts of virtue and patriotism became increasingly popular, the former championing all that was antithetical to the old practices, the latter urging or legitimizing intervention to save the body politic or body social, by empowering virtuous citizens. The new discourse of virtuous patriotism now provided a standpoint from which to evaluate politics.[43] A good illustration of this development is the way the words *cabale* and *intrigue* are used, first in Retz, and then by later authors. What is most striking is the way Retz uses them neutrally, in a matter-of-fact way. By the mid-eighteenth century the phrases in which these words are used are overwhelmingly pejorative and increasingly associated with courtier corruption and inefficiency of government, because they had become morally wrong. The revolutionaries continued this perspective of course. Although the *idea* of conspiracy still remained strong in prerevolutionary political culture, it was in some ways strengthened by a new climate. Conspiracy stemmed from moral corruption, it was believed. Courtiers were of course perfectly suited for this nefarious role. For example, on the subject of *courtisan*, we have in the *Encyclopédie* the following diatribe:

> [Courtier] is the epithet given to those sorts of people that the misfortune of kings and peoples has placed between kings and the truth to prevent it from reaching them, even when they are expressly charged with making it known to them: the foolish tyrant listens to and likes these sorts of people; the clever tyrant uses them and despises them; the king who knows how to behave like

one, dismisses them and punishes them, and the truth then reveals itself, for
it is only hidden from those who do not truly seek it.

This characterization draws upon an important discourse of anti-courtier
sentiment that goes back to the sixteenth century. For more than a century
from La Bruyère to Mercier courtiers are condemned in literature, and
Beaumarchais had numerous forerunners. But the criticisms found even
more fertile soil on the high moral ground of the eighteenth century moral
philosophy.

How was this understanding to be developed by future revolutionaries?
Jean Paul Marat, and Jacques-Nicolas Billaud-Varenne provide revealing
prerevolutionary examples. Marat's *Chains of slavery*, published in 1774,
is an interesting case. Although he barely deals explicitly with France,
where his diatribe was not published until 1792, the subtext suggests it is
heavily inspired by the question of despotism raised by the affair of the
Jesuits in 1762 (when Marat was first living in France) and the Maupeou
coup, even though it is more explicitly addressed to an English audience.
The whole book is an exposé of what we could call the 'conspiracy' of
princely government against liberty.[44] He discusses the procedures of the
exercise of power, drawing heavily for examples on the classics, but also
on Swedish politics, much earlier French history, and Cromwell's England.
Notable is the way in which those techniques of government, that a
historian today might attribute to the existence of a long-standing political
culture, are attributed to the scheming of princes, to their individual
agency. Marat and Pidansat de Mairobert share the same assumptions.
From this we might reflect that conspiracy accusations in the Revolution
are often a case of overinterpretation, for they attribute motive to actions
that resemble those of the old political *mores*; they deduce motive from
actions, so the action itself becomes sufficient proof.

Billaud-Varenne's *Despotism of the ministers of France* (3 vols, 1789,
but written in July 1788) also arrived at a conspiratorial understanding
of politics through the interaction of events and his reading, as an
important article by John Burney shows.[45] Drawing upon the Jansenist
version of parlementary history and an ancient constitution, Billaud
attacked the treasonable despotism of corrupt ministers. 'That's how for
nearly two centuries an odious despotism, to consolidate its tyrannical
authority, undermines the basis of the constitution.'[46] As Burney says,
Billaud had already identified his conspirators before the autumn of
1788: 'ministers, the administration, capitalists, financiers, rentiers.'[47] To
avoid the machinations of aristocrats and ministers, transparency was
needed: 'All is lost if the veil of mystery envelops once again government
operations.'[48]

Old practices in a new light

On the eve of 1789, a vision of politics which attributed policy- and decision-making taking place behind closed doors to influence, faction, ambition, and corruption was surely highly *rational*, or at least understandable on the part of these commentators, given the perspective and the kinds of information to which such observers had access, and their own limited political experience. Moreover, lawyers, who were used to putting together imperfect evidence to construct a case, and indeed anyone with a rhetorical training (which meant almost every educated person), would have been highly adept at such interpretations. That is why we must remember that although many radicals were convinced that there was an inherent tendency to conspiracy in politics, there was a *rhetoric* of conspiracy during the Revolution, for it was also a question of marshalling a useful and populist argument, believed by the people but manipulated by the deputies. It can be no accident that during the Revolution it was mostly lawyers who made such use of the rhetoric of plots in politics. Did they really believe in all the plots that were denounced, or was it merely a deadly rhetoric? As Marisa Linton shows in Chapter 6 of this volume, there was a great deal of knowing exploitation of this rhetoric, sometimes under pressure from popular beliefs. On the other hand, that 'politics' (which they were in the process of inventing or engaging in for the first time) was often not an act of will by decision-makers, who were often caught up in ongoing affairs and previous commitments, probably never occurred to some of them. Given these assumptions, and the lack of hard facts, they believed that actions were the best clues to motives.[49]

What we have, therefore, is a perception of the way politics worked which was based upon the several elements that soon would be considered indicative of conspiracy – in another world, that of the Revolution. Under the ancien régime, since the rest was normal practice, it was a question of degree, and only the most extreme elements would be considered 'plots' or 'conspiracy.' For example, both the Maupeou and the Lamoignon coups against the parlements easily lent themselves to interpretation as a conspiracy of despotic ministers against ancient liberties. The crisis of 1787–88, with its 'despotic' reforms, intimidation of the courts, exiles, *lits de justice*, published remonstrances rebuffed, pamphlets, and widespread public discussion, brought observers into closer contact with the political processes and gave them an opportunity to reflect on what was happening. Many did discern intrigue and corruption. The great plot of the 1780s was that developed by vile courtiers and corrupt ministers to make France into a despotism, and the parlements were seen as heroic defenders of the liberties of an ancient constitution subverted.[50] The Estates General was

believed necessary not just to solve fiscal problems but to bring about a
moral regeneration of a plainly political life. But on 25 September 1788,
the parlement of Paris appeared to side with the nobility against the Third
Estate, and by January 1789 the example of noble intransigence in
Brittany set the scene for a reinterpretation of events as a struggle by the
Third Estate to free itself from the domination of the nobility if it was to
achieve its dream of regeneration. Minor conspiracies could be discerned,
about bread, or wages: according to one observer, the Réveillon riots were
provoked by the deliberate misreporting of a speech by the factory owner
about wages.[51] During the Estates General the intransigence of the noble
order, whose dominant faction was influential at court, fueled suspicions
that the nobility and upper clergy were trying to undermine any
opportunity for reform and regeneration.[52] The attack on the Bastille grew
out of the fears of a counter-revolutionary coup by the king and his
ministers beginning with the dismissal of Necker on 11 July, and sinister
troop movements around Paris. The constitutional decisions on the veto
and single chamber saw a significant minority convinced that to create a
strong executive would lead to the suppression of the Revolution by an
authority that would use intrigue and corruption to manipulate the
deputies. The October days originated from the suspicion of a
counterrevolutionary policy by the king who was trying not to ratify the
Declaration of Rights, and certain noble regiments, although it was also
widely believed that an Orleanist conspiracy was behind them (See David
Andress in this volume, Chapter 4, pp. 87-90.) In the absence of hard
facts, people resorted to the old schema of conspiracy to explain what
they could not verify.

It is not hard to discern the continuities between this memoir-based
vision of corrupt politics and a relabeling of the practices of ancien régime
politics. The idea of the conspiracy of a despotic power against the liberties
of a people became a key element of revolutionary rhetoric, while the
idea of the machinations of individuals to acquire power was the other
aspect that could be imagined through, for example, *libelles* and memoir
literature. The two elements come together in that minor but revealing
personage of J. L. Giraud Soulavie, naturalist, collector, historian, and
minor diplomat, who as we have seen was responsible for many volumes
of genuine and apocryphal memoirs published from 1788 onward. As
chargé d'affaires for the Republic in Geneva, he wrote to Robespierre:

> I have sent you my dear Robespierre, some notes on the different kinds of
> conspirators . . .
>
> After these observations, I must inform you that in Europe, in Paris, a
> terrible coup is being plotted: I do not know what it is; but it is a conspiracy
> against the Republic and the Convention.[53]

Then consider Saint-Just:

> Another faction existed which schemed and was involved with all the others, which sometimes wanted to usurp [power], sometimes was royalist, sometimes wanted riches, sometimes thought to acquire a great authority, whatever the regime in place, sometimes served foreign states: this faction, like all the others, without courage, led the Revolution like the plot of a play. Fabre d'Eglantine was at the head of this faction; he was not alone there; *he was the cardinal de Retz of today.*[54]

Retz of course provided a model of conspiratorial politics – his memoirs were a sort of manual.[55] From reading this accusation by Saint-Just, and his earlier one against the Hébertistes, it is clear that there is considerable carry-over between a tacit sense of what ancien régime politics was all about (which he assumes his audience shares) and the activities of these alleged conspirators.[56]

The revolutionaries thus inherited a rich tradition of conceiving of court politics as essentially corrupt and subject to conspiracy, faction, intrigue, and cabals. The revolutionaries were not altogether inventing the centrality of conspiracy to politics, and were right to be worried by these *ci-devant* practices. For historians of the Revolution, the question is therefore less one of explaining the roots of their 'obsessions' – which were in fact not so irrational given their experience and the existence of real plots – than of explaining how and why they made political capital out of what can be seen as a quite natural and even justified fear of past practices that were a constant danger, and would undermine their revolutionary attempt to create virtuous citizens.

Notes

1 For some recent attempts at defining politics and the state, see Roger Mettam, *Power and Faction in Louis XIV's France* (Oxford, 1988); Peter. R. Campbell, *Power and Politics in Old Regime France 1720–1745* (London and New York, 1996); and John Hardman, *French Politics 1774–1789: From the Accession of Louis XVI to the Fall of the Bastille* (London and New York, 1995).

2 On the use of the classics in the Revolution see Harold T. Parker, *The Cult of Antiquity and the French Revolutionaries* (Chicago, 1937; reprint New York, 1965).

3 P. Richelet, *Dictionnaire portatif de la langue française: Nouvelle édition entièrement refondue et considérablement augmentée par M. de Wailly* (A. Lyon, chez J.-M. Bruyset père et fils, rue St Dominique, 1775).

4 Jean-Claude Waquet, 'La politique des dictionnaires: Langue royale et idiomes monarchiques dans la France moderne,' *Società e storia* 87 (2000), pp. 19–36. The article focuses on the area of meaning around *cabale*,

complot, conjuration, and *conspiration.* See Waquet's book expanding on these views, *La Conjuration des dictionnaires: Vérité des mots et vérités de la politique dans la France moderne* (Strasburg, 2000).

5 In his thought-provoking contribution toward our understanding of conspiracy, Timothy Tackett suggested that belief in conspiracy had declined by the late ancien régime: 'Conspiracy Obsession in a Time of Revolution: French Elites and the Origins of the Terror, 1789–1792,' *American Historical Review* 105(3) (2000), 691–713, pp. 696–699. Tackett bases his view partly on a search for the word *conspiration* in the ARTFL database, but apart from the database's relative lack of political material, the search for one word when several were used, could surely not give useful results.

6 Y.-M. Bercé, ed., *Complots et conjurations dans l'Europe moderne* (Rome, 1996), pp. 1–5.

7 Tackett, 'Conspiracy Obsession,' pp. 697–699.

8 We know today that they indeed often did involve planning by the lower orders (so regarded as conspiracy by their superiors) who might get together at the fair or carnival time, to consider protests. But many were unpremeditated, the product of a culture of revolt.

9 L. Biollay, *Le Pacte de famine* (Paris, 1901); Steven L. Kaplan, *The Famine Plot Persuasion in Eighteenth-Century France* (Philadelphia, 1982).

10 Abbé C. A. de Montgon, *Recueil des lettres et Mémoires écrits par M. l'abbé de Montgon* (n.p., 1731) and his *Mémoires de Monsieur l'abbé de Montgon, publiez par lui-même: Contenant les différentes négociations dont il a été chargé dans les cours de France, d'Espagne, et de Portugal; et divers événemens qui sont arrivés depuis l'année 1725 jusques à présent,* 8 vols (Lausanne, 1748–1753).

11 Arlette Farge and Jacques Revel, *The Vanishing Children of Paris: Rumor and Politics before the French Revolution* (Cambridge, MA, 1991).

12 Dale Van Kley, *The Damiens Affair and the Unravelling of the Ancien Régime 1750–1770* (Princeton, NJ, 1984).

13 *La réalité du projet de Bourg-Fontaine, démontrée par l'exécution,* two vols in one (Paris, 1787).

14 Dale Van Kley, *The Jansenists and the Expulsion of the Jesuits from France, 1757–1765* (New Haven, 1975).

15 See John Rothney, *The Brittany Affair and the Crisis of the Ancien Régime* (Oxford, 1969), and Julian Swann, *Politics and the Parlement of Paris under Louis XV, 1754–1774* (Cambridge UK, 1995).

16 Thomas E. Kaiser, 'Who's Afraid of Marie-Antoinette? Diplomacy, Austrophobia, and the Queen,' *French History* 14 (2000), pp. 241–271; Kaiser, 'Ambiguous Identities: Marie-Antoinette and the House of Lorraine from the Affair of the Minuet to Lambesc's Charge,' in Dena Goodman, ed., *Marie Antoinette: Writings on the Body of the Queen* (London and New York, 2003).

17 The best recent analyses are by R. A. W. Browne, 'The Diamond Necklace Affair Revisited: The Rohan Family and Court Politics,' *Renaissance and Modern Studies* 33 (1989), pp. 21–40; Sarah Maza, *Private Lives and Public*

Affairs: The Causes Célèbres of Prerevolutionary France (Berkeley and Los Angeles, 1993), chapter 4.

18 Julian Swann's forthcoming study of disgrace will add to our understanding of royal strategies and policies with regard to exiled ministers, courtiers, and magistrates.

19 See J. D. Woodbridge, *Revolt in Prerevolutionary France: The Price de Conti's Conspiracy against Louis XV, 1755–1757* (Baltimore, Maryland, 1995).

20 *Caractères*, 'De la cour,' Nelson edn (London, 1945), p. 254.

21 At village level this is illustrated by N. Rétif de la Bretonne, in *La vie de mon père*.

22 This elite was often composed of magistrates and judicial officers, with strong ties of vertical solidarity: see for example M. Gresset, *Gens de justice à Besançon, 1674–1789*, 2 vols (Paris, 1978), 2, part III, book III; M. Cubells, *La Provence des Lumières: Les parlementaires d'Aix au XVIIIe siècle* (Aix-en-Provence, 1984); J. Meyer, *La Noblesse bretonne*, 2 vols (Paris, 1966).

23 See especially W. Beik, *Absolutism and Society in Seventeenth-century France* (Cambridge, UK, 1985) and S. Kettering, 'Patronage in Early Modern France,' *French Historical Studies*, 17 (1992), pp. 839–862; on Burgundian connections to the governors, the ducs de Bourbon, up to 1740, see P. Lefebvre, 'Aspects de la fidélité en France au XVIIe siècle: le cas des agents du prince de Condé,' *Revue historique*, 250 (1973), pp. 59–106. During the eighteenth century these links were no doubt conceived of less in terms of clientage and more in terms of sociability, as expressed through provincial academies, freemasonry, and philanthropic societies.

24 *Mémoires et journal inédit du marquis d'Argenson*, Janet edn, 5 vols (Paris, 1858), 5, p. 350.

25 T. J. A. Le Goff, 'Essai sur les pensions royales,' in Martine Acerra *et al.*, eds, *État, marine et société* (Paris, 1995), pp. 252–281.

26 Besenval, *Mémoires*, ed. Diesbach (Paris, 1987), pp. 369–370.

27 T. Tackett, *Becoming a Revolutionary: The Deputies of the French National Assembly and the Emergence of a Revolutionary Culture (1789–1790)* (Princeton, 1996).

28 See the statistics denoting the increase in publications of classics during the century from Jean-Louis and Marie Flandrin, 'La Circulation du livre dans la société du 18e siècle: un sondage à travers quelques sources,' in M. T. Bouyssy, ed., *Livre et société dans la France du XVIIIe siècle*, 2 (Paris, 1970). On the revolutionaies and the classics, see H. T. Parker, *The Cult of Antiquity and the French Revolutionaries: A Study in the Development of the Revolutionary Spirit* (Chicago, 1937). On the use of classics in ancien régime schools, see P. François de Dainville, 'Livres de comptes et histoire de la culture,' *Arch. hist. S. J.*, 18 (1949), pp. 226–252, esp. pp. 227–229 for lists of classics sold for classes in the collège de Rodez.

29 René Louis de Voyer de Paulmy, marquis d'Argenson, *Considérations sur le gouvernement ancien et présent de la France* (Amsterdam, 1765) and *Les Loisirs d'un ministre, ou essais dans le goût de Montaigne*, 2 vols (Liège, 1787).

30 This paragraph is drawn essentially from the chapter by Jean-Claude Perrot, 'Nouveautés: l'économie politique et ses livres,' pp. 298–325, R. Chartier and H.-J. Martin, eds, *Histoire de l'Edition française, 2, Le livre triomphant* (Paris, 1990). For the complex relationship in practice between authors and the ministry, see also Joël Félix, *Finances et politique au siècle des Lumières: Le ministère L'Averdy, 1763–1768* (Paris, 1996).

31 Necker, *De l'Administration des finances*, 3 vols (1784), 3, chapter 32, pp. 392–394.

32 See the analysis by F. Furet, 'La Librairie du royaume de France au XVIIIe siècle,' in G. Bollême, J. Erhard, F. Furet, D. Roche, and J. Roger, *Livre et société dans la France du XVIIIe siècle* (Paris, 1970), pp. 3–32.

33 The period after Sully could be read about in P. Phélypeaux, *Mémoires concernant les affaires de France sous la Régence de Marie de Médicis . . . depuis 1610 jusqu'en 1620*, 2 vols (La Haye, [1720] 1729).

34 The chevalier de Poissens, *Mémoires de la Régence*, 3 vols, (The Hague, [Rouen] [1729] 1730), and an augmented edition in five vols (Amsterdam [Paris] 1749). See also the anonymous *Mémoires de la régence de S. A. R. Mgr. Le Duc d'Orléans, durant la minorité de Louis XV, Roi de France*, 3 vols (The Hague, 1742).

35 *Collection universelle des mémoires particuliers relatifs à l'histoire de France*, 72 vols (London, 1785–88).

36 Maza, 'Diamond Necklace affair', has an interesting discussion of libeles and the feminining of power, to which one could add the example of Pidansat de Mairobert's *Anecdotes sur Mme la comtesse du Barri* (Paris, 1776), discussed from a different perspective, however, by Robert Darnton in *Forbidden Bestsellers*, chapter 5.

37 *Mémoires secrets*, 33, p. 21.

38 Darnton's figures for 1769–89 show several of these to have been best-selling underground texts: The STN had 1,071 copies of the *Anecdotes* ordered, 561 of the *Journal historique*, 198 of the *Vie privée*, 189 of the *Correspondance secrète*, 175 of the *Fastes*. The *Mémoires secrets* with 404 and *L'Observateur anglois* with 150, were the top two orders for *chroniques scandaleuses*, though La Beaumelle's *Mémoires* of Madame de Maintenon were sixth with 69. See Darnton, *The Corpus of Clandestine Literature* (New York, 1995), pp. 213–228.

39 Allonville, *Mémoires*, 1, pp. 256, 259. For the argument that many pamphlets stemmed from the court, see J. D. Popkin, 'Pamphlet Journalism at the End of the Old Regime,' *Eighteenth-Century Studies*, 22 (Spring 1989), pp. 351–367; and 'The Prerevolutionary Origins of Political Journalism,' in Keith Baker, ed., *The French Revolution and Origins of Modern Political Culture*, vol. 1, *The Political Culture of the Old Regime* (Oxford, 1987), pp. 203–223.

40 J. M. Augeard, *Mémoires secrets de J. M. Augeard, secrétaire des commandements de la reine Marie-Antoinette, 1760–1800*, ed. E. Bavoux (Paris, 1866).

41 On newspapers and politics, see above all Jeremy D. Popkin, ed., *News and Politics in the Age of Revolution: Jean Luzac's* Gazette de Leyde (Ithaca, NY,

1989); and Jack Richard Censer and Jeremy D. Popkin, eds, *Press and Politics in Pre-revolutionary France* (Berkeley, CA, 1987).

42 See Maza, *Private Life and Public Affairs*, pp. 62–63.

43 The rise of virtuous discourse is particularly important in this period, providing as it does a moral basis for criticism of political practice. See the important new study by Marisa Linton, *The Politics of Virtue in Enlightenment France* (Basingstoke and New York, 2001).

44 Louis R. Gottschalk, *Jean Paul Marat: A Study in Radicalism* (Chicago and London, 1967), pp. 14–22.

45 John M. Burney, 'The Fear of the Executive and the Threat of Conspiracy: Billaud-Varenne's Terrorist Rhetoric in the French Revolution, 1788–1794,' *French History*, 5(2) (1991), pp. 143–163.

46 Cited in Burney, 'Fear of the Executive,' p. 149.

47 Ibid., p. 150.

48 Ibid., p. 151.

49 G. S. Wood, 'Conspiracy and the Paranoid Style: Causality and Deceit in the Eighteenth Century,' *The William and Mary Quarterly*, 3rd Ser., 19 (1982), pp. 401–441.

50 On the interpretation of this situation developed by one important terrorist, Billaud-Varenne, see Burney, 'Fear of the executive'. Tackett's evidence, 'Conspiracy Obsession,' p. 698 – that almost all of the 32 Third Estate Deputies who wrote prerevolutionary pamphlets did not reflect conspiracy theories – is debatable for two reasons. First, because their writings were not transparent expressions of views, and would-be deputies might not have felt in 1788 and 1789 that conspiratorial denunciations of the executive or nobility were the best way to get elected or promote their career ambitions. Secondly, because as we have seen some pamphlets written by deputies later elected to the Legislative Assembly and Convention but not in the Constituent Assembly were more openly radical. We might add that Breton deputies arrived at Versailles in 1789 already suspicious of the nobility and the ministry.

51 Marquis de Bombelles, *Journal*, ed. J. Grassion and F. Durif, 4 vols (Geneva, 1978), 2, 1784–89 (1982), pp. 300–301.

52 On how the nobility became a conspiracy, see Thomas E. Kaiser, 'Nobles into Aristocrats, or How an Order Became a Conspiracy,' in Jay Smith, ed., *The French Nobility in the Eighteenth-Century: Reassessments and New Approaches* (University Park PA, 2006).

53 Courtois, ed., *Pièces inédites*, 3 vols (Paris 1828), vol. 1, p. 125.

54 My italics Saint-Just, 'Rapport sur la conjuration ourdie pour obtenir un changement de dynastie; et contre Fabre d'Eglantine, Danton, Philippeaux, Lacroix et Camille Desmoulins,' in C. Vellay, ed., *Oeuvres complètes de Saint-Just*, 2 vols (Paris, 1908), 2, pp. 305 332, quotation from p. 312.

55 Colin Jones, 'The Organization of Conspiracy and Revolt in the Mémoires of the Cardinal de Retz,' *European Studies Review*, 11 (1981), pp. 125–150.

56 The official accusations of the Hébertistes presented by Saint-Just to the convention was entitled 'Rapport sur la faction de l'étranger.'

2

Conspiratorial thinking in the Constituent Assembly: Mirabeau and the exclusion of deputies from the ministry

Barry M. Shapiro

'This conspiracy of well-intentioned men will accomplish more than you might think, and as much as the public interest properly understood will want it to accomplish.'[1] So wrote the Comte de Mirabeau to the Duc de Lauzun in November 1788 regarding the meetings of the Society of Thirty, which, of course, would soon accomplish quite a bit. In enthusiastically embracing a word that normally conveyed just as strong a connotation of moral opprobrium in the eighteenth century as it does today,[2] Mirabeau, described by Lafayette as the kind of person who 'sometimes liked to boast about how bad he was,'[3] was undoubtedly indulging in some mischievous posturing. More importantly, however, the rhetorical reversal performed here by Mirabeau serves to remind us that the root meaning of the word conspire, 'to respire or breathe together,' is devoid of moral valuation and that the notion of conspiracy is itself, in many ways, an inherently ambiguous one. In this chapter, I will explore how certain forms of 'breathing together' – which, in other times and places, have been regarded as generally legitimate political activities – were seen, from a very early point in the French Revolution, as illegitimate and potentially criminal. More specifically, I will examine how suspicion and mistrust of Mirabeau's intentions drove his colleagues in the Constituent Assembly to derail any possibility that, as a royal minister, he could become the lynchpin of an attempt to develop a workable relationship between the Assembly and the Crown. With this case study serving as a prototype for an analysis of how the Assembly reacted to any deputy who seemed interested in 'breathing together' with the Crown, I will attempt to point to some of the psychological factors which may have helped to undermine the Assembly's efforts to establish a stable constitutional régime.

If Mirabeau was far from the only early revolutionary leader who sought, as François Furet put it, 'to reconcile the Revolution with the monarchy in order to safeguard liberty,'[4] he does seem to have had the most fully developed conception of a set of particular institutional arrangements through which the possibility of cooperative Crown/ Assembly relations could perhaps have been maximized. More specific- ally, he was the principal advocate in the Assembly of a system of parliamentary government in which the ministers would need to maintain the simultaneous confidence of both the Assembly and the king and in which they would maintain an everyday presence in the Assembly itself.[5] Coupled, moreover, with the institutional pluralism of this approach, Mirabeau's ideas on parliamentary government also reflected a tendency toward a kind of ideological pluralism, as indicated by his suggestion that fallen ministers need not be treated as potential objects of criminal proceedings. Thus, he argued that a minister who loses the confidence of either the Assembly or the king should be seen as having committed a political mistake rather than a crime, stating on 16 July 1789: 'I warn before denouncing, criticize before accusing, and offer retirement before treating ineffectiveness and incompetence as crimes.'[6] Indeed, as one of the rare revolutionaries who was capable, as Camille Desmoulins noted, of acknowledging that those who disagreed with him could 'make rational sense and be logically correct if not politically astute,'[7] Mirabeau had a much less extended conception, in general, of political crime than most of his colleagues, and was therefore much less disposed to construe unwelcome political activity as criminal conspiracy.

Now Mirabeau's vision of containing revolutionary energy through the workings of the kind of parliamentary system then emerging in Britain did not, of course, find fertile ground within the Constituent Assembly. Generally inclined to what has been termed a 'pure' or 'republican' version of the idea of separation of powers, one which, as J. K. Wright has noted, implies a notion of legislative supremacy,[8] the Assembly tended to be suspicious of any arrangement that threatened to impinge upon its own independence. In particular, it was especially hesitant to embrace any proposal, deriving from what Wright refers to as a more 'mixed' or 'balanced' conception of separation of powers, that seemed to imply any kind of regularized association or collaboration between itself and the Crown. To be sure, the Assembly had declared on 13 July 1789, following the dismissal of Necker and three other 'patriot ministers,' that these dismissed ministers 'carry with them the esteem and regrets of (the nation)' and that the reactionary ministers appointed to replace them were 'responsible for the present misfortunes.'[9] However, this clear expression of lack of confidence in a ministry occurred in the midst of the full-blown revolutionary crisis of mid-July, a crisis that had, in fact, been triggered by the dismissal of the patriot ministers. Having departed from a rigid adherence to separation of powers doctrine in the exceptional circumstances surrounding this particular case,[10] the Assembly remained consistently reluctant thereafter to make any similar declarations, preferring to maintain a more indirect method of controlling increasingly irrelevant ministers through the threat of penal rather than political responsibility. Indeed, in the most clear-cut and perhaps ultimately most significant example of its espousal of a 'pure' version of the separation of powers, the Assembly declared, on 7 November 1789, that none of its members could henceforth become ministers.

This edict, however, seems, at least at first glance, to have been as much the product of immediate jockeying for political position as it was a reflection of ideological principle or, for that matter, a reflection of Anglophobe sentiment within the Assembly. As part of the ministerial restructuring that followed the resolution of the July crisis, three members of the Assembly had, in fact, been named as ministers in early August, including, most prominently, the Monarchien cleric Champion de Cicé as Keeper of the Seals. Though no objections to this violation of strict separation seem to have been voiced at the time, all three of these deputy/ministers, perhaps out of deference to unstated concerns about the 'mixed' nature of their positions, immediately ceased to attend Assembly meetings. Seeing this withdrawal as a dangerous precedent that would seriously undermine any possibility of implementing his ideas for cooperation between the Assembly and the ministers and, of course, directly compromise his own ambition to become the deputy/minister who would orchestrate this cooperation, Mirabeau was moved to undertake a campaign advocating a ministerial presence in the Assembly. 'In vain,' declared his house organ, the *Courrier de Provence*, 'can a narrow and suspicious doctrine pretend that the independence of the legislative body would suffer from this presence, of which a neighboring state offers an example and of which the salutary effects are proven by experience . . . and by practical results superior to the sublime theories of our Utopians.'[11] Carrying this campaign to the floor of the Assembly, Mirabeau argued, on 29 September, that 'we need the assistance of enlightened ministers,' while stating, in a rhetorical nod to the lurking and widespread fears of 'ministerial despotism' that he surely realized could easily torpedo his project, that he was 'not afraid of ministerial influence, as long as it does not operate in the secrecy of the cabinet.'[12] But his proposal that the deputies debate the question of whether a minister should have any role to play within the Assembly was quickly tabled on that day, and the issue did not arise again until the first week of November, in the aftermath of the October Days Insurrection.

With the reshuffling of the political deck that followed the October Days, Mirabeau's long-standing dream to become a minister of the king, which had been nourished even as a paternal *lettre de cachet* confined him to a dungeon at Vincennes from 1777 to 1780,[13] seemed to be on the verge of becoming a reality as he engaged in a series of discussions with Lafayette and other patriot leaders on the creation of a new royal government.[14] Welcoming the apparently imminent accession of the celebrated Great Tribune to a central position within a new ministry, the deputy Adrien Duquesnoy wrote on 28 October that 'this giant among pigmies' was the only one with 'the genius, the talents, and the force of character to save us from the horrible chaos into which we have plunged.'[15] But even as the patriotic majority within the Assembly appreciated Mirabeau's talents, agreed with most of the views he expressed in his speeches, and recognized the political weight of his enormous popularity, his scandal-ridden past and corrupt reputation ensured that he would never be trusted. As Guy Chaussinand-Nogaret has written: 'His influence was immense because many deputies saw him as a man of great ability who was capable of conducting the Revolution in a reasonable direction. But his past, the rumors which spread about questionable scheming, his ambition and his need for money provoked scorn and suspicion.'[16] Coupled with the more wide-ranging fear of royal power and royalist conspiracy that was driving the Assembly's inclination toward a 'pure' version of the separation of powers (and which will be highlighted shortly), this irreducible sediment of particular scorn and suspicion, this 'lack of confidence,' as Alexandre Lameth put it, 'which his character inspired,'[17] would help generate Mirabeau's most bitter political defeat at a moment when triumph seemed so close.

As negotiations regarding the formation of a new ministry continued into the first week of November, Mirabeau renewed his public arguments for ministry/deputy cooperation, formally proposing on the 6th that the ministers be provided with what he called a 'consultative voice' within the Assembly.[18] After a brief discussion in which support for Mirabeau's proposal was voiced by a number of prominent deputies from across the political spectrum, two preliminary procedural votes seemed to indicate that sentiment within the Assembly was fairly evenly divided on this specific point.[19] However, the danger that was lying in wait surfaced when, after asserting that a ministerial presence would facilitate the 'venality and corruption through which the ministers assure their control and influence in the British Parliament,' the Breton physician Blin, moving seamlessly to a related but at least theoretically separate issue, announced his intention to propose that deputies be barred from the ministry.[20] Heralding the sharp backlash against the Great Tribune that would crystallize on the next day, Blin's announcement dramatically increased the stakes in this debate for Mirabeau, as a rather desultory discussion on a seemingly relatively minor aspect of governmental process was suddenly transformed into a barely disguised political power play, engineered, it would seem, by the Keeper of the Seals, Champion de Cicé.

Though some of the early discussions on a new ministry had apparently focused on the possibility of a slate that would include both Mirabeau and himself, de Cicé seems to have concluded by early November that he would have a better chance of retaining his position if Mirabeau were eliminated. This, at least, is what can be construed from the testimony of Lafayette and the right-wing deputy Montlosier, who both identify de Cicé as the prime mover behind the passage of the decree of 7 November. Thus, Montlosier reported being 'warned,' as he put it, by the Keeper of the Seals about how close Mirabeau was to entering the ministry. Thus prompted to take the floor in support of Blin's *démarche* of the previous day, Montlosier described how the Assembly instantly shot to attention when he declared on the 7th that Mirabeau's proposal for a ministerial 'consultative voice' had a 'mystic sense.'[21] Through a similar warning, de Cicé was also able, in the words of Lafayette, 'to activate the probity' of one of the leading lights on the left, the Jansenist law professor Lanjunais, who seems to have had links with the minister from earlier days together in Britanny.[22] After explicitly invoking the 'principle' of the separation of powers against Mirabeau's proposal for a ministerial consultative voice, Lanjunais argued, in a curious reversal of the usual fears of 'ministerial despotism,' that the presence of the ministers 'would expose them to become the playthings of ambitious men, if there are any of them in this Assembly.' Lanjunais then went on, for those few who might have missed it, to decipher the 'mystic sense' just referred to by Montlosier: 'An eloquent genius leads you on and subjugates you . . . What could he not do if he became a minister?'[23]

In contrast to the close division of the previous day, Mirabeau's proposal for a consultative voice was then voted down almost unanimously. Shortly thereafter, with the Assembly 'impatient to come to a vote' and with Mirabeau himself as the lone unimpeded voice of opposition, Blin's motion to exclude deputies from the ministry was quickly adopted.[24] With Mirabeau and other prominent deputies whose names had been mentioned as possible ministers thereby eliminated, de Cicé and his colleagues, including the by-then thoroughly discredited Necker, were able to hang on to their increasingly inconsequential positions for another year. More significantly, taking on a life of its own that transcended the immediate circumstances of its enactment, the exclusion of deputies from the ministry remained in place throughout the tenure of the Constituent Assembly and was pointedly reaffirmed on 7 April 1791 as a means of thwarting the ministerial designs of the Duport/Barnave/Lameth 'triumvirate,' which, by that period, had more or less assumed the political role played by Mirabeau in 1789.[25]

Now if, as it appears, the parliamentary victory scored by de Cicé and other supporters of the incumbent ministry on 7 November 1789 was predicated on their ability to activate and turn to their advantage a combination of particular suspicions about Mirabeau and general suspicions about executive/legislative cooperation, it should be possible to shed further light on the decision taken that day by looking more deeply into the nature of these suspicions. One text which – in bringing together suspicions of Mirabeau with more generalized suspicion of royal and ministerial power – is especially useful for such purposes is Duquesnoy's *Journal*, which, as we have already seen, described Mirabeau in late October as the only one capable of 'saving us.' But Duquesnoy, a mainstream patriot of decidedly moderate temperament who in many ways reflected majority opinion within the Assembly, was not always so complimentary toward the Great Tribune. Initially frightened by the revolutionary vehemence of a Mirabeau whom he described as 'a ferocious beast' and an '*enragé*,' Duquesnoy was by mid-June persuaded, on the basis of the 'ardent zeal with which he defends royal authority,' that Mirabeau was literally 'sold to the Court.'[26] (Indeed, Mirabeau's 15 June proposal – that the Third Estate constitute itself as the 'Representatives of the French People' rather than as the 'National Assembly' – produced among the deputies a firestorm of suspicion and indignation that echoed Duquesnoy's assumption.[27]) Moreover, even as Duquesnoy gradually came to appreciate the political subtlety of the peculiar balance between populism and royalism that Mirabeau was attempting to develop, he continued to regard this 'giant among pigmies' as an essentially dangerous man. Hence, his embrace of Mirabeau as a potential savior was always tempered by the fear that, as minister, 'he would amplify royal power and employ to the establishment of despotism all the resources which he used to annihilate it,' or, alternatively, by the fear that, if he did not become a minister, he would mobilize all of his 'immense means' to cause further unspecified mischief. Indeed, his ambivalence toward both Mirabeau's ministerial ambitions and royal power in general is reflected in his ambivalence toward the decree of 7 November, which he described as 'necessary' because those with 'ministerial pretensions could be so dangerous' and, at the same time, as 'bad in itself because it limits the king's options.'[28]

For Duquesnoy, it would seem, Mirabeau was dangerous precisely because of his unique political talents and resources, precisely, that is, because the 'immense means' that were available to him were always susceptible to being used for ominous ends. Moreover, as a person of 'known immorality' who 'always prefers his own petty personal glory to the public good,'[29] he was capable, at least in Duquesnoy's eyes, of intriguing and conspiring with any and all political forces and, ultimately, of making use of any potential route to power. In fashioning this larger than life and, however much rooted in reality, ultimately overblown image of a totally unscrupulous 'giant among pigmies' endowed with an immense capacity to foment disaster, Duquesnoy appears to be expressing himself, in at least one important respect, in tones that sound very much like what might be termed classical conspiratorial thinking. For as Richard Hofstadter pointed out more than 40 years ago, the conspiratorial thinker always attributes vast and exaggerated powers to those 'amoral supermen' and 'demonic agents' who are seen as relentlessly and ruthlessly preparing to 'deflect the normal course of history in an evil way.'[30] Psychologically speaking, moreover, the opposite side of the coin of exaggerating the power and capabilities of unfathomable and uncontrollable forces outside of oneself is minimizing one's own power and capabilities, or, to put it another way, seeing oneself as a weak and helpless pigmy. Thus, it can be suggested that, to the extent that Duquesnoy's comments reflected general sentiment within the Assembly, the edict of 7 November may have represented a kind of instinctive defensiveness on the part of deputies who, in trying to cope with the inevitable feelings of uncertainty, insecurity, and lack of control over events that were an important part of the revolutionary experience, felt particularly fearful of an individual like Mirabeau who seemed so at home in the revolutionary cauldron and who presented himself as someone more than capable of taking control of and directing the course of events.[31] Moreover, it might further be suggested that the general fear of power or what might be called the 'defensive liberalism' that was so characteristic of the Constituent Assembly, its 'distrust,' as Chaussinand-Nogaret put it, 'of all men who began to become ascendant' can, at least in part, be attributed to a visceral urge to 'cut down to size' any political figure who seemed to have the potential to master events.[32]

But all this supposition, plausible as it may be, only begs the question of why the deputies seem to have been, to use Timothy Tackett's word, so 'wary' of any colleague who seemed prepared to assume any kind of leadership role.[33] If the swirl of revolutionary uncertainty indeed provoked intense feelings of vulnerability and insecurity, why not, as the French seem to have done in 1799, look to strong leadership to provide some assuagement for these feelings? Or putting it more bluntly, why, during a period of profound political instability in which the Assembly was, to all intents and purposes, serving as a de facto governing institution as well as a legislative and constitution-formulating body, does this group of essentially quite moderate individuals seem to have been so afraid of anyone who actually seemed capable of governing?

A large part of the answer to these questions can, I believe, be found in the emotional dynamic of the original revolutionary confrontation of June and July 1789 between the deputies and the royal government. Whereas the legions of revolutionary activists who have challenged the forces of authority in a wide variety of settings in the past two centuries have seldom been under any illusion as to the life-and-death nature of revolutionary struggle, the eminently respectable and reputable representatives of French society who gathered in Versailles in late April and early May for the meeting of the suddenly revived Estates-General had little inkling of the wrenching circumstances into which they would soon be plunged. In particular, the lawyers, government officials, and other 'establishment types' who predominated in the delegation of the Third Estate and who, almost to a man, undoubtedly thought of themselves as veritable pillars of society were almost totally unprepared for a situation in which the coercive forces of the State would be mobilized against them and in which their behavior would be viewed by the authorities as criminal rebellion. Indeed, one indicator of just how unprepared the more than 600 Third Estate deputies were to envision themselves as potential victims of armed or judicial repression is the fact that the only one of them who seems to have had spent a significant portion of his life incarcerated in a royal prison was none other than the thoroughly disreputable Mirabeau.[34] Yet, within weeks of their arrival in Versailles, many of these deputies would feel that they were in grave danger of being arrested and put on trial, or, by the time the confrontation with the monarchy reached its climax in mid-July, of being killed outright by the king's soldiers. As the royal judge Lofficial wrote to his wife on 17 July: 'During the night of Tuesday the 14th, they drew up the plan to slaughter us. M. le maréchal de Broglie ordered that 22 pieces of cannon be directed against our meeting hall, but he was disobeyed. Irritated, he ordered the Hussards and the King's Bodyguards to surround us. We would be held as hostages while they bombarded Paris, and massacred if Paris refused to capitulate.' 'We were resigned to perishing in this meeting hall,' wrote the businessman Gantheret on 15 July, 'for rumors were flying that we would have our throats cut or at the very least [that we would] be carried off to prison.'[35]

Now the fears of many deputies that they would be arrested or even killed, their 'trepidation,' as Michelet put it, that each moment 'might be their last,'[36] have long been incorporated into the standard narrative of the legendary events that launched the French Revolution.[37] These fears, however, have generally been presented as little more than fleeting emotions and, as a result, there has been little serious effort by historians to consider their long-term political ramifications. Yet, it would not seem unreasonable to suggest the possibility that, to take the words of trauma researcher Daniel Weiss, the 'disruption of the working model of the world as a relatively safe and non-threatening environment' to which the deputies were exposed might well have had some impact on their future behavior,[38] especially considering how unprepared these hitherto law-abiding 'establishment types' were for this disruption.[39] In particular, it would not seem unreasonable to suggest that traumatic recollections of the terror that the monarch and his agents had provoked in June/July 1789 might well have had some impact on political and constitutional decisions that they would be making over the next two years regarding the place of the monarchy in the new political order.

In contrast to the recent emphasis of many historians on the prerevolutionary 'desacralization' or 'dethronement' of the monarchy,[40] my own research on the deputies of the Constituent Assembly indicates that, on the eve of the meeting of the Estates-General, the vast majority of them, and in particular those representing the Third Estate, retained a strong emotional and ideological attachment to Louis XVI as an individual and to the monarchy as an institution.[41] Thus, for example, the Le Mans magistrate Ménard de la Groye depicted the king 'tenderly' gazing upon the deputies 'as his cherished children' at the 5 May opening session of the Estates, and, in the same diary entry, looked forward to the representatives following the lead of the government, which 'will direct our work' and 'put into our hands the basic outlines of a reasonable legislation which will ensure public happiness.' Along the same lines, to provide only two additional illustrations of what deputy letters and diaries reveal to have been widely held sentiments as the Estates opened, the Troyes businessman Camusat de Belombre stated that he had been 'deliciously affected' by the acclamations and tears 'of a huge crowd eager to give witness of its gratitude toward its king,' while the future Jacobin Club president Gaultier de Biauzat, wrote that a cry of '*vive le roi*' that had been uttered 'may have seemed to have come from a single mouth, but it was a mouth which carried with it the voice of the entire kingdom.'[42]

Given the degree of positive affect invested in the monarch before the meeting of the Estates, the deputies of the Third were left, in the aftermath of the crisis of summer 1789, with the difficult psychological task of processing an emotional experience in which a benign and protective paternal figure who had hitherto largely evoked feelings of gratitude and affection suddenly and unexpectedly emerged as the source of an enormous threat. To be sure, a large number of deputies sought to displace conscious blame or hostility away from Louis himself by resorting to some version of the proverbial 'good king, evil advisers' motif to explain what had happened in June and July, with Delandine's assertion that 'the best of kings' had been 'led astray by the arrogant aristocrats who surround him' and Nairac's accusation that 'plotters' had employed 'criminal means' to convince the king that the Third Estate was seeking 'to make him lose his crown' being two fairly typical examples.[43] Indeed, as Norman Hampson has noted, 'it was to be an extraordinarily long time' before Louis was definitively repudiated by a group of men 'who were determined to believe that, at heart, he was on their side.'[44] Yet in the aftermath of the July crisis, however stubbornly many deputies may have attempted to cling to some residue of the positive feelings toward the king which they had brought with them to Versailles, and to banish from consciousness any thoughts or perceptions that clashed with these positive feelings, it would be difficult to imagine that they did not, in some corner of their minds, think of the king as someone who had been prepared to have them killed. Or, putting it in even more blunt terms that probably better reflect the broad-stroke 'primitive thinking' that psychoanalysts attribute to the unconscious, it would seem reasonable to assume that, in their heart of hearts, many deputies saw the king as someone who had literally tried to kill them.

In trying now to connect this analysis of the emotional impact of the events of summer 1789 upon the deputies to the Assembly's visceral fear of Mirabeau or of any other potentially ascendant colleague, let us begin with an observation made by Louis XVI biographer John Hardman. According to Hardman, all revolutionary figures who came into close political contact with the king soon found that such contact caused revolutionary authority and influence to 'melt from them.'[45] Indeed, from the Monarchien and 'Anglomane' faction of Mounier and Malouet to Mirabeau and Lafayette to the Duport/Barnave/Lameth 'triumvirate,' the mere suspicion that a deputy trying to play a leadership role within the Assembly was prepared to enter into any form of association or negotiation with the king seems to have been sufficient to render that leader vulnerable to repudiation by moderate Assembly 'back-benchers' with whom he was actually in basic philosophical and ideological agreement.[46] More than the embodiment of an anti-revolutionary or anti-patriotic political principle or institution, the monarch, it seems, had also become a source of contamination who, in a curious reversal of the king of France's mythical power to cure scrofula through the 'royal touch,' was capable of infecting all those he touched politically. But how would it have been possible in 1789, 1790, or 1791 for any would-be political leader in France to work toward the establishment of some kind of effective governing system without being prepared to associate in some way with a monarchy that, however weakened, still exercised some control over the levers of administrative power and still commanded a significant amount of ideological loyalty among the citizenry? In this sense, the 'defensive liberalism' displayed by the Constituent Assembly, its instinctive recoil from any association with the 'royal leper,' and its instinctive fear of anyone thought to have been infected by him under-mined any possibility of stabilizing the system of Constitutional Monarchy to which the deputies were ostensibly committed.

Seen from this perspective, the 7 November edict barring deputies from the ministry appears as a particularly spectacular example of the Assembly's urge to confine the executive power to a 'quarantined zone.' Indeed, the use of the term 'urge' here is explicitly meant to suggest the visceral emotional energy, the intense fear and suspicion of royal power that de Cicé seems to have been able to activate in order to secure the passage of this measure. Similarly, the use of the term 'quarantined zone' is meant to add an emotional charge to the more emotionally neutral description provided earlier of the 7 November edict as an example of the Assembly's devotion to a strict version of separation of powers, thereby suggesting that, far from emerging from what historians often present as a kind of political philosophy seminar, the 'principle' of separation of power was largely invoked in this case, to take Jean-Paul Clément's phrase, as 'an instrument of war against royal authority.'[47] Moreover, the visceral urge to conduct this essentially defensive war, the urge, in effect, to disarm the Crown and ensure that it would not be able to join forces with dangerous 'giants' like Mirabeau, can, I would suggest, be largely seen as a psychologically rooted protective mechanism that was being deployed against any possible repetition of the terrifying experience that the deputies had endured the previous summer. While prerevolutionary attacks on 'ministerial despotism' and other manifestations of the eighteenth-century ideological assault on absolutism undoubtedly helped to make such political warfare 'thinkable,' as Keith Baker might put it,[48] it was, I would argue, the wrenching experience of June and July 1789 that was largely responsible for giving the idea of such warfare its emotional resonance and turning it into a living reality.

Yet, though ordinary conscious suspicion of royal power among the deputies obviously increased significantly as a result of their experience of the events of summer 1789, important aspects of that experience seem to have been, as already noted, banished from the deputies' conscious awareness. In particular, we have seen how anger and hostility toward the king as the ultimate source of the dangers to which many felt they had been exposed seem to have been deflected onto 'evil advisers,' most of whom, as the 'vanquished' of summer 1789, had been effectively removed from positions of authority and influence after Louis XVI's 15 July pledge to cooperate with the Assembly. Of course, despite optimistic deputy assertions that the 'aristocratic cabal is totally defeated' and that the king was 'now surrounded only by honest men,'[49] this purge of the Court and the accompanying tearful reconciliation with the monarch that was supposedly sealed by Louis' visit to Paris on 17 July did not entirely dispel fears of the possibility of further royal aggression. Nevertheless, the months of relative calm that followed the resolution of the July crisis were marked, as Timothy Tackett has recently shown, by a significant reduction in overt references in deputy correspondence to anti-revolutionary plots and conspiracies.[50] As the deputies focused their attention on fashioning a constitution, the strong attachment to the king and to the monarchy that they had brought with them to Versailles – and their own rather moderate ideological and temperamental proclivities – seemed to come to the fore on many important occasions as they sought to create a delicate balance between emerging democratic sentiment and traditional monarchical authority. For example, the granting on 21 September 1789, in direct opposition to the principle of separation of powers, of a suspensive royal veto that could only be overturned if contradicted by *two* succeeding assemblies should be seen, in my view, as a reflection of a powerful inclination among the deputies to allow the king to maintain a significant degree of independent leverage in the lawmaking process.[51]

But if what Tackett calls 'a persistent longing for the patriarchal leadership of a good king' helped ensure that the deputies would seek to provide a significant place for the monarch in the new constitutional system and if the king, 'like a father in the midst of his children,' remained intermittently capable through most of the tenure of the Assembly of inspiring 'tears of joy and tenderness' among the representatives,[52] the traumatic residue of the frightening sense of vulnerability experienced during the original revolutionary crisis would, it can be suggested, also take its toll. While a large number of deputies continued to feel some degree of conscious affection for and loyalty to the king, Louis was also, I have been suggesting, being thought of by many of the same deputies, on some level of psychic reality, as their potential murderer. Coming a month and a half after the same Assembly had granted the executive power the ability to delay the passage of legislation for up to six years (that is to say, three 2-year legislative sessions), the sudden invocation on 7 November of the principle of separation of powers to block the possibility of a dangerous and potentially criminal alliance between an untrustworthy executive and ambitious legislators might be construed as an impulsive 'correction' in which a powerful sediment of unconscious anger and hostility exacted its due.[53]

Now it might be objected at this point that even if there is a certain plausibility to envisioning the edict of 7 November as a kind of counter-balance to the Assembly's decision on the veto issue, couldn't this 'correction' have easily resulted from a shift in the ebb and flow of political forces that had nothing to do with the unconscious feelings being posited here? Indeed, isn't it entirely possible that a significant proportion of deputies reached an entirely conscious and 'rational' conclusion that, given the terms of the suspensive veto, such a 'correction' was necessary to prevent the king from having *too* much influence in the legislative process, that the right to delay legislation, for however long, was one thing and the opportunity to exercise decisive influence over the legislature through compliant deputy-ministers quite another? But while such considerations would obviously have to be taken into account in any effort to provide a comprehensive analysis of the passage of the 7 November edict, one key indicator seeming to point to the influence of unacknowledged traumatization is the manner in which this measure was passed. Whereas the veto question was discussed in depth on the Assembly floor over the course of several weeks while simultaneously being the subject of intense public debate outside the Assembly, the deputy/minister edict seemed to come literally 'out of the blue,' being decreed almost unanimously after a bare minimum of debate. Further indicating the apparent impulsivity of the rush to quarantine the executive power is the contrast between the near unanimity manifested by the deputies on 7 November and the close division of the previous day on the question of providing a 'consultative voice' for ministers within the Assembly. Though some of the Assembly's most influential orators, including Lanjunais' Breton Club colleague Le Chapelier, had spoken in favor of Mirabeau's consultative voice proposal on the 6th,[54] no one seemed to feel the need to explain the sudden disappearance of support for this measure on the 7th. Rather, it is as if Montlosier's reference to the 'mystic sense' of Mirabeau's motion and Lanjunais' allusion to the potential damage that an 'eloquent genius' in the ministry could wreak were sufficient to trigger a wave of visceral fear and revulsion, a wave that swept away any distinction that might have been noted between allowing a ministerial presence in the Assembly and allowing deputies in the ministry, while, at the same time, sweeping away virtually all favorable sentiment that might have existed for either.

But even if a visceral sense of fear of what an eloquent genius like Mirabeau could do with the reins of royal government in his hands was indeed largely responsible for the passage of the edict of 7 November, the suggestion being made here about the possible role of unconscious motivation would seem to imply that the deputies were responding to something 'inside themselves' rather than to the realities of their situation, that their fear, in other words, was largely 'imaginary' rather than 'real.' Yet, it is quite clear that, far from their suspicion about the kind of machinations in which Mirabeau was likely to engage being nothing more than an internal 'figment of a frenzied preoccupation with power,'[55] the deputies had good reason to be fearful of royal power in general and Mirabeau's politically promiscuous schemes for advancing royal power in particular. After all, the dangers to which the representatives had been exposed in June and July 1789 had been anything but imaginary, and the presumption that the Crown might again seek to make use of its military assets or otherwise engage in further counterrevolutionary plotting could hardly be regarded as irrational or unreasonable. As for Mirabeau, though he does not seem to have actually received money from the king until spring 1790, his questionable relations with members of the royal family certainly date from much earlier. Indeed, even as he was promoting his plans for parliamentary government within the Assembly and discussing the formation of a new ministry with other deputies, he was cultivating a close political relationship with the king's brother, the Comte de Provence (the future Louis XVIII), to whom he submitted a memorandum on 15 October 1789 proposing that the royal family relocate to Rouen. Prefiguring, to some degree, the abortive flight to Varennes of June 1791, this memorandum argued that the king needed to get away from Paris in order to deal with the Assembly from a position of strength. At the same time, to round out an astonishingly versatile catalogue of intrigue and maneuver, Mirabeau was maintaining his pre-October Days relations with the Duc d'Orléans, considered then by many to be a major promoter of revolutionary radicalism, and would soon, along with Orléans, be a central target of a judicial investigation into plotting against the revolutionary régime from the left.[56] Clearly the deputies' fears of the Great Tribune did not arise from thin air.

However, though much historiographical and polemical energy has been expended in recent years in discussing the question of whether French revolutionary conspiracy fears were primarily 'real' or imaginary,'[57] it would perhaps be more helpful to focus on the mutually-reinforcing relationship which often exists between 'real' and 'imaginary' terrors. As the aftermath to the events of 11 September 2001 has once again made clear, ordinary human beings react to real disasters and real threats with a complex mixture of prudence and alarmism, coupled with a difficulty in distinguishing one from the other. As part of this complex mixture, real events that are particularly frightening and stressful frequently spawn a significant growth of exaggerated or imaginary fears. Haunted by the memory of what has happened to them and subject, through a process of 'hyperarousal' or 'hypervigilance,' to what psychiatrist Judith Herman calls the 'persistent expectation of danger,' individuals who have experienced such traumatic events tend to continually relive and reproduce aspects of that experience in the present.[58] Thus, shaken more than they realized by their original encounter with the king and his soldiers, many deputies of the Constituent Assembly were, it can be suggested, henceforth prone to react to any manifestation of royal political activity – and, in particular, to any hint of collaboration with the Crown – with a measure of alarmism and exaggerated suspicion. Or putting it another way, any manifestation of royal political activity would henceforth tend to carry with it a whiff of illegitimacy, and any form of 'breathing together' with the Court was henceforth subject to being construed as a form of criminal conspiracy. As reasonable as Mirabeau's ideas for Assembly/Crown cooperation may appear to observers accustomed to regard some degree of behind-the-scenes negotiation and discussion among all viable political forces as part of the normal political process in a parliamentary régime, these ideas may ultimately have been held hostage to the poisonous strain of fear and alarmism injected into the Revolution at its very outset.

Given the degree of emotional ambivalence toward the monarch and the monarchy that prevailed among the deputies as they worked to construct a new political order for France, it is hardly surprising that the Constituent Assembly was far from consistent in its efforts to delineate the position of the king in this new order. Indeed, the Assembly's ambivalent approach to the question of the monarchy might, with some justice, be seen as a reflection of the profound emotional ambivalence toward the king felt by many of the deputies. Since, however, a significant portion of the negative side of this ambivalence appears to have been banished to the realm of the unconscious, many of the deputies, it would seem, were not consciously aware of how deeply they had been affected by their initial confrontation with royal power and how deeply fearful of the monarch they actually were. As a result, it can be suggested, a low-grade but usually relatively quiescent apprehension of what the Crown and anyone associated with it might do could flare up and have an unacknowledged impact on policy-making at any moment.[59] Perhaps the insurrectionary energy of the October Days brought the memories of what had been experienced in

June and July closer to the surface. Perhaps the imminent accession to governmental power of Mirabeau helped trigger these recollections by reminding the deputies of the suspicious nature of the Great Tribune's efforts in mid-June to dissuade the Third Estate from proclaiming itself the National Assembly. For whatever reason or combination of reasons, it appears that the decision to exclude deputies from the ministry was just such a moment.

As for Mirabeau himself, in further elaboration of the symbiotic relationship between real dangers and imaginary ones, the post-November 1789 career of the Great Tribune provides an apt illustration of how imaginary or exaggerated fears of evildoing and conspiracy can sometimes contribute to the emergence in reality of the very things that are feared. For Mirabeau's parliamentary defeat of November 1789 led him to an ever more intense and more definitive involvement in clandestine and extra-parliamentary plotting and maneuvering. Barred from openly serving as a minister of the king, he instead became the king's secret paid adviser. Frustrated in his efforts to promote the development of the kind of parliamentary system in which politicians largely operate in public with the understanding that it is inevitable that some business will be conducted in private and blocked in his attempts to involve the Crown in such a system, he moved further and further into the shadows of counter-revolutionary conspiracy, culminating in his celebrated 47th note to the Court of December 1790 in which he presented a complex Machiavellian scheme to subvert the work of the Assembly.[60] Thus, just as realistic perceptions of Mirabeau's penchant for political scheming seem to have fueled exaggerated suspicions of betrayal and subversion, so did these suspicions themselves, in provoking a decree which made it harder to 'work within the system,' help generate actual betrayal and subversion. Though Mirabeau's ideas on parliamentary government were designed to allow him to become a kind of Horace Walpole or, speaking anachronistically, a kind of Lyndon Johnson of the French Revolution, the edict of 7 November helped ensure that, if he hadn't succumbed to an early natural death, he would almost certainly have become either an *émigré* or a victim of the guillotine.

Notes

1   *Mémoires biographiques, littéraires et politiques de Mirabeau*, ed. Lucas de Montigny (Paris, 1835), 5, p. 199. My translation here of '*honnêtes gens*' follows that of D. Wick, *A Conspiracy of Well-Intentioned Men: The Society of Thirty and the French Revolution* (New York, 1987).
2   See J. Dubois and R. Lagne, *Dictionnaire de la langue française classique* (Paris, 1960), p. 105.

3 *Mémoires, correspondance et manuscrits du général Lafayette* (Brussels, 1837), 4, p. 142.
4 F. Furet, 'Mirabeau,' *A Critical Dictionary of the French Revolution*, eds Furet and M. Ozouf, trans. A. Goldhammer (Cambridge, MA, 1989), p. 270.
5 For the most comprehensive analysis of Mirabeau's advocacy of British-style parliamentary government, see R. K. Gooch, *Parliamentary Government in France: Revolutionary Origins, 1789–1791* (Ithaca, NY, 1960).
6 *Archives parlementaires de 1789 à 1860 (Première série [1787–1799])*, 82 vols, eds J. Mavidal and E. Laurent (Paris, 1867–1913), 8, p. 243 (hereinafter *AP*). In J. J. Chevallier's view, Mirabeau was the only deputy 'who could distinguish between the penal responsibility of ministers and their simple political responsibility.' ('The Failure of Mirabeau's Political Ideas,' *Review of Politics,* 13 [1951], p. 95.)
7 *Révolutions de France et de Brabant*, 1 (late November 1789), p. 39.
8 See J. K. Wright 'National Sovereignty and the General Will,' in *The French Idea of Freedom: The Old Regime and the Declaration of Rights of 1789*, ed. D. Van Kley (Stanford CA, 1994), pp. 216–222.
9 *AP* 8, pp. 229–230.
10 Mounier, for example, declared on 13 July that 'in this moment of crisis, wouldn't the representatives of the nation betray their duty if they didn't warn the monarch of the dangers which imprudent advisers have not feared to visit on all of France' (ibid., p. 223).
11 *Courrier de Provence*, 11–14 September 1789, as found in *Select Documents Illustrative of the History of the French Revolution*, ed. L. G. Legg (Oxford, 1905), p. 131.
12 *AP* 9, p. 212.
13 See Furet, 'Mirabeau,' p. 269.
14 These negotiations can be followed most easily in L. Gottschalk and M. Maddox, *Lafayette in the French Revolution: From the October Days Through the Federation* (Chicago, 1973), pp. 26–41, 70–89.
15 *Journal d'Adrien Duquesnoy*, ed. R. de Crèvecoeur (Paris, 1894), 1, p. 493.
16 G. Chaussinand-Nogaret, *Mirabeau entre le roi et la Révolution* (Paris, 1986), p. 19.
17 A. Lameth, *Histoire de l'Assemblée constituante* (Paris, 1828), 1, p. 241.
18 See *AP* 9, p. 711.
19 Ibid., p. 714, where two voice votes on tabling Mirabeau's motion are termed 'inconclusive.'
20 Ibid., pp. 712–713.
21 See *Mémoires de M. le comte de Montlosier* (Paris 1830), 1, pp. 338–339; and *AP* 9, p.716.
22 Lafayette, *Mémoires*, 4, p. 154. For the prerevolutionary links between de Cicé and Lanjunais, see F. Cadilhon, *L'Honneur perdu de Monseigneur Champion de Cicé* (Bordeaux, 1996), pp. 192–193; and N. Aston, *The End of an Elite: The French Bishops and the Coming of the Revolution* (Oxford, 1992), pp. 219–220.

23 *AP* 9, p. 716; and *Journal des Etats-généraux* (Le Hodey) (7 November 1789), 5, p. 399.

24 See *AP* 9, p. 718; *Révolutions de Paris*, 7–14 November 1789, p. 42; and *Patriote français*, 8 November 1789, p. 2.

25 See for example G. Michon, *Essai sur l'histoire du parti feuillant: Adrien Duport* (Paris, 1924), pp. 313–318.

26 Duquesnoy, *Journal*, 1, pp. 9, 96.

27 See for example E. Dumont, *Souvenirs sur Mirabeau* (Paris, 1951), pp. 70–72. Cleverly trading on the ambiguity conveyed by the word '*peuple*,' which could have been construed as referring to all the people in France or only to the 'common people,' Mirabeau's designation amounted to a form of waffling on the central question of whether the Third Estate should declare that its assembly represented the entire nation.

28 Duquesnoy, *Journal*, 1, p. 463; 2, pp. 24–25.

29 Ibid., 1, p. 336.

30 R. Hofstadter, *The Paranoid Style in American Politics and Other Essays* (New York, 1965), pp. 31–32.

31 A more detailed analysis of the palpable fear that Mirabeau aroused among his colleagues from the very beginning of the Estates-General might take the following as its keynote: 'The comte de Mirabeau's experience of the Ancien Régime was thus without parallel. His future colleagues in the Constituent Assembly were lawyers, judges, and magistrates. He had been a defendant, a convict, a litigant.' (Furet, 'Mirabeau,' p. 265). Indeed, if the unusual circumstances of Mirabeau's early life had left him uniquely marginal with respect to pre-revolutionary society, these same circumstances seem to have rendered him uniquely equipped to thrive, or at least give the appearance of thriving, in the cauldron of the Revolution. As one who seemed to be operating so comfortably 'within his element,' Mirabeau might well have appeared even more dangerous to other deputies.

32 Chaussinand-Nogaret, *Mirabeau*, p. 18.

33 See T. Tackett, *Becoming a Revolutionary: The Deputies of the French National Assembly and the Emergence of a Revolutionary Culture (1789–1790)* (Princeton, 1996), p. 226.

34 Such at least is the conclusion that emerges from a perusal of the thumbnail sketches of the deputies provided by E. Lemay, *Dictionnaire des Constituants*, 2 vols (Paris, 1991).

35 'Lettres de Lofficial,' ed. Leroux-Cesbron, *La nouvelle revue rétrospective*, 7 (1897), p. 90; and Gantheret, letter to his brother-in-law, private collection of Françoise Misserey, Dijon. References to rumors of impending arrests three weeks earlier include J. P. Bouillé, letter of 28 June 1789, 'Ouverture des Etats généraux de 1789,' ed. A. Macé, *Revue de la Révolution: Documents inédits* 14 (1889), p. 26; and J. F. Gaultier de Biauzat, *Gaultier de Biauzat, député du Tiers état aux Etats généraux de 1789*, ed. F. Mège (Clermont-Ferrand, 1890), letter of 25 June 1789, 2, p. 141.

36 J. Michelet, *History of the French Revolution*, trans. C. Cocks (Chicago, 1967), p. 183.

37 For one of countless examples, see G. Lefebvre, *The Coming of the French Revolution*, trans. R. R. Palmer (Princeton, 1947), p. 92.

38 See D. Weiss, 'Psychological Processes in Traumatic Stress,' *Journal of Social Behavior and Personality*, 8(5) (1993), p. 14. In suggesting in the pages that follow that many of the deputies may well have been 'traumatized' by the sudden feeling of endangerment and vulnerability that they experienced during the summer of 1789, I am by no means asserting that any of them developed anything comparable to what would be known today as 'post-traumatic stress syndrome.' Indeed, the evidence available to us in deputy letters and diaries and in other sources is hardly sufficient to allow even the most experienced of clinical professionals, let alone the present writer, to make such an evaluation (though it is entirely possible that some deputies may have been affected in such a way). Rather, for purposes of this chapter, the relevant point to be made is that certain symptoms associated with being traumatized seem to be part of a 'normal' reaction to intensely stressful events, especially to events in which one feels that one's life is in danger. In particular, as will be seen later in this chapter, those exposed to such events frequently manifest 'hypervigilance' or 'hyperarousal' long after the event is past, acting, as Judith Herman puts it, in terms of a 'persistent expectation of danger.' See Herman, *Trauma and Recovery* (New York, 1992), pp. 35–36, and L. S. O'Brien, *Traumatic Events and Mental Health* (Cambridge, UK, 1998), pp. 44–46.

39 For lack of preparation for a stressful event as a significant factor in increasing the psychological impact of such an event, see A. Shalev, 'Stress versus Traumatic Stress,' as found in *Traumatic Stress: The Effects of Overwhelming Experience on Mind, Body, and Society*, eds B. A. van der Kolk *et al.* (New York, 1996), p. 87.

40 See for example D. Van Kley, *The Damiens Affair and the Unraveling of the Ancien Régime, 1750–1770* (Princeton, 1984), pp. 246–255; R. Chartier, *The Cultural Origins of the French Revolution*, tr. L. Cochrane (Durham NC, 1991), pp. 111–135; and F. Furet and R. Halévi, *La Monarchie républicaine: La Constitution de 1791* (Paris: 1996), p. 56.

41 This research forms part of a manuscript now in preparation, the working title of which is 'Living the Revolution: Trauma and Denial in the French Constituent Assembly.'

42 F. R. Ménard de la Groye, journal entry of 5 May 1789, *Correspondance (1789–1791)*, ed. F. Mirouse (Le Mans, 1989), pp. 21–22; N. J. Camusat de Belombre, letter of 9 May 1789, 'Le Journal de Camusat de Belombre,' ed. H. Diné, *Annales historiques de la Révolution française*, 37 (1965), p. 263; and Gaultier de Biauzat, letter of 4 May 1789, 2, p. 26.

43 A. F. Delandine, entry of 20 June 1789, *Mémorial historique des Etats généraux* (n.p., 1789), 2, p. 169; and P. P. Nairac, entry of 22 June 1789, 'Journal,' *Archives départementales d'Eure*, 5 F 63, fol. 84.

44 N. Hampson, *Prelude to Terror: The Constituent Assembly and the Failure of Consensus, 1789–1791* (Oxford, 1988), p. 53.

45 See Hardman, *Louis XVI* (New Haven, 1993), p. 207.

46 For a more detailed analysis of this point, see B. Shapiro, 'Self-Sacrifice, Self-Interest, or Self-Defense? The Constituent Assembly and the "Self-Denying Ordinance" of May 1791,' *French Historical Studies*, 25 (2002), pp. 625–656.

47 See Clément, *Aux sources du libéralisme français: Boissy d'Anglas, Daunou, Lanjunais* (Paris, 2000), p. 99.

48 See K. Baker, 'The French Revolution: Possible Because Thinkable or Thinkable Because Possible: A Response to William Doyle,' *Proceedings of the Western Society for French History: Selected Papers of the 2002 Annual Meeting*, ed. B. Rothaus (Greeley, CO, 2004), pp. 184–190.

49 J. F. Palasne de Champeaux, letter of 19 July 1789, 'Correspondance des députés des Côtes-du-Nord aux Etats généraux et à l'Assemblée nationale constituante,' ed. D. Tempier, *Bulletin et mémoires de la Société d'émulation des Côtes-du-Nord*, 26 (1888), p. 238.

50 See Tackett, 'Conspiracy Obsession in a Time of Revolution: French Elites and the Origins of the Terror, 1789–1792,' *American Historical Review*, 105 (2000), pp. 702–704.

51 For a very different reading of the meaning of the granting of the suspensive veto, see K. Baker, *Inventing the French Revolution* (Cambridge, UK, 1990), pp. 252–305; and F. Furet, *Revolutionary France*, p. 77. In this regard, also see B. Shapiro, 'Opting for the Terror?: A Critique of Keith Baker's Analysis of the Suspensive Veto of 1789,' *Proceedings of the Western Society for French History: Selected Papers of the 1998 Annual Meeting*, ed. B. Rothaus (Greeley, CO, 1999), pp. 324–334.

52 Tackett, *Becoming a Revolutionary*, p. 79; and P. F. Lepoutre, letter of 5 February 1790, *Député-paysan et fermière de Flandre en 1789: La Correspondance des Lepoutre*, eds J. P. Jessenne and E. Lemay (Lille, 1998), p. 189. Lepoutre is referring here to the Assembly's reaction to the king's appearance before it on 4 February 1790.

53 In the larger work mentioned in note 41 above, I discuss the 'correction' described here in terms of the tendency of trauma victims to oscillate between denial of what has happened to them and various forms of 're-living' of the trauma that they have experienced, a pattern of behavior that Judith Herman calls the 'dialectic of trauma.' (See Herman, *Trauma and Recovery*, pp. 42–47.)

54 See *AP* 9, pp. 711–714; and *Patriote français* (8 November 1789), p. 1.

55 See F. Furet, *Interpreting the French Revolution*, trans. E. Forster (Cambridge UK, 1981), p. 54.

56 See Gottschalk and Maddox, *Lafayette: From the October Days*, pp. 14–24, 36–39; and B. Shapiro, *Revolutionary Justice in Paris, 1789–1790* (Cambridge, UK, 1993), pp. 118–120.

57 See for example R. Spang, 'Paradigms and Paranoia: How Modern is the French Revolution?', *American Historical Review*, 108 (2003), pp. 127–129.

58 See Herman, *Trauma and Recovery*, pp. 35–36; and O'Brien, *Traumatic Events*, pp. 44–66. Also see D. LaCapra, *Writing History, Writing Trauma*

(Baltimore, 2001), p. 21: 'Tenses implode and it is as if one were back there in the past reliving the traumatic scene.'

59 According to trauma researchers, thoughts and images associated with previously experienced traumatic events usually make their presence felt only intermittently in the mental life of traumatized individuals, often alternating, as indicated in note 53 above, with periods in which denial of what has happened predominates.

60 See Chaussinand-Nogaret, *Mirabeau*, pp. 173–231.

3

The real and imagined
conspiracies of Louis XVI

John Hardman

Introduction

Hours before his death Louis XVI scoffed at the paranoia of his enemies: 'These men see daggers and poison everywhere!' Yet many would share the view of T. C. W. Blanning that the 'paranoid' fear of betrayal by the court was justified because it '*was* conspiring against the Revolution and it *was* seeking the armed intervention of the European powers'.[1]

The question of the extent of Louis XVI's conspiratorial activity must be considered from a double perspective: that of his contemporaries and that of the present day. In particular we need to distinguish between the evidence that was available to contemporaries – at the trial of the king, for example – and the evidence available to the modern historian. For example, people rightly assumed that Marie-Antoinette was in treasonable correspondence with her Austrian family to overthrow the Revolution but they lacked the evidence we have, especially that she betrayed the French war plans.

A fortiori, they produced no evidence that the king himself was engaged in such activities but assumed an identity of policies between Louis and Marie-Antoinette symbolized by their mealy-mouthed use of the phrase 'the court'. Most modern historians such as Tim Blanning and Munro Price also take this view, which we seek to modify. This assumption did immense damage to the king because, as Tom Kaiser has demonstrated, it tapped into a centuries-old hatred of Austria as the traditional national enemy which was intensified rather than diminished by the 'diplomatic revolution' of 1755, symbolized by the marriage of the Austrian Archduchess Marie-Antoinette to the future Louis XVI.[2]

Marie-Antoinette's influence on policy fluctuated over the years. In the period 1774–87 it was negligible, especially in foreign policy, the field in which the conspiracy was couched. In the period 1787–88 it was considerable. Louis was completely demoralized after the defeat of his reform program by the Assembly of Notables, and under Brienne and Necker – for both of whose appointments she was responsible – she attended ministerial *comités*. During the Revolution itself her influence was mixed: one of her adherents referred to 'the mass of cases where . . . [the king] eludes the queen', and she had no protégés as ministers.[3]

Then there is the question of the interpretation of given evidence. At his trial, the prosecution produced little or no evidence of Louis' dealings with the foreign Powers – or Marie-Antoinette's for that matter. They were both careful to burn any compromising papers. What the documents in the *armoire de fer* do reveal is how Louis used the money from his civil list – over which he exercised complete personal control – to mount an elaborate propaganda and secret-service machine with an extensive network of secret agents; he subsidized royalist journals and bought politicians, notably Mirabeau for 5,000 francs a month plus a lump sum in the case of success. It was this information which created the climate in which the trial of the king could proceed. And yet under different assumptions such evidence could be taken as proof that Louis was acting as an eighteenth-century constitutional monarch – La Porte, the Intendant of the Civil List playing John Robinson to Louis's George III! And did not the private notebook which Robespierre kept in 1793 reveal similar ambitions of political management? *Autres temps, autres moeurs.*

This chapter will explore these themes through three linked episodes in the Revolutionary career of Louis XVI. The first is the summoning of troops to the Paris region in the period 22 June to 14 July 1789. The second is the 'flight to Varennes' on 20 June 1791 –so-called after the little town or rather village where Louis and his family were stopped and sent back to the Tuileries palace whence they had 'escaped' some 18 hours earlier. But by definition, Varennes was not his destination, and the debate centers on what that destination was because the place suggests the motive. The third matter is the king's relationship to the war that France declared on Austria on 20 April 1792. We will try to ascertain both what the king's motives and plans actually were and those that the various pamphleteers and politicians attributed to him.

In all three cases the king's plans were kept secret, and in the climate of the times, when transparency and virtue were deemed to go hand in hand, that in itself constituted a conspiracy. And 'conspiracy' was – is – always used in a pejorative sense: Mirabeau's characterization of the *Society of Thirty* as a 'conspiracy of well-intentioned men' is presented as a bold paradox. So even if Louis's opponents had accepted our contention that the king left Paris on 20 June 1791 simply to renegotiate the constitution

– and not to flee France and restore the ancien régime – that would for them be no less a conspiracy. But we would argue that 'Varennes' was a well-intentioned conspiracy because Louis was right in declaring that France could not be governed under the proposed Constitution.

Conspiracy theories thrive on paucity of evidence or evidence which is difficult to interpret. This paucity is particularly acute in the three cases under study. In that of 1789 the only concrete evidence we have is the orders given to the troops. For Varennes, as one pamphlet admitted, the only concrete evidence is the declaration Louis left behind in the Tuileries and the direction in which Louis was travelling when he was stopped at Varennes. The evidence for Louis's dealings with the foreign powers in 1791–92 is confined to a single letter which could be a forgery. But this in itself could be suspicious: the king being careful to cover his conspiratorial tracks as when, according to once account, he burnt a whole box of papers in the house of the deputy mayor of Varennes.

Troop movements on the eve of the fall of the Bastille

The trigger for the rising symbolized by the storming of the Bastille was the dismissal of the popular minister Necker on 12 July, which seemed to be the final proof that the troops which the king had been summoning to the Paris Basin over the previous month were to be used against the Capital. It was commonly believed that the administration which succeeded Necker's, headed by the baron de Breteuil, planned to dissolve the National Assembly, arrest its leaders by *lettres de cachet*, and subdue Paris by force of arms. In fact we know little of Breteuil's plans – the main evidence adduced by Munro Price in his article on the Breteuil ministry relates to plans for raising money from loyal bankers. Price further stresses that Breteuil sought to negotiate with the Assembly in general and in particular with the duc d'Orléans (with whom Breteuil had family connections[4]). He probably wanted to enforce the provisions of the *séance royale* of 23 June 1789, in which the king sought to enforce a messy compromise which sacrificed the royal prerogative in a vain attempt to retain the society of orders in the régime of the Estates-General. Support for the last supposition comes from the retention of Laurent de Villedeuil, the minister for the interior, and Barentin, the Keeper of the Seals who tried to promulgate the provisions of the séance in the provinces even after the king had ordered the nobility and clergy to sit with the third estate on 27 June.

Nevertheless we do have the orders given to the troops: their destination and, in some instances, what they were to do when they reached it. Some of these were published by P. Caron in 1906[5] and the material at

Vincennes has been used by J. Godechot in *The Taking of the Bastille*.[6] Both authors, however, draw perverse conclusions from the valuable evidence they present and stick to their *arrière-pensée* that the king was planning a coup d'état. How, for example, can they ignore the implications of the following purely defensive order from Broglie, the king's generalissimo to Besenval, his field commander in Paris dated 1 July:

> The king consents that you assemble all the forces on which you can rely to safeguard the Royal Treasury and the Discount Bank and that you confine yourself to defending these two positions ... at a time when we are unfortunately not in a position to look to everything. I shall authorize the marquis d'Autichamp to remain in his command at Sèvres and then, if it becomes necessary, to bring up the Salis regiment *as reinforcements to protect Versailles, falling back on the palace if necessary*.[7]

So even as early as 1 July, when the insurrection in Paris and the 'conspiracy' of the king were both in their infancy, the maintenance of law and order, as the king told the Assembly on 10 July, was the priority. And the defense of Versailles. If one can impute any strategy to the king it might be this: to neutralize any attempt by the National Assembly, faced with the reintroduction of the program of the *séance royale*, to call Paris to its assistance as it was to do the following October to resolve a deadlock in proceedings in its favor.

But above all it was simply the safety of Versailles that was at stake. Godechot goes into some detail about where the troops are to be placed. Three cavalry regiments are to be stationed at La Muette; two regiments of dragoons are to go to Rambouillet; and a further cavalry regiment is to go to Marly. These orders were given between 22 and 28 June. But then 'on June 29 and 30, fresh orders were sent, proving that the king's plans were taking shape.' The troops were to get 'as close as possible to Paris.' The regiment of Nassau-Infanterie was to speed up its progress and go to Choisy-le-roi instead of Charenton while the Royal-Allemand was also to go to Choisy. Finally on 7 July Lauzun's hussars were summoned from Verdun to Marly. What did all these places have in common: La Muette, Rambouillet, Marly, and Choisy? Why does Godechot neglect to say that they were all royal châteaux? The troops were there to prevent their being sacked.[8]

This was not what was believed at the time. The author of *LE FUYARD ou le Baron de Besenval, général sans armée*,[9] believed that the plan concocted by Broglie and Besenval had been to invade Paris via the Champ de Mars, the Invalides and the Faubourg Saint-Germain, peopled by aristocratic accomplices, murder the population and hang their dismembered but still palpitating limbs from the trees lining the route to Versailles.

All this was done, however, 'without the king's knowledge' and at the risk of disturbing his serenity. The Assembly at first granted Besenval's request for safe passage to his native Switzerland, rescinded it under popular pressure and allowed him to be put on trial, when he was acquitted of all charges.

The respected *Le Moniteur* was scarcely less fanciful than *Le Fuyard*. On 11 July it regaled its readers with the story that the conseil d'état had debated:

> How to wind up the Estates-General and abduct its deputies at midnight . . .
> The sale of Lorraine to the emperor, who naturally will pay for it with the 6 millions which have been sent to him [by Marie-Antoinette].
> The holding of a séance royale at which the king will present four declarations.
> A declaration which will instantly dissolve the Estates-General.[10]

On 8 July the National Assembly, after an angry speech in which Mirabeau denounced the 'warlike preparations of the Court', petitioned the king to withdraw his troops from the Paris region. The king's reply, on the 10th, stressed that the troops 'were only intended to . . . maintain law and order.' If, however, the Assembly found their 'necessary presence' offensive he would, 'at the request of the Estates-General [sic]', transfer the Assembly to Noyon or Soissons and install himself in the nearby chateau of Compiègne to keep contact with it.'[11] This offer was variously regarded as a gibe tipped with irony, insulting, or sinister. Godechot considered that it 'redoubled' the 'apprehensions' of the Assembly. If so, it was because it would remove the pressure of Paris on the king. That was why he made the suggestion, in a letter which he drafted himself. And the idea remained at the heart of the king's plans in the next episode we consider, the flight to Varennes, and surfaced in the very last days of the monarchy.

Varennes

On the night of 20/21 June 1791 the king and the royal family secretly and in disguise left the Tuileries and were conveyed eastward in a large coach or berline, passing through Châlons and Sainte-Ménéhoude. Arriving at Varennes-en-Argonne, they were prevented by the inhabitants from crossing the River Aire to the other half of the town where their change of horses lay. They were detained in the house of the deputy mayor until commissioners from the National Assembly arrived with orders to take them back to Paris. These facts alone are agreed; and also that whatever Louis's destination, it wasn't Varennes, though David Jordan makes the somewhat disturbing mistake of thinking that the river Aire, which divided Varennes, formed the frontier with Luxembourg![12] This may be a Freudian slip, since many historians believe that Louis's intention was to emigrate. This leads them either to deny or circumvent another fact as solid as the details of Louis's journey, namely that the king's destination was the fortified hill town of Montmédy in Lorraine; and the debate centers on what that destination was because the place suggests the motive. If Louis was planning to emigrate then his enterprise acquires a foreign, treasonable tincture.

Louis considered flight on two occasions before 'Varennes': on 15 July and 5 October 1789, when the women were marching on Versailles. In July flight would have been futile, for as his commander-in-chief put it, 'we can certainly go to Metz but what do we do when we get there?'[13] If Louis had left on 15 July, he would have had no party. But having made concessions, like Charles I in 1640–41, he could on 5 October, like Charles, have raised his standard with some hope of success.

Flight from Versailles, Louis considered, would have been ignoble in a king, and shown cowardice. But it would have been open, no conspiracy. Leaving Paris, however, where he rightly regarded himself as a prisoner, would have been not flight but escape, and a prisoner of war has a duty to escape. But precisely because he was a prisoner, the escape would have to planned secretly, to be a conspiracy. And when he finally escaped from Paris it was in the dead of night, if the shortest one, 20–21 June, when it never becomes truly dark.

Darkness was the cloak of the conspirator. Mirabeau understood that when he warned La Marck, his interlocutor with the court:

> Remember . . . that you must never under any pretext be an accomplice or even a confidant in a secret escape [*évasion*] and that a king must leave in broad daylight if he wants to continue as a king.[14]

To appreciate the force of these words it must be remembered that Mirabeau at the same time was advocating a royal breakout to Compiègne under military escort. Instead Louis went 'at night like a broken king' – the words T. S. Elliot applied to Charles I in 'Little Gidding.'

Broken, it seemed to his subjects and his historians, by his deception. The deception was not just the cloak of darkness, nor his disguise as a servant. (Why, Michlelet asked, did Louis not wear instead the red uniform of an admiral with gold braid he had worn when inspecting the naval works at Cherbourg instead of packing it away in the carriage box?) It was also the communiqué that Louis sent to all the French diplomatic agents after the abortive Saint-Cloud departure stating that he was free, that he was no more than the 'first functionary' of the people and that he rejoiced in the constitution and the Revolution.

In fact when the crowd abetted by the National Guard forced the royal family to get out of their carriage and abandon the attempt to go to the château of Saint-Cloud on the outskirts of Paris for Easter 1791, the king finally made the decision to escape. Yet at precisely this moment he dissembled to cover his tracks and issued the circular, 'the entirely novel language of which,' as Michelet rightly says,

> Wherein everybody perceived the stamp of falsehood, and this false, jarring voice, did the king incredible harm; and whatever attachment was still felt for him could not withstand the contempt inspired by his duplicity.[15]

Indeed the parallel actions of the circular and urgent preparations for flight mirror Louis's simultaneously calling for the union of the orders in June 1789 and summoning troops to the Paris basin. But even here appearances can be deceptive: the circular was sent on the insistence of Montmorin, the foreign secretary whom Louis could not tell he had already decided on flight.

What did Louis hope to achieve by flight? Evidence was and is scanty. As one otherwise hostile pamphlet put it, 'His [the king's] intentions are his own, they are his secret; he has not revealed them in any way. There are presumptions against him but presumptions are not proofs.' The same pamphlet asks the question, 'how far has . . . [the king] acted culpably?' and concludes, 'It is in the manuscript he left behind that the measure of the reproach to be made against him is to be found.'[16] This has to be the basis of any analysis.

Another pamphlet, the *Opinion d'un publiciste*, also thought it was idle to speculate on where Louis's coach was heading: 'All we know for certain is that he was within France and indeed well within its frontiers when he was stopped.'[17] We do in fact know Louis's destination: the hill fortress of Montmédy in Lorraine. For this there is abundant evidence and as Louis said any doubters had only to inspect the accommodation which had been arranged for housing the royal family in the town.

A recent author has discovered a memorandum which the baron de Breteuil intended to be delivered to the king on his arrival at Montmédy. This advocates a restoration of the ancien régime *tout court* –even the compromise of the *séance royale* of 23 June was rejected. Breteuil intended to be Louis's prime minister and had the queen's support, but the force of the discovery is softened by the same author's conclusion that the letter from Louis giving Breteuil plenipotential powers is probably a forgery.[18]

So we are left to piece together the scanty evidence. The spur to flight was the abortive Saint-Cloud departure but there was also a deadline– a point after which flight would lose its purpose. Louis had to get out of Paris before the constitution was finalized in July. Otherwise he would be forced either to accept the constitution as it stood or reject it, which meant abdicating. There was no possibility of his negotiating its clauses from the Tuilieries.

At the same time the primary elections to the successor assembly, the Legislative, were under way in which, as the historian of the Jacobin clubs puts it, 'never before had Jacobin intervention in the electoral process been so flagrant.'[19] In possibly the first sustained analysis of how the Jacobin Clubs worked, Louis expresses the fear that as a result of their influence,

> if one can detect any disposition on the part . . . [of the primary assemblies] to go back on anything it is in order to destroy the remains of the monarchy and set up a metaphysical and doctrinaire form of government which would not work.[20]

The influence of the Jacobin Clubs had also destroyed Louis's chief hope in the period 1790/91: that the 'wise men of the Assembly' would off their own initiative strengthen the executive. This was not a vain hope. On 23 September 1790 Le Chapelier had proposed that seven new members be added to the constitutional committee to give a coherent final draft to a constitution which had been voted piecemeal over the previous twelve months. Among the seven were Barnave, Alexandre de Lameth, and Adrien Duport – dubbed the 'triumvirs' – who quickly established control over the committee. These men had been the leaders of the Left in 1789 but now they wanted to 'stop the Revolution,' as Barnave put it on 15 July 1791, before it turned to the redistribution of property.

In the spring of 1791 they made contact with the Court. Two members of the group, Beaumetz and d'André, probably saw the king on 19 April while Montmorin, the foreign secretary, Mirabeau, Barnave, and Lameth had several meetings.[21] They probably simply discussed the revision of the constitution but after the king's flight many, including Robespierre, thought they were conspiring to plan or at least turn a blind eye to the flight itself.

The spring discussions would have centered on how the constitutional committee's initial successes in strengthening the executive had, under pressure from the clubs, been reversed with for example the king's loss of the prerogative of mercy, which was dear to him, and a clause stipulating that he must reside not more than 20 leagues from the Assembly –which meant, however, that flight to Compiègne would still be legal. As Louis puts it in his declaration,

> The nearer the Assembly approached the end of its labours, the more the wise men were seen to lose their influence, together with a daily increase of clauses which could only make government more difficult . . . the mentality of the clubs dominated everything.

The king's declaration offers a detailed and specific critique of the new constitution, beginning with the general observation that, 'in contempt of the *cahiers*,'

> The Assembly has denied the king any say in the constitution by refusing him the right to grant or withhold consent to the articles which it regards as constitutional [and] by reserving for itself the right to place such articles in that category as it sees fit.

Apart from an input into framing the constitution, Louis asks for the right to initiate legislation, an absolute veto and, possibly, the right to dissolve parliament – i.e., the English system. He wants the power to negotiate peace treaties subject to ratification by the assembly – again as in England. But he accepts the loss of the power to declare war as a corollary of the surrender of the power of the purse which he intended to make to the Estates-General before they opened. He wants to negotiate the religious settlement with the Pope and end the schism. And he wants a bodyguard to protect him from pressure from the crowd.

Louis's 'Declaration to all Frenchmen' would have been his manifesto if he had recovered his liberty. But the document did not by the fact of his recapture fall to the ground. The *Opinion d'un publiciste*, offered an intriguing analysis of the posthumous status of the text *'if the king persisted in his Declaration.'*[22] Louis, it argued, had been misled by evil advisers into thinking that by giving his consent willy-nilly to all the legislation presented to him between 5 October and his flight he could taint the whole constitution with nullity on the grounds that he was not a free agent. This deep game, however, was futile because Louis properly had no role in the making of the constitution: he merely had to be informed of the laws so he could execute them – the extreme crown lawyer view of the role of the parlements in the ancien régime. Or, as Prudhomme put in the *Révolutions de Paris*, the king was no more than a herald-at-arms patiently waiting outside the legislature to learn what decrees he had to proclaim.[23]

As regards ordinary legislation, however, the *publiciste* has a more nuanced view. True the king could not have his cake and eat it:

> There is no provision in the constitution for the king to be able to sanction decrees . . . and then subsequently announce in a private document that he no longer adheres to them when he could in the first place have suspended their operation by a manifest veto.

However, it was open to the king to tell the subsequent legislature and even the one after that he had not been free and wished to exercise his suspensive veto retrospectively. And if the subsequent legislatures concluded that this had been the case or that the legislation was otherwise defective they could rescind it. Only with the third legislature could the matter rest, and that because the king's veto was only for two legislatures in any case.[24]

The duplicity of the king in sanctioning decrees of which he did not approve was matched, however, by a similar duplicity – even conspiracy – on the part of the Assembly: to turn a blind eye to the fact that the king was, as one deputy put it, 'playing possum.' After the king's flight, Adrien Duport told the Assembly that had the king refused his sanction to any of the decrees, 'you would have declared what you declare now that you had no need for any sanction on the king's part to establish your constitution.' But he added, it was fortunate that the king had not spoken his mind because his sanction had smoothed the passage of legislation which the country would otherwise have regarded as too radical 'until it was ready to entrust its destinies to your zeal.'[25]

It could also be argued that the Assembly was engaged in a conspiracy against the nation in drawing what was termed 'a religious veil' over the fact that it was denying the king the role which the country, in its *cahiers*, had demanded for him. Pétion, for example, who travelled with the royal family on its humiliating return from Varennes, wrote in a private letter to Brissot:

> The people would complain if the king were stripped of all his prerogatives. There aren't twenty *cahiers* which don't instruct the deputies to make laws in conjunction with the king. The suspensive veto only leaves him with the appearance of power which I think it is impossible that he can abuse given permanent assemblies.[26]

Louis considered that Pétion was his personal enemy, yet his private analysis is identical to Louis's public one in his Declaration.

Perhaps out of guilty conscience, the National Assembly while suppressing the king's declaration revised the constitution in the light of it: the civil constitution was removed from the constitution and made subject to repeal, as was the king's loss of the prerogative of mercy, and the king was given his own bodyguard. The revisions were limited because of an unholy alliance between the Right, who were playing a *politique du pire* and the Left. On 26 August the constitutional committee's proposal to restore the initiative in financial legislation was rejected.

The opposition to the revision was led, on the Left, by Robespierre. Robespierre's analysis of the king's objectives in leaving Paris is similar to my own, though naturally he condemns them. Robespierre did not think that the king's flight was designed to bring about the restoration of the ancien régime. Nor, he adds, 'could it have been upon Leopold and the King of Sweden and on the army [of *émigrés*] beyond the Rhine that he placed his hopes.' No, Robespierre argued, a deeper conspiracy was afoot: the king intended to do a deal with the Assembly which would enable the *émigrés* to return voluntarily to France. (Louis mentions this objective in his manifesto.)[27]

Louis's escape, Robespierre asserted, was effected either in collusion or at least in connivance with leaders of the Assembly such as Barnave, Lameth, and Duport, and with Lafayette. 'The king,' Robespierre proclaimed, 'fled with the consent of Lafayette.'[28] No evidence for this assertion has survived but on 21 June one deputy said Lafayette should be interrogated by the president of the Assembly as to whether for several weeks he had given orders that the king was not to leave the palace after midnight. Barnave said this was a slur on the actions of a man who was needed to restore order and carried the day.[29]

The 'triumvirs' according to Robespierre would 'at first ask for very small sacrifices to bring about a general reconciliation;' and they would have 'little trouble in inducing a weary people to accept a deal, a half-way compromise.' 'You will have observed,' he added, 'how . . . [the king] distinguishes between those things in the constitution which he finds offensive and those he deigns to find acceptable'. Robespierre also appreciated the timing of the king's flight: four times he employs the rhetorical refrain, 'why did he choose this precise moment to go?' And answers: 'he chose the moment' when the primary assemblies were in progress and with the prospect of a successor Assembly more radical than its predecessor and prepared to 'revoke a portion of its measures' – just as Louis had said in his declaration.[30]

For Robespierre, the attempt by the king to modify the constitution was just as much a 'conspiracy' as would have been an attempt to flee France and restore the ancien régime by force of arms. Indeed it was worse because it involved corrupting men who had made the Revolution. Robespierre could understand why men like the prince de Condé, who had lost everything in the Revolution, should oppose it but he could never forgive those who had benefited from the Revolution and then turned against it. These were the real traitors.

Others, though, assessed Louis's guilt in more conventional terms. Nevertheless, the Assembly came up with the most far-fetched conspiracy theory of all; namely that the king had been 'abducted' on the night of 20/21 June. Not only did they not believe this – for one thing Louis would have had to have been forced to change into his servant's costume at gunpoint – but they did not expect anyone else to either. It was a purely conventional abduction – no one even pretended to explain what had taken place, for example whether the royal family had been drugged or held at knifepoint – and was a concept which was deeply insulting both to the king and the people.

Yet others went along with it in varying degrees; and first and foremost Bouillé. In a letter to the Assembly designed to deflect popular wrath from the king toward himself, Bouillé claimed not indeed that he had physically abducted the king – that would have been difficult from Lorraine – but that he had subjected the king and queen to constant and unendurable pressure to leave by observing that the alternative was civil war and foreign invasion. For months the king and queen had resisted on the grounds that they had sworn to stay in Paris next to the Assembly. Only after the Saint-Cloud departure did Louis yield to Bouillé's redoubled pressure. The king would go to Montmédy and issue a proclamation summoning a new legislature which would base its work 'on the execution of the *cahiers*, which alone expressed the wishes of the nation.' These measures would be announced to the foreign powers which would 'suspend their vengeance.'[31]

This was largely fiction. Bouillé had been considering plans for Louis's escape but Louis first approached him not vice versa, and in any case Bouillé preferred Mirabeau's scheme for an open breakout and only fell in with Louis's plan out of obedience. He may have believed – as Louis also may have believed – that the Austrians/*émigrés* were about to invade, acting on the misinformation in the so-called 'Mantua forgery.' Nevertheless, Bouillé's letter may have achieved something of its purpose. At least the 'publiciste' thought that Bouillé was now 'dishonored in the eyes . . . of the royal family which has been seduced and led into a trap.'[32]

A variation on the *enlèvement*/Bouillé theme was provided by the pamphlet *Ce qu'il convient de penser du départ du roi*. This has no truck with a literal abduction, given that there were 'no external signs of violence.' Moreover, the plan was long meditated and the recent assurances of 'complete adherence to the constitution' 'were designed to lull the Nation into a false sense of security.' Therefore one of two things followed: 'Either the king is guilty of this inconceivable deception or – the writer's preferred version – someone has gained an ascendancy over all his decisions, directing them invincibly.' This succubus was the queen and the solution was to incarcerate Marie-Antoinette in the convent of Val-de-Grace.[33]

Louis XVI and the foreign powers

On 13 August, Barnave told the Assembly that the previous evening the Constitutional Committee had discussed whether it should resign in view of the Assembly's rejection of so many of its proposed revisions.

Nevertheless on 13 September, Louis accepted the constitution and was restored as head of the executive. He had suffered agonies of indecision which made him ill but he had no real choice but to accept. Nevertheless his letter of acceptance to the Assembly did not pull any punches: the constitution had been improved by incorporating some of his suggestions. Nevertheless, he added, 'I should be telling less than the truth if I said that I perceived in the executive and administrative resources sufficient vigor' to govern 'so vast an empire' as France. But he concluded: 'since opinions are at present divided I consent that experience alone shall decide.'

By this he meant that he hoped that the constitution would in time be amended, something which was difficult but technically possible. The debate now was whether Louis intended to abide by the verdict of the nation or whether he secretly sought to change – or rather, overthrow – the constitution by force. If the latter it would have to be foreign force (the *émigrés* and/or the Powers) for, as Marie-Antoinette confided, Varennes had demonstrated that, 'there is not a single town, not a regiment on which we can rely.'[34]

The best evidence that Louis both eschewed force and intended to give the constitution a go is found in a secret letter he wrote to his *émigré* brothers explaining why he had accepted the constitution. Since he didn't trust his brothers and knew that they would insist that his acceptance of the constitution was insincere so that they could claim to act in his name, he sent a copy of his letter to his brother-in-law, the Emperor Leopold II. This enabled Leopold to catch Artois and Provence in a lie:

> Not only do I believe that my brother-in-law, the king has genuinely accepted the constitution and is against any idea of counter-revolution but I have positive proof. So do Your Royal Highnesses: he has communicated his real intentions to you in a secret memorandum etc.[35]

This 'secret memorandum' points out that war will not be the walkover the *émigrés* imagine because, 'The leaders of the Revolution, those who control the levers of power both in Paris and the provinces, are committed up to the hilt to the Revolution.'[36] And, he added prophetically, 'They will use the national guards and arm the citizenry and they will begin by massacring those who are called aristocrats.' The war would be 'terrible because it will be motivated by violence and despair. Can a king contemplate all these misfortunes with equanimity?' And even if the invaders won, they would need to maintain an army of occupation because 'one can never govern a people against its inclinations' – even in despotisms such as that at 'Constantinople.'

People wanted the constitution because the 'lower portion of the people see only that they are reckoned with, [while] the bourgeoisie sees nothing above them. Vanity is satisfied.' So the 'sole means remaining' to the king was 'the junction of his will to the principles of the constitution' until the people of themselves saw the need for change, that it was 'impossible' to govern France by it. Meanwhile,

> Let the princes conduct themselves in such a way as to spare me the decrees against them that the Assembly may present for my sanction . . . . The courage of the nobility would be better understood if it returned to France to augment the forces of the men of good will . . .The true nobility would then have a splendid opportunity or regaining all of its prestige and a portion of its rights. What I say of the nobility could equally be applied to the monarchy.

It is a great pity for Louis's reputation that this letter was not intercepted and published. In the light of it, it seems perverse to doubt Louis's sincerity at least *at this point*. However the above paragraph contains the Cassandra-like prophecy of how the constitutional monarchy would be destroyed, the prospect of 'decrees against . . . [the *émigrés*] that the Assembly may present for my sanction.' For here we have the germ of a counterconspiracy, this time against the king himself.

On 31 August Marie-Antoinette had asked Barnave,

> Despite the decrees, the Constitution and the oaths, who can guarantee that . . . [the next legislature] will not want to change everything and that the republican party will not regain the upper hand? If that happens, where is the force to prevent it?[37]

The political grouping which has come to be known as the Girondins were not a majority in the Legislative Assembly, but the constitutional monarchists did not have sufficient moral fiber to shield the king from their attempt to de-popularize him by presenting him with legislation – against the non-juring clergy and against his own brothers – which they knew he was bound to veto. By these means, as T. C. W. Blanning has it, they sought 'the subversion of the constitution which had just been introduced.'[38]

And, *pace* Blanning, the only grouping which was unequivocally seeking 'the armed intervention of the European powers' was precisely the Girondins.[39] Their aim was to drive France into declaring war on the Emperor with the sole aim of placing his sister, Marie-Antoinette in an impossible position. As Brissot put it in December 1791,

> I have only one fear; it is that we won't be betrayed. We need great treasons; our salvation lies there, because there are still strong doses of poison in France and strong emetics are needed to expel them.[40]

Although the Girondin leaders worked out tactics in dinner parties (parties which Robespierre, who opposed war, thought in themselves to constitute conspiracies), their objectives themselves were quite open, advocated in parliament and the press, notably Brissot's *Patriote français*, and so lacked one essential ingredient of the true conspiracy. But this is splitting hairs.

The diplomat Bigot de Saint-Croix, in his *Histoire de la conspiration du 10 août 1792*, published days after Louis's execution, argued that 'without the war France would not be a republic.' His thesis is that as early as 1789 there was a faction conspiring to destroy the monarchy. The result of its efforts was that 'The first Assembly had deprived the king of the power to resist the incursions of the second.' In order to further their designs, the assemblies 'invented a raft of new oaths in order to supply the legislators with acts of resistance to punish or perjuries to presume.' The emigration achieved the dual purpose of creating both 'an imaginary connivance [on the king's part] with those who aspired to save the king' and 'the external threat which was necessary in order to propagate terror at home.'[41]

Bigot knew whereof he spoke. He was the envoy of the foreign secretary de Lessart to the electorate of Trier, the epicenter of the conflict between France and the Empire because the small army of French *émigrés* had taken refuge in the elector's dominions. The Girondins had been stridently demanding their dispersal but Louis wrong-footed them by informing the Assembly on 14 December that he had already given the elector an ultimatum. Bigot supervised the evacuation of the *émigrés* from the electorate. His mission accomplished, he wanted to return but de Lessart told him to stay put to give the lie to any Girondin claims that the *émigrés* had returned.

However, the Girondins' conspiracy to destroy the constitutional monarchy was matched by a parallel conspiracy by Marie-Antoinette and Breteuil who were secretly canvassing support for an 'armed congress' of the Powers to modify the constitution, perhaps in accordance with the *séance royale* of 23 June 1789. The armed congress – 'not war but the threat of war' – as she put it was very much the hobby horse of Marie-Antoinette and of her long-time favorite minister Breteuil, who had organized the Congress of Teschen in 1777 and had a great belief in the efficacy of congresses. No one else believed in an armed congress, not Mercy-Argenteau, the Austrian ambassador, not Leopold, not Frederick William II of Prussia.[42] Did Louis XVI? That is the question.

The correspondence relating to the congress was conducted entirely by Marie-Antoinette, though she claimed she was acting in the name of the king. Evidence that the king supported the idea is confined to a single letter to Frederick William II of Prussia dated 3 December 1791, which may be a forgery, and Fersen's account of a conversation with Louis in

February 1792.[43] This must be set against his secret memorandum to his brothers, for if Louis argued that the revolutionary leaders would not cave in before a full-blooded invasion, *a fortiori* they would not be swayed by the mere 'threat of war.' On the other hand the memorandum was written before the bad faith of the Girondins and the supine behavior of the constitutional monarchists in the Legislative Assembly became apparent, and it may be that by the winter of 1791 Louis had concluded that the constitution could not protect the monarch and the monarch could not protect the constitution.

Yet again Louis's triumph of 14 December when he announced the dispersal of the *émigré* concentrations may suggest that there was all still to play for in putting peace at the disposal of the constitutional monarchy. That hope, however, was soon dispelled by a blunder by the pacific Austrian chancellor Kaunitz when he sent France a note threatening to send in troops if it invaded the electorate of Trier. Kaunitz was secretly delighted that the *émigrés* had been dispersed and he knew that there was no risk of a French invasion since its objective had already been achieved. But he disliked French involvement in the affairs of the Holy Roman Empire and his clumsy response allowed the Girondins to ratchet up the conflict. A string of consequences was to follow: the queen was accused in the Convention of organizing an 'Austrian Committee;' the impeachment of the pacific de Lessart led to the resignation of the Feuillant ministry; the appointment by the king of a ministry of Girondin complexion then entailed the French declaration of war on Austria on 20 April.

The conspiracy-minded thought the king was playing a deep game – since the appointment of the Girondin ministry guaranteed the war which, at the risk of his life, might rescue him and restore him to the plenitude of his authority. But there is no evidence that Louis desired war nor that Marie-Antoinette for that matter worked for it. But though hitherto Marie-Antoinette had condemned both civil and foreign war, when her enemies brought it about she rejoiced, thinking they had fallen into a trap from which they could not extricate themselves. Louis certainly did not rejoice: when, on the advice of his Girondin ministers, he went down to the assembly to propose the declaration of war against Austria he was white as a sheet and stammered. He feared war and especially taking responsibility for it, even going to the lengths of making the ministers sign their individual advice and publishing it at the Imprimerie Royale. But he may have realized that the war could improve his position either in the case of an unlikely French victory or of defeat. His attitude to a foreign war can perhaps be summed up by what he had said to Mirabeau in the summer of 1790 concerning civil war: 'provided it arises neither through the king's wishes nor through his actions, he will prepare to face it'.[44]

As for the 'Machiavellian' appointment of the Girondin ministry, he had little alternative since few constitutional monarchists were keen to join de Lessart in an accusation of *lèse-nation*, the new crime voted by acclamation from which Vergniaud had pointedly observed the queen would not be exempt. Although the Girondins' notion of an 'Austrian committee' was pure fantasy, they were on the mark when their decree stipulated that 'anyone who participates . . . in a congress with the object of obtaining modifications to the constitution' would be guilty of the new crime.[45]

Louis sanctioned the decree immediately, whereas he had vetoed those aimed at his brothers and appointed its sponsors to the ministry, whether out of fear, a desire to give them enough rope to hang themselves, or the hope that, as Mirabeau had said, 'a Jacobin in the ministry is not a Jacobin minister,' that they would take responsibility for their power.

He was wrong. The Girondins acted as an opposition party in power, asking the king to sanction three decrees abolishing his constitutional bodyguard, placing him thus unarmed at the mercy of a camp of 20,000 *fédérés* at Paris, and ordering the deportation of non-juring priests. Louis responded by replacing the Girondin ministry by one of Feuillant complexion. This, together with the worsening military situation (Prussia having entered the war in July poised to invade France), ushered in the end game.

In these, the last desperate weeks of the monarchy, two conspiratorial episodes illustrate our story: the two opposing factions, the Girondins and the Feuillants with Lafayette both secretly asked the king to appeal personally to Frederick William to halt his advance. The king replied to Vergniaud, who had threatened the life of Marie-Antoinette, with cold contempt and frozen admonition: a cease-fire could only be effected by 'les moyens généraux' – that is, official diplomacy; he would not make that personal intervention which alone might have stopped the Prussian advance. And he could not refrain from the sub-acid observation that 'we owe the declaration of war entirely to the self-styled patriot ministers.' In which Louis was right. However, Vergniaud was equally right in reminding the king that 'he had been sadly deceived if he had been led to believe that not to depart from the letter of the constitution was to do all that he should.'[46]

Here Vergniaud put his finger on what is to my mind the biggest crime committed by the king during the period of the constitutional monarchy. Louis was quite open about his attitude which is summed up in his words to the naval minister Bertrand de Moleville on his appointment: 'My opinion is that the literal execution of the constitution is the best way of making the nation see the alterations to which it is susceptible.'[47] He was involved in a point-scoring exercise as if there were prizes in politics for being right; yet all the time he knew how desperate the situation was and that the constitution needed all the help he could give it. As his young cousin the future Louis-Philippe put it, Louis XVI possessed two kinds of authority: that which he derived from the constitution and that which he inherited and which no revolution could abolish overnight. His failing was in not putting the latter at the service of the former.

The Girondins entered into secret negotiations with the king and indeed staved off the popular insurrection which exploded on 10 August three times because they were outflanked on the Left by factions led by Danton and by Robespierre. In this they resembled the Feuillants who thought they could 'stop' the Revolution at a point of their choosing, as if it had been a local bus; or as if they had hired it like a cab. But the king gave them, in the words of the go-between, a 'dry and negative' response which would not have 'satisfied either a friend of liberty nor a man of ambition'.[48]

However, he was interested in the Feuillant conspiracy and disposed to join it. This conspiracy, like so many others, centered on Compiègne, this time dignified with a coded description: the 'invalid' (i.e., the king) must, 'choose a healthy place for himself on his estates – he has plenty to choose from – but the airiest and most exposed to the north wind would be best.'[49] This comes from several letters found in the possession of the ex-triumvir Adrien Duport when he was arrested after the fall of the monarchy. They relate to the (unsuccessful) attempt by the Feuillants to get Austrian backing for an English-style constitutional monarchy with a bicameral parliament and the restoration of a titled nobility without material privileges.[50]

The plan was that Lafayette's Army of the Rhine and Luckner's Army of Flanders should exchange positions, intersecting at Compiègne. This happened to be within the 20 leagues from the Assembly within which the constitution obliged the king to remain. Lafayette would tell the Assembly that the king was going to his palace at Compiègne and he would proceed thither under the escort of the Swiss and loyal units of the national guard. From Compiègne Louis would issue a proclamation forbidding his brothers and the foreign armies to advance further.

On 11 July Marie-Antoinette gave details of this plan which was to have been executed on the 15th to Fersen and added, 'The king is disposed to lend himself to this project; the queen is against it. The outcome of this great venture which I am far from approving is still in doubt.'[51] The choice was one of high symbolism: whether to trust to the resources of the constitutional monarchy, such as they were, or to the Prussians even though the royal couple may be dead and the Tuileries sacked before they arrived. In the end the king, against his better judgement, yielded to the pleadings of his wife – to his wife who earlier, and surely without his knowledge, had betrayed the French military plans to the Austrians.

Conclusion

Was Louis XVI a conspirator? His opponents would have said so even on the hard evidence which we have attempted to provide. After all, he secretly summoned troops in 1789 and he secretly planned his escape from Paris in 1791, leaving behind an instrument which criticized a constitution he had seemed to accept. So he was both secretive and duplicitous, *le roi parjuré*. Curiously, there is little or no evidence that he was a conspirator, even by the lights of the Jacobins, after his acceptance of the constitution, except for his dalliance with the late Feuillant conspiracy of July 1792; and did his final rejection of the plan, under the influence of Marie-Antoinette, make him more or less of a conspirator?

The king's instinctive response to the Revolution was that passivity which had characterized his reign ever since the rejection of his reform program by the Assembly of Notables in 1787 had plunged him into a depressive apathy from which he never entirely emerged. He was reluctant to act – even in the face of the October Days which he regarded as a heinous and unforgivable crime against his family and the state. He moved only because the situation was deteriorating so rapidly even before the flight to Varennes which, in some ways, made it worse. The Saint-Cloud departure symbolized this but the essence was that the rise of the Jacobin network was threatening not just the revision of the constitution on which Louis had pinned all his hopes, but the very survival of the monarchy.

After the October Days Louis acted secretly because there is no other way that a prisoner can act. He gave his sanction to decrees which he believed to be disastrous because his resistance would have been ignored, as Adrien Duport conceded, or overcome by force: it shouldn't be forgotten that the primary purpose of the October Days was to make the king sign legislation with which he disagreed but which he sanctioned, with tears streaming down his eyes, under mob pressure.

In a sense a discussion of the evidence – whether Louis was a real or an imagined conspirator – is immaterial, or was at the time, when it mattered. Appearances were against the king. It was not just that there was a general climate of suspicion, paranoia if you will. There was also a sense that Louis in particular had betrayed his people because, having proclaimed a programe of equality (if not liberty) before the Assembly of Notables in 1787, he appeared – in 1789 when he was expected to redeem his pledges – to have 'sold out to the magnates,' as Mirabeau put it. This betrayal injected a poison into the body politic to which even the king's death was no antidote.

I have argued that when Louis left Paris on 20/21 June 1791 his intention was to modify the constitution away from Paris but not away from France.[52] But whatever his intentions, if a king leaves his capital at dead of night and heads East and is stopped within 50 miles of the frontier, it is a reasonable assumption that he is planning to cross it and enlist foreign troops. One way of determining criminal intent today is to ask what a reasonable man would deduce if a silent film were made of the activities concerned.

Moreover, while it is indisputable that Louis's destination was Montmédy, it is legitimate to ask what would have happened if he had got there? Unless there had been a swift and satisfactory renegotiation of the constitution with the Assembly, Louis would have found himself in hostile ultra-revolutionary territory protected by an army of dubious and decreasing loyalty and might have been forced to cross the border for his personal safety. Then the project which began as a counter-constitution could have become one for counter-revolution.

Notes

1   T. C. W. Blanning, *The Origins of the French Revolutionary Wars* (London, 1986), p. 99; J.-B. Cléry, *Journal de ce qui s'est passé à la tour du Temple pendant la captivité de Louis XVI, roi de France* (London, 1798), pp. 211–213, 220.

2   Thomas E. Kaiser, 'Who's Afraid of Marie-Antoinette? Diplomacy, Austrophobia, and the Queen,' *French History* 14 (2000), pp. 241–271; *Kaiser*, 'From the Austrian Committee to the Foreign Plot: Marie-Antoinette, Austrophobia, and the Terror,' *French Historical Studies*, 26 (2003), pp. 579–617.

3   Vienna, 88FFA, dossier 3, fos. 143–146, cited in P. and P. Girault de Coursac, *Enquête sur le procès du roi Louis XVI* (Paris, 1982), p. 262.

4   Ibid.

5   P. Caron, 'La tentative de contre-révolution de juin–juillet 1789', *Revue d'histoire moderne et contemporaine* 8 (1906–7), pp. 5–34 and pp. 649–678.

6   J. Godechot, *The Taking of the Bastille: July 14th, 1789*, trans. J. Stewart (London, 1970).

7   P. Caron, 'La tentative de contre-révolution', p. 25. My italics.

8   J. Godechot, *Bastille*, 178–181.

9   *LE FUYARD ou le Baron de Besenval, général sans armée criminel de lèze nation, prisonnier à Brie Comte-Robert* [1789].

10 Cited in Girault de Coursac, *Enquête*, 177.

11 Godechot, *Bastille*, 182.

12 David Jordan, *The King's Trial* (Berkeley, CA and London, 1979), p. 26.

13 R. M von Klinckowström, *Le comte de Fersen et la Cour de France*, 2 vols (Paris, 1877–78), 2, p. 6.

14 Mirabeau to La Marck, 4 June 1790, in *Correspondance entre le comte de Mirabeau et le comte de La Marck*, ed. A de Bacourt, 3 vols (Paris, 1851), 1, p. 331.

15 J. Michelet, *History of the French Revolution*, trans. C. Cocks (Chicago, 1967), pp. 580–595.

16 *Ce qu'il convient de penser du départ du roi* (Paris, 1791), pp. 14, 8.

17 *Opinion d'un publiciste* (Paris, 1791), p. 10.

18 M. Price, *The Fall of the French Monarchy: Louis XVI, Marie-Antoinette and the baron de Breteuil* (London, 2002), pp. 192–205 and Appendix.

19 M. Kennedy, *The Jacobin Clubs in the French Revolution: The First Years* (Princeton, 1982), 220–222.

20 All quotations from the king's declaration are taken from J. Hardman, *The French Revolution Sourcebook* (London and New York, 1999), pp. 128–136.

21 *Marie-Antoinette et Barnave*, ed. O. G. Heidenstam (Paris, 1913), pp. 39, 79.

22 *Opinion d'un publiciste*, p. 5, my italics.

23 Cited in *Le Trait de lumière ou le roi considéré au milieu de périls avant son départ pour Montmédy* (Paris, 1791), 10.

24 *Opinion d'un publiciste*, pp. 1–8.

25 Cited in P. and P. Girault de Coursac, *Sur la route de Varennes* (Paris, 1984), p. 228.

26 Ibid., pp. 229–230.

27 M. Robespierre, *Oeuvres*, ed. Société des études Robespierristes, 10 vols (Paris, 1912–67), 7, pp. 518–523.

28 Ibid., 8, p. 383.

29 *Déclaration de l'Assemblée nationale à tous les citoyens du royaume sur le départ du roi* (Paris, 1791), 5 pages, pp. 2–3.

30 Robespierre, *Oeuvres*, 7, pp. 518–523.

31 *Lettre de M. le marquis de Bouillé, Général de l'Armée françoise etc. à l'Assemblée Nationale*, [1791] 8 pages.

32 *Opinion d'un publiciste*, p. 13.

33 *Ce qu'il convient de penser du départ du roi* (Paris, n.d. [1791]), 19 pages.

34 J. Hardman, *Louis XVI* (New Haven and London, 1993), p. 208.

35 Archives of Austria, Frankreich Hoffcorrespondenz, 7.

36 Archives of Austria, Familien Acten 88.3 fos. 108–125.

37 Hardman, *Louis XVI*, 208.

38 T. C. W. Blanning, *The Origins of the French Revolutionary Wars* (London, 1986), p. 98.

39 Ibid., p. 99.

40 Hardman, *Sourcebook*, p. 141.

41 L. C. Bigot de Saint-Croix, *Histoire de la conspiration du 10 août 1792* (London, 1793), pp. 80, 87, 88.

42 J. Hardman, *Louis XVI*, p. 203.

43 J. Flammermont, *Négotiations secrètes de Louis XVI et du baron de Breteuil avec le cour de Berlin (décembre 1791–juillet 1792)* (Paris, 1885); Girault de Coursac, *Enquête*, p. 290; Price, *Fall*, Appendix; Klinckowström, *Fersen*, 2, p. 6.

44 Munro Price, 'Mirabeau and the Court: Some New Evidence,' *French Historical Studies*, 29 (2006), pp. 37–77, 56.

45 Price, *Fall*, pp. 255–257.

46 *Annales Historiques de la Révolution Française* (1931) pp. 198–201, 207; *Annales Historiques de la Révolution Française* (1946), pp. 353–354.

47 A. F. Bertrand de Moleville, *Mémoires secrètes*, 3 vols (London, 1797), 1, p. 210.

48 *Annales Historiques de la Révolution Française* (1946), pp. 353–354.

49 Price, *Fall*, p. 291.

50 Price, *Fall*, pp. 285–290.

51 *Lettres de Marie-Antoinette*, ed. M. de la Rocheterie and the marquis de Beaucourt, 2 vols (Paris, 1895–96), 2, p. 415.

52 This idea was first suggested to me many years ago, by the realization that Robespierre, no less, believed this to have been the case (while significantly thinking such conduct just as bad as an attempt to subdue the Revolution with foreign troops). Later I developed this idea further in my *Louis XVI* of 1993. This interpretation has been challenged by such historians as Blanning and Price but accepted, even uncritically in view of its controversial nature, by Timothy Tackett, *When the King Took Flight* (Cambridge, MA, 2003).

4

'Horrible plots and infernal treasons': conspiracy and the urban landscape in the early Revolution

David Andress

As other chapters in this book have shown, the national political class of eighteenth-century France needed no encouragement to see political action as conspiracy. Engagement with the complex conduits of Court politics, memories of traumatic clashes between Jesuits and Jansenists, and the resonances of a classical education were among many factors combining to give the elite strong reasons for resorting to conspiracy as an explanation for opposition and setbacks. To address the development of conspiratorial thinking through the Revolution, however, to the point at which it became a driving force in the descent toward Terror, we must also consider the weight of this mode of thought among the wider population. In exploring a revolutionary process so often animated by movements of crowds and communities, the extent to which such communities shared the elite's commitment to a rhetoric of conspiracy – and indeed may have adhered to it even more passionately – must be a central concern. This chapter addresses the particular political environment of Paris, which cannot hope to stand in for the rest of France, but which in itself must be recognized as a central element in the course of the Revolution as a whole. It will show how conspiratorial thinking shaped local responses from the very opening of the Revolution, how that thinking drew on a well-established heritage of such beliefs, and how it developed, interpenetrating with the elite world through press commentary and political responses, as Parisians dealt with the vicissitudes of the Revolution. It will conclude by showing how the chain of events that led to the September Massacres of 1792 was intimately associated with these beliefs, but that they also drew strength from very real threats, and at the same time served to feed still further the conspiratorial paranoia of an elite primed for further mutually destructive conflict.

On the part of both people and authorities, Paris was subject to a decades-long tradition of invoking the plots of 'brigands' and the 'ill-intentioned' to do harm. The capital's citizens had long made a habit of gathering unprompted at any unexpected event, and showed little hesitation in spreading the wildest rumors about such events even as the police struggled to close down the avenues of speculation. These police actions, almost uniquely paternalist and pervasive for a city of this period, themselves relied on patterns of thought that encompassed conspiracy and plot as near-natural explanations for irregularity or conflict.[1] As Arlette Farge and others have documented extensively, the ancien régime ideology that posited the necessity of unconditional love and obedience from subject to king resulted in the relentless official pursuit of those whose speech wandered into the wide realm of the seditious.[2] Individuals suspected of plotting against the king could be incarcerated for decades, trapped in a labyrinth of interrogations and attempted self-justification, as authorities strove to extract from them the apparently carefully-hoarded (and generally non-existent) details of accomplices, goals, and influential contacts – for like much popular activity across the century, it was generally assumed by the police that only the intervention of a senior political figure or faction could summon forth dissent from the shapeless mass of the people.[3]

Of all the conspiratorial modes of explanation circulating in the eighteenth century, perhaps the one with the greatest resonance for the revolutionary future was the 'famine plot persuasion.' This complex of beliefs about the food-supply embroiled king, court, ministers, and merchants in a network of crimes against the people believed in implicitly at almost all levels of society.[4] In every decade from the 1720s on, the same elements of alleged conspiracy reappeared. Underpinning the whole framework was the universal assumption that France was a land of boundless fertility, where any dearth that arose must be due to deliberate agency. This tendency was augmented by the reluctance of the police apparatus to admit that difficulties might be caused by factors outside their control, such as the weather, rather than by miscreants that could notionally be brought to book. When shortages emerged, the first assumption of people from all social classes was that there was some organized body profiting from the resultant price-rise: often such accusations embraced unpopular Court factions, royal or ministerial mistresses, bankers, or tax-farmers. While crowds across the Paris basin acted out the consequences of these beliefs in the widespread unrest of the 1775 'Flour

War,' the beliefs were stoked further for the urban population by their constant recirculation in pamphlets and rumors.[5]

Arlette Farge has noted just how significant was the Parisian population's constant suspicious search for information about material and political conditions. Forever alert for threats and in search of reinforcement, 'it was looking for equilibrium at the heart of a fragility . . . a precariousness which permanently threatened its stability.' Thus, 'the whole of its intelligence was put into not being abused or deceived.'[6] Inhabiting a vast metropolis utterly reliant on the goodwill of its rural food-suppliers, and on the similar goodwill of the authorities who controlled the influx of such necessities, Parisians routinely conflated material well-being or hardship with political events – and thus, inevitably, with conspiracy. The completion of a wall around the city only a few years before 1789, intended to secure customs-revenue by blocking all unmonitored access, had seemed to consolidate this link, as a contemporary ditty noted, *le mur murant Paris rend Paris murmurant*: 'the wall around Paris set Paris murmuring.'[7]

In coming to the events of the Revolution itself, it is almost impossible to avoid the impact of the form of conspiratorial thinking to which these conditions gave birth. Much of the massive upheaval that preceded the gathering of the Estates-General through the winter and spring of 1789 had at its core the popular conviction of a massive famine plot among the privileged orders.[8] The almost hysterical expectations of that summer are inseparable from a sense of palpable dread at what might be done to the people. Paris had felt the force of this as early as April 1789, when imprudent remarks by the employer Réveillon at a public meeting were turned by rumor into a plot to starve the wage-dependent workers, bringing thousands onto the streets in two days of riotous protest (to explicitly political slogans of 'Long live Liberty! Long live the Third Estate!') that left Réveillon's factory in flames. Military action to suppress the violence left hundreds of protestors dead.[9] By July, the atmosphere in Paris was even more explosive.

Rumor was not the prerogative of the untutored or the illiterate – and in any case, most Parisians could read by 1789, as the explosive growth of the popular press would demonstrate. Anonymous pamphlets that claimed to speak on behalf of the people, while clearly produced by writers with a wide political vocabulary, spewed contradictory allegations. One claimed to address the king, defending the news-hungry crowds who gathered at the Palais Royal against charges of sedition. Such charges, it said, were spread by 'those beings whose very breath is disorder . . . who seem to wish in their hearts to send our deputies back to the provinces, across rivers of blood.'[10] The 'wicked and cabalistic suggestions of satraps' were behind claims that the people intended harm to the monarchy, and reported troop-movements around the capital should be reversed to restore harmony. On the other hand, another pamphlet of the same time proclaimed unambiguously that such rumors of military maneuvers were themselves the products of 'despicable emissaries' sent at great expense by 'the aristocrats' into public places to 'drive the people to actions which could lead to their destruction, and cause the triumph of the enemies of the state.'[11]

In such circumstances, it is scarcely surprising that disorder grew steadily within the Palais Royal, so that by 6 July troops had to clear it at the personal request of the duc d'Orléans himself.[12] The famous events that followed within the week would often be blamed on the duke, even though, as many accounts demonstrate, it was a substantial and effectively spontaneous uprising by all ranks of the population against a feared conspiracy by the court, and a military suppression of the capital, that set in train the events leading to the seizure of the Bastille on 14 July 1789.[13]

The origins of the Parisian Revolution are thus inseparable from belief in conspiracy, and the fate of the duc d'Orléans over the following few months demonstrated how these beliefs ricocheted up and down the social and political ladder. Orléans was a popular hero, thanks to a long history of liberal opposition to royal policies, and a vast expenditure on public charity in the preceding harsh seasons. Unsurprisingly, he was himself the target of numerous conspiracy-allegations from those further to the right. Given his undeniable links with a wide range of radical politicians and journalists, he seemed to fit perfectly into the pattern of a meddling grandee, at the heart of so many conspiracy-fears in earlier decades. Formation of what one sympathetic observer has dubbed a political 'machine' around d'Orléans was indistinguishable in the context of the times from such a conspiracy.[14] This led the duke, himself a largely indolent dispenser of funds through his more scheming secretary, Choderlos de Laclos, to be blamed for the October Days that brought the royal family to Paris, after threatening them with crowd violence.

D'Orléans remarked morosely, on hearing of the dramatic events, that it was all a plot by his arch-rival, the other great aristocratic liberal, the marquis de Lafayette – but that nonetheless he, d'Orléans, was sure to be blamed. Thus it largely transpired, resulting in a diplomatic exile for the duke to London for several months.[15] Upon d'Orléans's return, Lafayette's powerbase in the Paris municipality and National Guard headquarters sponsored a barrage of propaganda denouncing his pernicious influence in stirring dissent among the lower orders. Whether there was any such agitation is unclear, since the evidence for it lies largely in blaming d'Orléans for the radical actions of those who had contacts with him, regardless of any other source there may have been for such people's activism. Any such activity, however, was viewed unambiguously by the 'Fayettists' as an illegitimate and conspiratorial manipulation of mob sentiments.[16]

The belief in such conspiracies, and in the continual manifestation of suspicious evidence for them, runs like a dark but consistent thread through the archival records of Parisian local government in these years. The unusually full surviving records of the Saint-Roch district, which embraced the Palais Royal within its borders, show plot-scares at every stage of the Revolution's first year. On 18 July 1789, for example, the moderate and prosperous local committee-men were alarmed enough at reports that a soldier found dead had been poisoned, that they deputed four of their own number to investigate.[17] By late September 1789 the committee thought it routine to dispatch two members to investigate a report that large quantities of silver were being sent out on the mail-coach for Lyons.[18] On 7 October, in the fevered atmosphere that followed the March on Versailles, two more *commissaires* were sent by the committee as far as St-Cloud, downriver outside the city, to investigate a rumor that loaves of bread had turned up drifting into fishermen's nets – and had therefore presumably been dumped by those seeking to starve the city.[19]

That many such rumors were insubstantial goes without saying, but it remains significant that a single district, of undistinguished political pedigree, thought it worth repeatedly exceeding any formal definition of its powers to investigate them. How easily rumor and suspicion could jump from vague evildoers to prominent individuals was shown on 5 October 1789, when a crowd of onlookers had forced the same district's general assembly to open and read a series of letters captured from couriers for the war, marine, and foreign ministries, along with other packets of letters addressed to the comte de Provence and the duc d'Orléans.[20] On 10 October the Saint-Roch district gave a flavor of the continued alarm felt within the capital. Noting that mysterious 'chalk-marks of various colors' had appeared on doors in the neighborhood, that 'packs of ill-intentioned people' had been seen in the streets, and that several 'alarming rumors' were running through the city, it imposed a curfew and invited all citizens to share anything they might learn, or discover, 'relative to the abominable plots which are woven in secret against the capital, and which . . . [threaten] the public safety, and above all [the safety] of a King beloved of the nation . . .' Addressing the municipal government of Paris, the district exhorted it

> to occupy itself, with all the prudence, activity and strength of which it is capable, in discovering, unveiling and publishing the horrible plots and infernal treasons that are unceasingly meditated against the inhabitants of

the capital; to denounce to the public all the authors, actors and adherents of such plots; of whatever rank they might be; and to assure itself of their persons, to pursue their punishment with all the rigor that such attacks deserve.[21]

The pretext for all this, the mysterious chalk-marks, was glossed ten days later by *Le Moniteur*, the Revolution's newspaper of record:

For several nights, suborned scoundrels marked houses with chalk; and in order to multiply alarm, it was, in some quarters, the houses of municipal and National Guard officers [that were marked], in others, those of financiers and men of the robe [i.e., judges and lawyers], and in many cases, those of simple citizens of every class. These various markings, whether white, black or red, designated, it was said, pillage, murder or arson.[22]

Here again, as in the district's pronouncement, the existence of plotters who have 'suborned', or bribed, 'scoundrels' into doing their dirty work is taken entirely for granted as a matter of fact. The penetration of this view into the urban mindset is illustrated by an irate letter that the Saint-Roch district received on 5 November 1789 from a local National Guardsman, complaining at the lack of official support for those individual soldiers forced to endure the hostility of crowds as they guarded bakers' shops. The rain of opprobrium, in which there very probably lay echoes of the classic and continuing alarm at a 'famine plot,' caused this Guard, Martin Delaigle, to ask ominously 'what we shall become, and whether we shall always be masters of our patience,' having been 'constantly exposed to the fury of the enemies of the public good, who suborn the unfortunate to insult us everywhere.'[23] In the minds of those who faced it on the urban front lines every day, public disorder was, in itself, evidence of counterrevolutionary conspiracy.

The connection came through a category of crime that had long been an obsessive fear of the French: brigandage. It was assumed, at all levels of the social and political hierarchy, that the very lowest ranks of society were permeated by vicious evildoers, ready to unleash chaos at any moment.[24] The soaring levels of poverty and dislocation created by the economic crisis of 1788–89 had already made brigandage into a political problem. The fear of wandering beggars and the complexities of the confrontation with privilege slid unstoppably into the Great Fear of July/August 1789, in which the key focus of alarm was the belief in aristocratically funded brigands roaming the countryside to attack the harvest. In Paris itself, the events of July 1789 were not seen unambiguously as a positive popular mobilization. The novelist Nicolas Restif de la Bretonne was traumatized by a series of threatening encounters on the night of 13/14 July with groups he denounced as 'brigands,' 'bandits,' 'ruffians,' and 'formidable rabble,' all claiming to be revolutionary militia.[25] One ex-officer who joined the National Guard of the Saint-Roch district recalled later how he had felt obliged to join the 'frightful league' of individuals who were running about under arms on 12 July – a 'murky cohort terrifying the capital' – and succeeded in collecting a number of weapons from them on the pretext of knowing better how to use them, weapons he subsequently hid at his home.[26] The marquis de Lafayette himself, installed a few days after these events as official commander of the new militia, stated unambiguously that thirty thousand 'outsiders and vagabonds' had flooded the city to play a dangerous role in unrest.[27] Even less ambiguously, at the end of the year a flyer denounced the marquis de Favras, recently arrested for plotting to rescue the royal family, 'for a plan he has made to raise up thirty thousand men to assassinate M. de Lafayette and the Mayor . . . and then to cut off the food supply' – royalist conspiracy, brigandage, and a famine plot in one neat package.[28]

What is perhaps most notable about all of these outbreaks is that it is effectively impossible to find a political level at which conspiratorial thinking was not evident. Although the involutions of plot-thinking cast different figures as villains for different agendas, each agenda shared the conspiratorial matrix of explanation. The rapidity with which the essentially ancien régime versions of famine-plot and political machination had become adapted to the revolutionary environment is also noteworthy: aristocrats and brigands had been the enemies of progress and good order long before 1789, and so they were the enemy now, too, but an enemy which acted in ever-innovative and ever-ramifying ways.

By the end of 1790, a year of relative calm in national politics, several strands of development were coming together to trigger an intensification of political hostilities, necessarily interwoven with a revival, and indeed a veritable explosion, in conspiratorial sensitivities. A small but significant detail shows the effective normalization of such concern, especially with brigandage. When in the first weeks of January 1791 the parochial clergy of the capital were summoned to take a loyalty-oath to the Revolution, all the neighborhood police officials of the city were given explicit instructions from the municipality to patrol lodging-houses on the Saturday evenings preceding such Sunday ceremonies. Their brief was to look out for 'extraordinary movements,' and although none seem to have been reported, it was clearly assumed that the rootless population of such lodging-houses, members of an 'undomiciled' underclass in contemporary perceptions, were ripe for use by aristocratic agents bent on disrupting the priests' oath-taking.[29] Despite the relative absence of immediate troubles, the fact that around half of the city's clergy refused the oath set them on a collision-course with both the authorities and more radical elements of the population. Within the grim nexus of dispute that rapidly emerged, conspiratorial explanation was always prominent. On 25 January a former prosecutor of the Châtelet court felt it was worth reporting to the *commissaire de police* of the Section du Louvre that 'small crosses' were on sale in the rue des Arcis, and that 'these sales and purchases may announce something dangerous.' One of the merchants confirmed 'that he had sold many of them over the last few days, even by the dozen.'[30]

Compounding the suspicions of many were the activities of a new organization, the Society of Friends of the Monarchical Constitution. Modelled on the already nationwide success of the Jacobin Clubs, the 'Societies of Friends of the Constitution,' in bringing together patriotic activists from the largely propertied classes, the *Club monarchique*, as it was universally dubbed, attempted to win similar influence for those who would defend the king's role in the new constitutional order. Among its efforts was a campaign to provide subsidized bread to the poor: conventional philanthropy in a winter of unemployment and economic uncertainty, it claimed, but others thought differently. Radical journalists, increasingly convinced that counterrevolution was not only flourishing, but perilously close to success in its mission to overturn the gains of 1789, leapt on the existence and activities of the *Club monarchique* as overt proof of conspiracy. The club's bread-scheme became rolled up into alarm that broke out after National Guards and customs officials skirmished at the town of La Chapelle on 24 January. A confused and pointless incident, where panic firing led to several deaths, became for the radicals an emblem of the nefarious plans of the counterrevolutionaries. According to one journalist, Stanislas Fréron, the Club had 'thirty thousand workers' enrolled, along with 'all the former royal bodyguards,' and the city was 'on the eve of the counterrevolution' when such forces would be unleashed. Camille Desmoulins, another noted firebrand, echoed the same total, while the reputable *Révolutions de Paris* opted for a more conservative fifteen thousand, but no less suspicion of the motives for the enrolment.[31] The penetration of this belief was shown as early as 20 January, days ahead of the La Chapelle incident, when a homeless beggar was jailed for ten days after loudly declaiming that 'M. de Clermont-Tonnerre [president of the *Club monarchique*] received at his home a quantity of persons that he enrolled for the counterrevolution.'[32]

In the course of the following month, nothing abated the widespread fears that drew together the royal family, counterrevolution, conspiracy, and brigandage. The continued resistance of the oath-refusing, or 'non-juror', clergy and their supporters raised tensions to a fever-pitch. A relatively moderate left-leaning journalist such as Antoine Gorsas was driven to accuse the priests of mobilizing bands of prostitutes to campaign for their cause, and to fulminate on whole series of conspiracies. On 22 February he wrote connecting the religious issue to a plot by the tax-farmers (who controlled the customs-guards incriminated at La Chapelle) to blow up the city's walls, and to a conspiracy for a counterrevolution that would use thirty thousand brigands, taking control of the queen and the dauphin, disposing of the king as a liability, and massacring the patriots of Paris in a new Saint Bartholomew's Day (the long-remembered 1572 massacre of thousands of Protestants by a scheming Church and queen).[33]

Popular and radical discontent combined with aristocratic agitation and alarm at counterrevolution to produce an explosion of activity on 28 February 1791, in a series of confused episodes which served to reinforce prejudices on all sides. The day began with an extraordinary mobilization by the population of the eastern Faubourg Saint-Antoine, most self-consciously radical of the city's suburbs. Alarmed at reports that the Municipality was remodelling the château of Vincennes, a few miles outside the city, the *faubouriens* and their radical allies had been contemplating action for several days. By late morning on the 28th, several thousand Parisians had occupied the courtyard at Vincennes, while a hard core of up to a hundred men set to work attacking the refurbishment work inside the keep.[34] Their motivation was straightforward: they did not want a 'new Bastille' to be raised and garrisoned on their doorstep, fearing that, as the *Révolutions de Paris* summarized, it 'could be dangerous for the success of the Revolution.'[35] The municipal plans, which intended to use Vincennes to relieve pressure on the overcrowded prisons of the city, were reinterpreted within a conspiratorial matrix that made them automatically dangerous to the liberty and lives of the capital's patriots.

Extraordinary in itself, the Vincennes expedition pales beside the second act of this day's drama. The Parisian National Guard was summoned to arms to defend the château, and thousands marched in their battalions out of the city. As they did so, news reached the streets that a *chevalier de Saint-Louis* had been arrested at the Tuileries, the residence of the royal family, carrying a dagger.[36] The undeniable fact of this man's existence made concrete a rumor that had run through the press and public for three days. On the 26th, at least one administrative Section of the city had met in general assembly, and voted formally to call for a ban on hidden weapons. They justified this with reference to 'the exposition made to the assembly that there existed in Paris factories and stores of mechanical daggers, spring-loaded stilettos chained to gauntlets, and other hidden and perfidious weapons.' This revelation was supposed to come from the radical Cordeliers Club, which had 'made the discovery of the model and the manufacture of these daggers,' the 'infernal invention' of which ought to be pursued by the rigors of justice.[37]

As news of the arrest spread, a chaotic mêlée developed around the Tuileries. Young royalists, possibly several hundred in number, flocked to the palace, managing to get inside. Their arrival was probably prompted by their own alarm that a rising number of other Parisians, gathering around the palace, intended harm to the king. The crowd outside, however, believed that the original *chevalier du poignard*, 'knight of the dagger,' and all his reinforcements could only bode ill for monarch and revolution. The absence of the National Guard, marched off to Vincennes, was interpreted by all as a necessary and planned precondition for plotted infamy. As the *Révolutions de Paris* said of this diversion, it was 'evident that it was provoked by the aristocrats' – this in the same paragraph that recorded approvingly the nature of fears over a 'new Bastille.'[38] The stand-off that ensued at the Tuileries was only broken by the Guard's return. Having faced down the crowd and arrested more than sixty men within the keep at Vincennes, the troops went on to take several dozen military officers and gentlemen of the court into custody at the palace. Dispute would rage for weeks as the aristocratic officers found more comfortable detention, and earlier release, than the Saint-Antoine militants, despite the latter being, as one of their home Sections phrased it on 3 March, only 'citizens seduced by the enemies of the public good . . . led on by a too-great zeal' for that same quality.[39]

It is hard to imagine how the events of 28 February could ever have happened, let alone unleashed the storm of controversy that they did, without an abiding and deep-seated fear of conspiracy throughout the Parisian population. The troubles of the Parisian body politic would only grow deeper and more agonizing as winter gave way to spring in 1791. The non-juring priests continued to raise resistance to their removal, occasioning violent responses from 'patriot' crowds.[40] The economy suffered as the assignat paper currency depreciated rapidly against metallic coinage, and brought forth new accusations of plot. Crowds in the Palais Royal and elsewhere regularly attacked the money-changers, and rumors of the nefarious intent of those who speculated on the currency were rife. The *Révolutions de Paris* summed up the views of many in early April: 'There is no more doubt that the three *caisses* [the central banking organs] are in league to block the sources of circulation for all kinds of currency.' Their tactics went as far as organizing mobs to crowd their doors, preventing honest citizens from transacting business and forcing them into the arms of the money-changers: 'Would not the share-out from these extortions be done each evening between the posted speculators, the clerks and perhaps the administrators?'[41] Forged assignats were becoming a plague, and few had any doubt as to their ultimate origin. In March one merchant denounced to the police a certain comte de Toussaint, who had, he claimed, 'enough paper to overturn everything' if he could find a good engraver to make the plates.[42]

Political events at the highest level continued to present Parisians with material ripe for translation into a conspiratorial matrix. The king himself took Palm Sunday communion from a non-juring priest in his private chapel on 17 April 1791, and the next day attempted to leave the city with his family, heading for their summer residence at Saint-Cloud, but thus absenting himself from public Easter communion. When word of the Palm Sunday event reached the streets, hundreds seized on it as evidence of counterrevolutionary conspiracy, and a large crowd blockaded the royal party in the Tuileries the following morning, eventually causing the king to abandon his plans.[43]

The municipal authorities used everything short of open violence to shift the crowd, only giving up when it became clear that many of the National Guards on duty shared their fellow citizens' disquiet. General Lafayette resigned in disgust at the appalling insubordination. He was soon back in office as a wave of petitions from the Guard's battalions begged him to resume his duties. Both these events occasioned a further flowering of plot-mongering. On 20 April the *Courrier de Paris* reported that Louis had been bound for a royalist army based in Rouen, and two days later noted that 'the rumor is current . . . that the king's departure was merely a planned ruse, and M de la Fayette's resignation the next stage of a plan' all leading toward the customary Saint Bartholomew's Day.[44]

Radicals in the press and on the streets were not the only ones succumbing to the lure of conspiracy theory. One anonymous pamphlet produced in late April, for example, blamed the crowd action of the 18th on a secret signal given to agitators by the jets of water pulsing from fountains in the Palais Royal – under the control, of course, of its proprietor, the duc d'Orléans.[45] Centre-right newspapers such as the *Feuille du Jour*, more-or-less in sympathy with the 'Fayettist' grouping that had been attacking Orléans and the radicals since 1789, noted rumors such as that about the fountains with a semi-cautious tone: 'we are assured that this is the signal which rallies the seditious.' However, continued radical attacks on Lafayette in the latter days of April were attributed by the same paper unambiguously to 'groups instructed by the infamous motors of the troubles that agitate us.'[46]

Meanwhile the Municipality of Paris united with its technical superiors in the departmental authorities to make a direct appeal to the National Assembly for urgent legislation to restrict the freedom of popular political activity. The heart of their argument was an unambiguous statement of conspiratorial assumption:

> For a long time, the enemies of the constitution have placed their hopes in anarchy; they have counted on the exaggeration of patriotism and on the excess of that impatient ardor produced by the rapid conquest of liberty. They have calculated on the habit of mistrust in a people always abused; that so-long repressed hatred of an oppressive government; those movements of fear and of scorn inspired by all acts of authority, when it is usurped. They have employed these sentiments, which they must have found everywhere, with the most fatal cunning against all the legitimate powers conferred by a free people.[47]

On 10 May 1791 the National Assembly passed a law against collective petitioning as a result of this lobbying: a measure designed to end the growing role of radical popular societies in haranguing the Assembly with their views. Such views included a significant freight of conspiratorial assumption, as events after the royal family's flight to Varennes would prove. This famous event, discovered in Paris on the morning of 21 June, and played out over the rest of that day further east in Champagne, is often portrayed as a turning-point in revolutionary politics. The most recent scholarly treatment highlights the shocked reaction of communities across the country, and suggests a turn to darker and more pessimistic views of the Revolution's prospects as a result.[48] In the Parisian context at least, there is substantial evidence for the event merely slotting into an established set of beliefs and confrontations. Crowds harassed military and National Guard officers, accusing them of complicity in the Flight; rumors spread that the population of the prisons was being agitated for an episode of brigandage, and lodging-houses were hurriedly checked, as in January; emergency recruitment of poorer citizens to the National Guard was tempered by fears that 'vagabonds . . . will not fail to profit from this occasion to spread themselves throughout the city under arms.'[49]

The king's dramatic seizure at Varennes did little to ease the conspiratorial tensions. One political gossip-sheet, which reprinted much of the talk of the cafés and open spaces, summarized in its issue of 25 June the current concerns:

> A vague, but terrible ferment is spread throughout the capital; all citizens of any quality are alarmed: they fear the arrival of the king. Already it has been insinuated to the paid Guard companies that their pay is to be cut, but that they will be supported by the faubourg St-Antoine and the workers on charity if they wish to get justice for themselves. The faubourgs are in fact in turmoil; everyone says that the enemy powers are stirring them, and wish for the Guard to remain under arms to impose themselves on the madmen . . . The delirium has reached the height of raising the price of coin to 27 per

cent; and, to embitter people's minds, the rumor has been spread that from the end of the month the assignats will no longer be valid. A thousand workers run through the streets in gangs. The market-women are assembling; their design is to fill the inns along the route of the king and queen, and not to go home until they have had satisfaction from them.[50]

In this analysis, rumor is never spontaneous, but always produced by unknown enemies to secure an effect, and the one constant is the presence of those enemies. Three weeks later, as Paris was rocked by further massive demonstrations, that analysis at last brought forth the significant violence it had always seemed to promise. The National Assembly's decision on 15 July 1791 to acquit the king and queen of any complicity in their flight brought a confused wave of protest onto the streets, coalescing into a movement to occupy the Champ de Mars, site of the Festival of Federation a year earlier, and sign a mass petition to refer the king's fate to a popular vote. This in itself was an eminently pacific way of proceeding, but in the surrounding turmoil the center-left journalist Gorsas scented death: 'it is possible that in a few days we shall see the people armed against the National Guard,' he wrote on the 17th, even as events were playing out elsewhere to accelerate confrontation dramatically.[51]

Around midday, two men had been found in the space beneath the wooden stage that held the Altar of the Fatherland, centerpiece of the Champ de Mars. They were apparently making holes in the planking. As a crowd of both men and women occupied the stage, it is now commonly supposed that they were little more than peeping-toms seizing an unusual opportunity to spy on female legs. After being discovered and hauled out, the two men were dragged by an irate crowd to the police authorities of the local Section, where after an interrogation the crowd was assured that justice would be done. The crowd, however, was convinced that the men were plotting to explode a bomb beneath the petitioners. Seized again from the hands of the authorities, they were hanged and then beheaded. This violence was the trigger for an investigation by two members of the Municipality, who found the situation restored to calm, but learned on returning to the Hôtel de Ville that the alarmed National Assembly had pressured the mayor into declaring martial law after the first reports of the deaths.[52] News of the lynching had spread far enough for Gorsas to comment on it – one of the two men, a military *invalide*, had been 'very suspect, even to his comrades,' and 'passed for being paid by the aristocrats,' but also 'has often been seen in the groups where inflammatory speeches' (by implication radical ones) 'are made.' Such instant analysis, committing hearsay to print, found the pairing of aristocratic subversion and radical provocation a natural conclusion.

The horrors of the actual 'Champ de Mars Massacre' that followed, a police riot in which enraged volunteer National Guard battalions shot at and charged down the crowd of some 20,000 petitioners, need not detain us. Though radicals would number the casualties at several hundred, no more than a dozen were definitively identified, and the real number is unlikely to have exceeded fifty. Nor does the response of those who ran through the streets or joined the famous 'groups' to tell of the events in the following days require detailed analysis. Their vision was a straightforward one in which the National Guard had attacked 'the people,' its motivation the same aristocratic subornation that had allowed the king to escape in June.[53] Though this is grist to the conspiratorial mill, the more significant revelation comes from examining the press coverage of this bloody day.

The relatively conservative *Feuille du Jour* had the easiest job: its editorial line had always represented popular action as a threat, likely one supported by counterrevolutionaries and the shadowy Orléanist faction. It could dwell on the details of the heroic deaths of two National Guards and note bluntly that 'on the side of the seditious are counted nine persons killed and about as many wounded . . . Factious men! The end of your successes approaches; they have lasted too long; but tremble!'[54] More radical journalists had a harder time: they had to weave the undoubted violence of the confrontation into a mindset that took the unity of the citizen body as an absolute. Conspiracy and brigandage, factors impinging from outside on that body, were inescapable conclusions. The firebrand Marat took the simplest line, reversing the suppositions of the right-wing press, and depicting the National Guard as penetrated by the agents of Lafayette, acting in concert with brigandish *agents provocateurs* among the crowd similarly paid by the marquis.[55] The *Révolutions de Paris* took a similar line, attributing the lynching that sparked the massacre to brigands, but going on:

> if force had been provoked by brigands, it is against the brigands that it needed to be used. But no, they knew them, the brigands, and had them left alone, and the blind fury of the National Guard was directed against the authors and subscribers of a petition which was going to have its effect, and which is a crime that the committees of the National Assembly find it impossible to pardon.[56]

Gorsas, who had written of looming confrontation between people and National Guard, was driven by news of the events to resolve the awful prospect of such a division, resorting, yet again, to the thesis of conspiratorial brigandage:

The popular execution which took place in the morning had pierced the good citizens with horror and disquiet. They saw with pain that the thousands of brigands that the aristocracy suborns in the heart of the capital, and who have for their lairs, not lodging-houses [hôtels garnis], but the town-houses [hôtels] of our emigrants, had mixed themselves with the multitude, whose sole object was to sign a petition, and they led them astray with inflammatory and fatal speeches.[57]

Overall, Gorsas wrote, the events had been a plot conceived by 'enemies of the public good,' intent on a restoration of despotism by means of unleashing anarchy. This was exactly the same analysis that the municipal authorities had used months before against the popular societies.

Pausing to review the conspiratorial matrix as it had evolved by late 1791, several key aspects for the political future can be identified. There is first the perpetual interaction of individuals, authorities, and commentators. Rarely is it possible to say that a conspiratorial explanation is being placed on events purely after the fact. Often, overt conspiratorial assumptions emerge in their most developed form in the writings of the press and pamphleteers, but in all the events reviewed above the actors themselves either clearly express, or by their very actions articulate, the same conspiratorial assumptions. Furthermore, authorities charged with keeping public order, from the neighbourhood guardians of Saint-Roch in October 1789 to the Municipality of Paris itself in May 1791, assert with equal clarity and vigor the nature of the conspiratorial threat, and do so publicly in ways which can only reinforce popular alarm. Where once, before 1789, there had been a Parisian 'public sphere' that circulated information between 'people' and elites relatively slowly, through gossip and rumor, there was now an intense and effectively institutionalized circulation. Radical clubs and neighborhood Sections were open forums for denunciations both vague and specific, while the talk of streetcorners and cafés was recycled into newsprint, often within the day, and from there on up to more elite organs such as the Jacobin Club, the Municipality, and the National Assembly itself.

   In discussing the beginnings of the Parisian Revolution, we noted the ease with which the capital's events were assimilated to conspiratorial thinking among the elite – in that case concerning the intentions of the duc d'Orléans. As politics evolved over the year after the Champ de Mars Massacre, this fundamental connection persisted. The emergent Brissotin faction in the new Legislative Assembly attacked all those who would cooperate with royal power, raising fears about the penetration of France by *émigré* networks and the supporters of the non-juring priests. Massive waves of popular discontent at high prices and shortages over the winter of 1791–92 evoked the return of the classic 'famine plot,' now associated intimately with the gathering counterrevolution on the borders, against whom the Brissotins hymned the virtues of war. The outbreak of war itself in the spring of 1792, accompanied at once by disastrous defeats, brought a splintering of conspiratorial alarm. While Brissotins continued to declaim against an 'Austrian Committee' piloting the country to its doom from within the Tuileries, centrist forces, continuing the argument of the Parisian authorities of 1791, blamed popular radicalism – on 3 June 1792 holding a 'Festival of the Law' explicitly to reject the 'anarchistic' (and hence brigandish) tendencies of those who had lynched suspected hoarders earlier in the year.[58]

The marquis de Lafayette, who had abandoned Parisian politics after losing a mayoral election in late 1791, and was now one of the generals desperately trying to hold together France's front lines, unequivocally blamed Jacobin radicalism for the current crisis, writing to the Assembly on 18 June 1792 that clubs were 'organized as a separate Empire within the capital . . . led blindly by a few ambitious chiefs . . . a corporation set apart at the heart of the French people, whose powers it usurps in subjugating its representatives and mandatories.'[59] Ten days later, the general abandoned his command to appear in the capital, reiterating his demand for the abolition of the clubs and censorship of the radical press. His actions over the next month proved how close to reality the conspiratorial fears of Parisians lay. Only a message from Queen Marie-Antoinette, causing the Jacobin mayor of the city to cancel a review of the National Guard in Lafayette's honour on 29 June, prevented the general from launching a *coup d'état* against radical influence on the Assembly. The queen's personal loathing of the man she blamed for the October Days blocked this conspiracy, as it did another less than three weeks later, when Lafayette plotted to unite the armies from the northern frontiers, escort the royal family out of Paris, and dictate peace to radicals and *émigrés* alike.[60]

For Parisian radicals, meanwhile, who increasingly used the demotic image of the *sans-culottes* to label and legitimize their wide coalition of artisans, businessmen, shopkeepers, professionals, and the occasional wage-laborer, Paris was dominated by the grand conspiracy that centered on the king's blatant refusal to do anything constructive toward the capital's military salvation.[61] And here, as with Lafayette, the striking consonance of paranoia and reality is visible. The king and queen, since the opening of the year, had been determined on an effort to lead France into military conflict, and to profit from that to use the threat of armed force to overturn the Revolution. The pathetic optimism of beliefs that, first, an 'armed congress' of the Great Powers would cause the revolutionaries to give way, or, secondly, that Louis XVI might be allowed out of the capital to take command of an army, cannot obscure the basic clear intent to betray the oath to uphold the Constitution that Louis had publicly sworn in September 1791. If the radicals of the capital only suspected and did not know of this treachery, their suspicions were nonetheless accurate, even if they then went on to extend the tentacles of this conspiracy far wider than the royal couple's actual inner circle of true believers.[62]

As so often in the past, the enemies of the Revolution delivered up new ammunition for the apocalyptic mindset of the *sans-culottes*. Vengeful *émigrés* drafted a manifesto for the advancing army of the Duke of Brunswick, promising that all who 'dare to defend themselves' against the Allied armies would be shot, and their homes demolished, and that Paris and its population would suffer an 'exemplary and ever-memorable vengeance' in 'military execution, and total destruction,' if the royal family were not safeguarded in the freedom 'which the laws of nature and of men oblige from subjects to sovereigns.'[63] The decision of the *sans-culotte* leadership, a week after this text was published in Paris, to launch an assault on the Tuileries can be seen in this light as their own desperate effort to escape the closing jaws of an internal and external conspiratorial trap. When the king fled to the safety of the Legislative Assembly on 10 August, but neglected to order his Swiss Guards to stand down, and when the latter were goaded into opening fire, killing some three hundred insurgents (before being themselves brutally massacred), all this could easily be read in the *sans-culottes'* context as continued plotting: as the seizure of yet another chance to cause unnecessary casualties among the patriots.

Yet more treachery continued to be exposed: on 17 August General Lafayette tried to order his troops to march against Paris, and when they defied him, fled to the Austrian lines. In the weeks that followed, the rapid collapse of France's fortified towns that stood in the way of Brunswick's advance signalled more betrayal, and in Paris the Insurrectionary Commune of *sans-culotte* leaders, sharing power uneasily with the rump of the Legislative Assembly, began on 26 August to search the city for 'aristocratic' arms caches, and to arrest non-juror priests as members of a counterrevolutionary fifth column.[64] The groundwork was thus laid for an event which has often been seen to mark the birth of the Terror, and was also the logical culmination of this phase of Parisian conspiracy-mania – the September Massacres.

What is most notable about these killings, which saw some 1,500 individuals, the vast majority of whom were common criminals, executed by sword- and axe-wielding *sans-culottes* between 2 and 6 September

1792, is that they remain outside the bounds of explanation for so many historians. For many on the right, they are of course the symbol of the savagery lurking beneath the surface of the popular cause, but even for those who take a more balanced view, there is rarely any effort to find a logic to the killings. The fact that only a small minority of victims had been locked up for 'counterrevolutionary' tendencies seems to make the events inexplicable except as an overreaction, an excess of pure violence.[65]

In truth, the September Massacres were the acting-out of the long-nurtured *sans-culotte* belief in an aristocratic plot, headed by nobles and priests, and with a rank and file made up of the brigands that had lurked dangerously in 1789, been suborned by the *Club monarchique*, flooded into the aristocrats' *hôtels*, and provoked the citizenry to mutual carnage on the Champ de Mars. To the radical patriots of Paris, long accustomed to seeing their welfare threatened by plotters above and criminal accessories below, the mixture of all these forces in the notoriously insecure prisons of the capital was both a deadly danger and a real opportunity. In almost all the diverse locations where prisoners were tracked down, processes of judgment took place, attempting to distinguish 'real' enemies from unfortunates. Thus the princesse de Lamballe, whose death became a veritable theater of cruelty in many accounts, was the only one of some 110 female prisoners in La Force to be killed. At La Salpêtrière, where some 270 women were detained, 87 branded felons were singled out for scrutiny, and of these 35 were killed. On the other hand, 72 of 75 male felons in one prison were killed, as were a party of Swiss Guards held at the Abbaye, judged guilty in advance of the killings on 10 August, no doubt. Again, by contrast, at the Abbaye overall, at least 250 of the 450 inmates were adjudged innocent. Nowhere was killing absolutely indiscriminate, overall the victims were a clear numerical minority of the prison population, and in every case where those detained for debts, minor public-order incidents, or anything else not suggesting either political motive or hardcore criminality were found, they were spared.[66]

It should not be suggested for a second that those killed in these events were in any sense 'deserving' of their deaths, or parties to any actual conspiracy. But they were undoubtedly the victims of the belief in conspiracy nurtured by an array of Parisians far beyond the bounds of the *sans-culotte* movement that carried out the killings. The Massacres also marked the moment when the conflict which was to shape the next year in politics, between radical Jacobins and Brissotins, took deadly shape under the banner of conspiracy. As the killings began on 2 September, Robespierre spoke in the Insurrectionary Commune of a Brissotin plot to put the Duke of Brunswick on the throne, and that night warrants were issued by the Commune's surveillance committee to arrest Brissot, Interior

Minister Roland, and more than two dozen other Brissotin members of the Legislative Assembly.[67] Moreover, it was not only on the side of Robespierre and his fellow radicals that the assumption of conspiratorial evildoing was made. Madame Roland wrote on 5 September to Jean-Henri Bancal des Issarts, a colleague of Brissot, that 'Robespierre and Marat have a knife to our throats ... they have a small army paid from the proceeds of what they found or stole from the [Tuileries] palace.' Asserting that the unfulfilled arrest-warrants were a plot to slaughter her friends in the prisons, she pleaded for a provincial guard to be organized to save them from the Parisians: 'So work rapidly to send us this guard, on the pretext of the external enemies against whom those Parisians who can bear arms are being sent.'[68] To combat one conspiracy, she effectively suggests another, to dispatch armed force to the capital under false pretences. While ultimately it was the commitment of Robespierre and his fellow Jacobins to a conspiratorial interpretation of the Brissotins that would, indeed, doom the latter, Madame Roland's words are a reminder that conspiracy was the sea in which all the revolutionaries swam.

Notes

1 For introductions to the policing of Paris in the eighteenth century, see A. Williams, *The Police of Paris, 1718–1789* (Baton Rouge, 1979); D. Garrioch, *Neighbourhood and Community in Paris, 1740–1790* (Cambridge, UK, 1986); Garrioch, *The Making of Revolutionary Paris* (Berkeley, 2002), chapter 5.

2 A. Farge, *Subversive Words; Public Opinion in Eighteenth-century France* (Cambridge UK, 1994), see especially chapter 4, and introduction to Part III, pp. 123–131.

3 For examples of the relentless pursuit of the conspiratorial 'impregnation' of the lower orders, see R. Darnton, 'An Early Information Society: News and the Media in Eighteenth-century Paris,' *American Historical Review*, 105 (2000), pp. 1–35.

4 S. L. Kaplan, *The Famine Plot Persuasion in Eighteenth-century France* (Philadelphia, 1982), p. 2.

5 Ibid., especially conclusion and pp. 63–64. For the 1775 troubles, see C. Bouton, *The Flour War: Gender, Class and Community in Late Ancien Régime French Society* (University Park, PA, 1993).

6 A. Farge, *Fragile Lives: Violence, Power and Solidarity in Eighteenth-century Paris* (Cambridge, UK, 1993), p. 285.

7 G. Rudé, *The Crowd in the French Revolution* (Oxford, 1959), pp. 10–11.

8 G. Lefebvre, *The Great Fear of 1789* (London, 1973).

9 J. Godechot, *The Taking of the Bastille, July 14th 1789* (London, 1970), pp. 135–140.

10 British Library (hereafter BL), R.231(1). 'Lettre adressée au roi, par tous les bons François frequentant le Palais Royal, Pour supplier Sa Majesté d'éloigner les troupes de sa Capitale.'

11 BL R.231(2), 'Fausse Alarme donnée le 2 juillet au Palais-Royal, par les aristocrates, ou Avis au peuple françois, sur le piège qu'on lui tend.'

12 Godechot, *Bastille*, pp. 176ff.

13 See D. Andress, *The French Revolution and the People* (London, 2004), pp. 105–109; M. Price, *The Fall of the French Monarchy: Louis XVI, Marie Antoinette and the Baron de Breteuil* (London, 2002), chapter 4.

14 G. A. Kelly, 'The Machine of the duc d'Orléans and the New Politics,' *Journal of Modern History* 51 (1979), pp. 667–684.

15 B.M. Shapiro, *Revolutionary Justice in Paris, 1789–1790* (Cambridge, UK, 1993), chapters 4, 9, 10, for the efforts to pin these events on d'Orléans; A. Castelot, *Philippe Égalité le régicide* (Paris, 1991), p. 185, for the duke's remark.

16 O. Elyada, 'L'Appel aux faubourgs: pamphlets populaires et propagande à Paris, 1789–1790', in M. Vovelle, ed., *Paris et la Révolution: actes du colloque de Paris I, 14–16 avril 1989* (Paris, 1989), pp. 185–200.

17 Bibliothèque nationale de France (hereafter BnF), Ms. n.a.f. 2665 f. 11.

18 BnF, Ms. n.a.f. 2670 ff. 152–153.

19 BnF, Ms. n.a.f. 2670 f. 176. See D. Garrioch, 'The Everyday Lives of Parisian Women and the October Days of 1789', *Social History*, 24 (1999), pp. 231–249.

20 Archives de la Préfecture de Police (hereafter APP) AA81 f. 16.

21 APP AA 81 f. 25.

22 *Le Moniteur*, 20–22 October 1789.

23 BnF Ms. n.a.f. 2670 f. 243.

24 Andress, *French Revolution*, pp. 57–59.

25 Ibid., p. 108.

26 BnF Ms. n.a.f. 2670 f. 88.

27 Rudé, *Crowd*, p. 19 n. 8.

28 N. Ruault, *Gazette d'un parisien sous la Révolution: lettres à son frère, 1783–1796*, ed. A.Vassal and C. Rimbaud (Paris, 1976), p. 174.

29 APP AA82, ff. 48, 60, 93, 111, 115.

30 APP AA182, f. 54.

31 D. Andress, *Massacre at the Champ de Mars: Popular Dissent and Political Culture in the French Revolution* (Woodbridge, 2000), pp. 41–42.

32 APP AB322, case 1015.

33 *Le Courrier de Paris dans les LXXXIII Départements*, 22 and 26 February 1791.

34 S. Lacroix, *Actes de la Commune de Paris*, 2nd ser., 2, pp. 763–764.

35 *Révolutions de Paris*, 26 February–5 March 1791.

36 APP AB322, case 1377.

37 Lacroix, *Actes*, 2, p. 796.

38 See Lacroix, *Actes*, 2, pp. 774–775; 3, pp. 10–14, for commentary.

39 Lacroix, *Actes*, 3, p. 14.
40 Andress, *Massacre*, pp. 104–8.
41 *Révolutions de Paris*, 2–9, 9–16 April 1791.
42 APP, AA82, f. 347; see also Andress, *Massacre*, pp. 127–128.
43 *Le Moniteur*, 19 April 1791.
44 Andress, *Massacre*, pp. 110–111.
45 BnF, 8–Lb39–4828.
46 *Feuille du Jour*, 28 April, 1 May 1791.
47 Lacroix, *Actes*, 4, pp. 6–7.
48 T. Tackett, *When the King Took Flight* (Cambridge, MA, 2003).
49 Andress, *Massacre*, pp. 148–150; *Feuille du Jour*, 23 June 1791.
50 *Le Babillard, ou journal du Palais-Royal*, no. 21, 25 June 1791.
51 *Courrier de Paris*, 18 July 1791.
52 For accounts of this process, see G. A. Kelly, *Victims, Authority and Terror: the Parallel Deaths of d'Orléans, Custine, Bailly and Malesherbes* (Chapel Hill, 1982), pp. 189–192, and A. Mathiez, *Le Club des Cordeliers pendant la crise de Varennes et le massacre du Champ de Mars* ([Paris] Geneva, [1910] 1975), p. 132.
53 For such an analysis see Andress, *Massacre*, pp. 174–212.
54 *Feuille du Jour*, 18 July 1791.
55 *L'Ami du peuple*, no. 524, 20 July 1791.
56 *Révolutions de Paris*, 23–30 July 1791.
57 *Courrier de Paris*, 19 July.
58 D. Andress, *The Terror: Civil War in the French Revolution* (London, 2005), pp. 66ff.
59 Ibid., p. 75.
60 Ibid., pp. 78–80.
61 R. B. Rose, *The Making of the Sans-culottes: Democratic Ideas and Institutions in Paris, 1789–1792* (Manchester, 1983), pp. 150ff.
62 Andress, *Terror*, pp. 68–70.
63 Ibid., pp. 82–83.
64 Ibid., pp. 91–92.
65 J. F. Bosher, *The French Revolution* (London, 1989), p. 178, dismisses the entire process as down to 'the violence of the populace'. D. M. G. Sutherland, *The French Revolution and Empire; the Quest for a Civic Order* (Oxford, 2003), p. 140, speaks of 'grisly slaughters' and denounces any notion of panic or a strike against feared insurrection as 'diminishing the responsibility of the perpetrators.' C. Jones, *The Great Nation: France from Louis XV to Napoleon* (London, 2002), p. 461, is slightly more sympathetic, but also speaks of 'the travesty of trial' and 'an ambience of pure carnage.'
66 See the detailed discussion of this episode in Andress, *Terror*, pp. 95–110.
67 J. Hardman, *Robespierre* (London, 1989), p. 56.
68 J. Hardman, ed., *The French Revolution Sourcebook* (London, 1999), p. 157.

5

Conspiracy in the village? French revolutionary authorities and the search for 'subverters of public opinion' in the rural south-west[1]

Jill Maciak Walshaw

In the summer of 1799, the district court judge in the region of the Adour, in the department of the Hautes-Pyrénées in south-western France, sat pondering an intriguing case. The incident concerned a woman named Jeannet Begarrie, a day-laborer from Argelès, a tiny mountain community of 210 inhabitants situated nearly on the Spanish border. According to the preliminary investigation which now sat on the judge's desk, Jeannet had been heard by numerous people, between 9 and 10 o'clock on the evening of 11 July, to have shouted many anti-revolutionary and royalist words, including 'long live the king, long live Louis XVII,' somewhat oddly, 'long live the Intendant of Pau,' and finally, 'down with the nation, down with the Republic.' The seven villagers whose testimony is preserved in the archives, mindful of the volatile political environment, appear to have tried to protect their friend and neighbor. Jean Mesailles, the local innkeeper, stated that he had stayed in with his sick wife that evening, and several others insisted that they had been too far away to see who was shouting. The few witnesses who did identify Begarrie qualified their statement by pointing out that she had been in a state of 'extraordinary drunkenness.' However, whether out of sincere conviction or the need to demonstrate sufficient patriotism, the district court judge wrote that 'outrageous' as these provocative shouts were, they were 'all the more seditious' in that they 'coincided with royalist conspiracies and attacks on liberty which were occurring at many other places in the Republic.' Probably warned by her neighbors, she was wisely not at home when the authorities came to arrest her, and the case was dismissed some weeks later.[2]

As we have seen, this 'paranoid style of politics'[3] is nothing new to historians of the French Revolution. Conspiracy theories became common and, after about 1792, even endemic, as the various contributions to this volume clearly demonstrate. Among the peasantry, who made up more than three-quarters of those denied a place in the political sphere, the idea that the secret machinations of a small group of self-interested individuals lay behind political events was not uncommon.[4] Rumors seemed to travel the countryside faster than messengers on horseback, and the marketplaces, fairgrounds and taverns echoed with villagers voicing aloud their opinions on matters of general concern.[5] Traditional views of the king as a benevolent father to his people were mixed with a deep-seated mistrust of the state, whose interference in local affairs was associated with tax increases and requests to billet soldiers. At times when government policies seemed at odds with the well-being of the population, it was suspected that the king had fallen under the influence of an ill-intentioned minister, or that other forces – perhaps local landowners, *seigneurs*, or the urban bourgeoisie – were responsible. By far the most prevalent manifestation of conspiracy fears was the idea of a 'famine plot,' in which various high-ranking groups were thought to conspire against the people by hoarding grain and keeping prices high. Such fears became endemic toward the end of the ancien régime, and while they clearly peaked during subsistence crises, they have also been linked, as Steven Kaplan has shown, to a more generalized disenchantment with the government and an emerging political consciousness in the countryside.[6]

The fear of famine plots and associated 'aristocratic plots' would resurface periodically during the Revolution, with the most obvious manifestation occurring during the Great Fear of July 1789.[7] The political consciousness, too, was to become a permanent feature: having remained largely on the sidelines for the preceding decades, rural dwellers were to take their place on the political stage during the French Revolution. This chapter, however, is not about the perception of plots by the peasantry itself. Rather, it is about the use of a model of conspiracy by revolutionary authorities to explain the inexplicable: the apparent expression of political consciousness in the countryside. In the course of my research on the efforts of the authorities to control what political information circulated in the countryside of the south-west, I have examined more than two hundred investigations and trials arising from the policing of 'seditious speech' in the countryside, of which nearly one-quarter make explicit mention of the notion of conspiracy. In fact, even when these incidents occurred in the tiniest, most isolated villages, authorities at the district level and above tended to exaggerate the situation, portraying minor anti-revolutionary outbursts as potentially threatening to the internal security of the state. Some statements to this effect, particularly during the Terror, appear to have been merely a prudent use of revolutionary rhetoric. However, in many instances, officials seem to have been genuinely concerned that counter-revolutionary agents at large in the countryside might be attempting to subvert rural public opinion.

The attitude of the authorities toward rural politicization led to an overzealous prosecution of seditious speech in the countryside. From the beginning of the Revolution, the legislation put in place to curb seditious activity led to mere words and expressions of discontent being pros-ecuted as signs of full-scale conspiracy or plots against the government. Revolutionary authorities were working under the assumption – fed by the myth of the 'good peasant' – that those who broke the laws would not be disgruntled rustics but, rather, relentless counterrevolutionaries or their agents. In the end, both local magistrates and legislators remained unreceptive to the possibility that rural laborers and artisans held their contentious opinions autonomously, preffering to explain rural dissent as evidence of a plot to subvert public opinion in the countryside.

Tools to root out sedition

The fear of dissent and conspiracy which plagued the members of the revolutionary assemblies is clear from the series of legislative texts put into place to guard against sedition and treason, and from the frequency with which these texts were cited. This frequency derives in part from the fact that, while the laws themselves were almost always drafted with actual attempts to overthrow the government in mind, they were worded vaguely enough that particularly zealous local officials were able to apply severe penalties to individuals who had only *talked* about such actions or complained about the state of affairs. Nor was this seen as contradictory: even mere words, spoken with enough conviction and by a determined counterrevolutionary, could have a damaging effect on public attachment to the Revolution.

The repression of words which were perceived to threaten the established order is, of course, far from being an invention of the French Revolution. The ecclesiastical authorities of the Catholic Church undertook the policing of speech as a means of rooting out and destroying heresy from the late Middle Ages onward, and early modern Britons experienced waves of prosecution for treasonous speech and political libel.[8] In ancien régime France, the crimes of verbal *lèse-majesté* and sedition were maintained on the law books, and police spies, or *mouches*, were sent to infiltrate the cafés, streets, and public squares of the capital, listening to the 'mauvais discours' of the populace and noting it down for the information of the king and his councillors.[9] However, such surveillance was largely concentrated on the urban lower classes: although rural subjects were monitored, they were rarely charged with serious crimes such as *lèse-majesté* in this period. When peasants do make an appearance in the archives for seditious activity, it is almost always as participants in illegal gatherings, rather than as political actors.[10]

However, the upheaval of the Revolution would unseat numerous elite assumptions about popular politics, and the threat of conspiracy from dissident elements along with the effervescence of Parisian crowds in the wake of the storming of the Bastille would soon force the members of the National Assembly to put new laws into place against treason. Since the nation had replaced the king as the embodiment of sovereign power, treachery against the state was rebaptized '*lèse-nation*,' a clever neologism which fired the popular imagination.[11] The *Comité des rapports*, which was established on 28 July 1789 and renamed the *Comité des recherches* on 25 August, was designed to receive and report on correspondence relating to troubles in the provinces, investigate charges of *lèse-nation*, and 'serve as a political police.'[12] A single *Haute-cour nationale* was proposed to act as a supreme court in cases of political justice.[13]

However, the vague definition of the crime of *lèse-nation*, which suited the political aims of the government, was difficult to put into practice. The Assembly's primary concern had been subversive activity of the sort that might bring down the revolutionary government, such as the actions of *émigrés*, both within France and abroad, and plots hatched in collusion with foreign powers. Indeed, among the high-level cases sent before the *Haute Cour*, we find the conspiracy of the cardinal de Rohan, the trial of the Minister of Foreign Affairs de Lessart, and the charges against the journalist Marat. However, in their company we also find provincial citizens arrested for much lesser crimes.[14] As one of the *Haute-Cour nationale*'s high officials wrote to the president of the National Assembly in April of 1791, it seemed a waste of time for the court to be judging cases such as that of Guillard, accused of 'insulting words spoken against the National Assembly', those of Lenormand and Tisset, each accused of having penned 'reprehensible writings', or that of a certain Sieur Marquenot, accused of having announced, to the sound of a drum, that the *champarts*, a feudal harvest tax, should no longer be paid. All of these, he argued, should be treated as simple 'disrupters of public order.'[15]

Although the *Haute cour nationale* had not been designed to judge village *curés* who spoke against the Revolution from their pulpits, or drunken rural artisans who publicly disparaged the government, its institution marked the beginning of a new era in the attitude of the French authorities toward the spread of political information throughout the nation. The Terror tends to spring to mind as the period in which people were arrested and even executed for unacceptable political statements made in public, but in fact, each phase of the Revolution had its 'enemies' and its 'state of emergency' which made verbal sedition a highly punishable offence. The first discernibly discontented words in the countryside came from parish priests. Across France, members of the clergy protested what they saw as the revolutionary government's interference in Church affairs. The nationalization of Church property on 2 November 1790 and the Civil Constitution of the Clergy which followed triggered an even greater number of outbursts from dissatisfied clerics, and as early as 26 November 1790, the deputies of the National Assembly gathered to consider what was to be done. 'The priest of Cambon,' reported M. Voydel in the name of several revolutionary committees, 'is publicly protesting the National Assembly's decrees from the pulpit . . . the priest of Noordpéene condemns any who acquire nationalized properties . . . [and] M. Lavallée, the regular priest in a Rouen parish, is preaching against the seizure of Church property and the printing of *assignats*.' The continued resistance of parish priests throughout France, Voydel concluded, would not only destroy the new social order, but would teach the people to scorn the work of their legislators, and encourage them to rise up in revolt.[16] The resulting decree, dated 27 November 1790, declared that those members of the clergy who disobeyed the laws of the National Assembly 'by forming or encouraging opposition' would be prosecuted by the courts as 'not amenable to the law' and 'disturbers of public order,' whether they had sworn the oath or not.[17]

The number of topics liable to elicit discontent increased with each passing year, and the *Comité de législation* had its hands full, as seditious words spoken by individuals of all walks of life echoed in the crossroads of rural society. The celebrated Penal Code of 1791 contained a series of clauses which would be used extensively to repress general cases of seditious words in the countryside, including a total of twelve articles devoted to crimes which were deemed to threaten the internal or external security of the state.[18] Any type of '*manoeuvre*' or '*intelligence*' with enemies of the nation was denounced, as were 'all conspiracies and plots designed to undermine the State.' While such provisions had clearly been designed to deal with the greatest threats imaginable, one clause left the door open for the prosecution of seditious words spoken by rural malcontents:

> *All schemes* and all intelligence with the enemies of France which tend to facilitate the entry of those enemies into the French Empire, whether by giving them access to French towns, fortresses, ports, ships, armories or arsenals, or by providing them with soldiers, silver, supplies or munitions,

or by aiding in any way the advance of their weapons across French territory
or against our land or sea forces, or by *shaking the loyalty of* officers,
soldiers, or other *citizens to the French nation, will be punished by death*.[19]

The article, as it was used, omitted the more serious forms of treason and
mentioned only those parts shown here in italics, allowing for mere
statements – if judged to have been seditiously intended – to incur the
death penalty.[20] The anti-royalist law of 4 December 1792 further opened
the door to the prosecution of words. During a session of the National
Convention in which the fate of the king was being debated, Reubell
argued that the assembly needed to take action against individuals who
might, in the meanwhile, attempt to restore the monarchy.[21] The resulting
text, which was passed after some discussion, decreed simply that anyone
who *proposed or attempted* to reestablish either the monarchy or any
other form of power which threatened popular sovereignty in France,
would be subject to the death penalty.[22] Clearly, it was felt that the mere
suggestion of a return to a royalist régime could be dangerous.

However, the greatest period of anti-sedition legislation occurred during
the six months from 10 March to 3 October 1793. By the early spring
of 1793, France had been at war for nearly twelve months, and the
accompanying shortages and hardships had begun to make themselves
heard in the seditious statements of provincial citizens. Many laws were
passed in response to discouraging statements on specific topics. The law
of 19 March 1793, for example, was put in place in order to calm the
unrest which had rippled through the countryside since the promulgation
of the levy of 300,000 soldier conscripts one month earlier, and another,
finalized on 5 September 1793, condemned those who made dissatisfied
remarks about the *assignats*. At the same time, judges and juries could
draw on a growing body of generic legislation for prosecuting unspecified
threats against the government, including the decree of 27 March 1793,
according to which ex-nobles and other enemies of the Revolution were
declared outlaws, and the vague crime of 'inciting the reestablishment
of the monarchy' which was listed among the 'counterrevolutionary
endeavors' covered by the laws of 7–9 and 11 April 1793.[23] The infamous
Law of Suspects of 17 September 1793 allowed even greater latitude in
identifying potential enemies, as it included as 'suspects' those who
'declare themselves partisans of tyranny and enemies of liberty, by either
their actions, their connections, their words, or their writings.'[24] Often,
however, the crimes of 'counterrevolutionary words' or of 'seditious
words' were simply understood as being of the utmost severity, and the
citing of specific legal texts was not always required.

Although the events of 9 thermidor II marked the end of a period
of exaggerated surveillance, the era which followed was by no means free

of dissent, and the government's fear of verbal opposition decreased remarkably little.[25] The containment of the conflict in the Vendée by November 1795 allowed the French army abroad to begin taking the offensive, marking the start of an era in which continuous warfare would sap both the strength and the goodwill of the provincial population. From 1794 to 1797, the revolutionary armies suffered heavily from desertion, reducing their total numbers by close to half, and the transient presence of deserters in the countryside added to the atmosphere of challenge, resentment, and opposition.[26] While the penal code continued to be cited in the courts, the laws drafted during the 1793–94 era were largely supplanted by the emergency measures of 27–28 germinal IV, which targeted the 'agents of royalism and of anarchy.' While the second of these two laws focused upon counterrevolutionary infractions via the press, the first law – that of 27 germinal – was an extensive piece of legislation, covering all manner of seditious words, activities, and gatherings. It was the first article of this law which was most often cited in cases of antigovernmental speech during this period:

> All those who, by their words or by their writings whether printed, circulated or posted, incite the dissolution of National Representation or of the executive arm of the Directory . . . or the reestablishment of the monarchy, or of the constitution of 1793, that of 1791, or of any government besides that established by the constitution of Year III, which was accepted by the French people . . . are guilty of committing a crime against the internal security of the Republic and against the individual security of its citizens, and will be punished by death, according to article 612 of the Criminal Code.[27]

Effectively, any political statement advocating, supporting, or even referring wistfully to any previous régime – indeed, any dissent at all – was punishable by death.

The usual suspects

Who were these country subversives, then, these outspoken critics of the new régime? Had they represented a faithful cross-section of rural society in the 1790s, they would have been approximately 90 percent peasants or rural artisans, with bourgeois, members of the liberal professions, clergymen, and nobility making up the rest. However, for the cases studied here, a full 40 percent of defendants were either members of the elite – usually nobles, doctors, or lawyers – or what we might call rural intermediaries: municipal officers, parish priests, and mobile individuals such as soldiers and pedlars. In the early years of the Revolution in particular, suspicions were aimed not at peasants but at the 'usual suspects': the ex-priests and nobles whose importance in society had been reduced under the new order. On the one hand, it is only logical that the authorities would be more attuned to the threat posed by these groups, and that they would target them accordingly in their search for dissenters. On the other hand, however, the government's priorities in their investigations reveal a great deal about their ideas of conspiracy in the countryside.

The assumptions of the deputies of the revolutionary assemblies regarding the political abilities of the rural population had their roots in generations of prejudice. Under the ancien régime, those who worked the land had been considered at best ignorant and simple-minded and at worst little more than animals: in the elite mind, they were 'the very antithesis of culture'.[28] The educated upper classes recoiled in horror at the thought of the barbaric lack of manners and unhygienic living conditions of the rural majority; the phrases used to describe the rural population included 'the masses,' 'the rabble,' and even 'the underworld.' This situation had begun to change during the eighteenth century, particularly with the influence of 'enlightened' thinkers such as Louis de Jaucourt and the Baron d'Holbach.[29] Attitudes of either contempt or indifference were gradually replaced with grudging respect, as the *philosophes* painted a utopian, rustic picture of the good farmers who provided for the nation.[30] While none advocated democracy or even mass education, preferring to keep the people in their place both socially and politically, their writings did much to rescue the rural population from a reputation for violence and ignorance, bestowing upon it a glow of usefulness and virtue.[31] The fact that the peasantry was seen as generally well-intentioned and wholesome, yet ignorant in matters of politics and easily led astray, largely explains why the authorities were so concerned that peasants might be 'seduced' by seditious words spoken in the countryside.

From an early modern perspective, such assumptions are not unreasonable. Throughout the seventeenth and eighteenth centuries, for example, it was commonly acknowledged that peasant uprisings were stirred up by local notables, and this model persisted into the revolutionary decade.[32] In the wake of the Great Fear, royal proclamations condemned the ill-intentioned individuals who had sown false rumors in the countryside in order to spread alarm. One such proclamation specified that wherever such individuals were found, copies of the investigations were to be forwarded to the National Assembly. The government could then compare the evidence from different parts of the kingdom and trace the events to their source, in order that 'the leaders of these plots might be shown exemplary justice, preventing similar attempts.'[33] The same assumption of ignorance and helplessness appears again several months later, in the codification of martial law: in difficult times, the proclamation read, 'people . . . become the instrument of plots they know nothing about . . .'[34] Further disorders in the spring of 1790, finally, were answered with a decree which placed blame with unidentified 'brigands,' rather than with the 'upstanding citizens,' invariably portrayed as the victims of the ill-intentioned.[35]

As we have seen, it was dissenting parish priests who alerted the National Assembly to the dangers of sedition in the countryside, and their role as traditional intermediaries between state and peasantry made them particular targets. Even before the drafting of the decree of 27 November 1790, above, reports of the 'seditious sermons' and 'anticonstitutional words' of village *curés* began to pour into the office of the *Comité des recherches*. One such account told of the outburst of Father Rives, the *curé* of the community of Estampures, in the Hautes-Pyrénées.[36] A sudden hailstorm had struck the village in late May, the report related, and as the inhabitants stared out balefully from the doors of their houses, their minister had jumped about in the streets, yelling, 'Look! It's raining decrees from the National Assembly!' Stooping to gather up some of the hard white pellets, he had thrown them at his parishioners, saying: 'Here's something to pay your taxes with. Go to the National Assembly, they will give you a decree to clear away the hail.' Across the nation, the pattern of rejection of the religious policy of the Revolution proved to be extremely complex, and the question of how to prevent refractory priests from poisoning public opinion in the countryside was raised in countless sessions of the National Assembly, with more than one speaker intimating that such schemes could only be a sign of conspiracy.[37]

However, even after the religious crisis had lessened, the members of the Paris assemblies continued to assume that dissent in the countryside was the work of clearly defined social groups, rather than of peasants themselves. The discussions which laid the groundwork for the law of 4 December 1792 leave no doubt as to its target: 'this law is needed,' Reubell had argued, 'to repress the audacity of those who dare to give the people the idea that they have only to resort to another revolt or to throw themselves into the arms of another tyrant.'[38] The law of 19 March 1793, concerned with negative statements made during recruitment ceremonies, was aimed specifically at 'the priests, ex-nobles, ex-seigneurs, *émigrés*, and the agents and servants of all of these people,'[39] and the law of 27–28 germinal IV, as we have seen, targeted 'the agents of royalism and anarchy.'[40] In every case, it was assumed not only that verbal dissent signalled a counterrevolutionary enterprise, but that this dissent could only come from the educated, traditional enemies of the new order. As keen propagandists themselves, the revolutionaries were aware that words could be a powerful weapon, and the traditional perception of peasants as childlike and unaware of the political sphere beyond the confines of the village made them seem an easy target. No local administrator or judge wanted his district to be the next Vendée; as the oft-repeated formula went, 'it was with similar words that they succeeded in leading the people astray in many departments where order has now been reestablished.'[41]

Besides the parish priests and local nobility, other members of the rural elite were also carefully monitored. The high incidence of seditious statements from municipal officers, for example, contributed to the purges of local authorities conducted under the Terror. In one case, Ganivet, the mayor of a small village in the Dordogne, had spoken out against the economic sanctions of the revolutionary régime. Since his fellow villagers – peasants who were suffering from the effects of those sanctions – were 'won over' to his point of view, Ganivet was accused of having 'indoctrinated' them with his sedition.[42] In another village in the same area, a *bourgeois* named Gauthier was indicted for having remarked, over a glass of red wine, that he would kill his oxen before he would allow them to be worked on a holiday like the *Fête de Notre Dame*, a comment which flew in the face of dechristianization laws. In his trial, however, it was the innocence and impressionability of his audience which held the attention of the public prosecutor. Gauthier's words, the court was told, were 'more than enough to lead the inhabitants of the commune astray' and 'maintain the fanatical prejudices' used by the enemies of the people in order to corrupt that mysterious element, '*l'esprit public*' and to bring about, if possible, a counter-Revolution in France.[43]

At the opposite end of the spectrum from the rural elite, those on the margins of rural society – foreigners, soldiers, pedlars, and beggars – were also closely monitored and sometimes used as scapegoats in cases of seditious speech. The presence of 'outsiders' in general, referring to anyone from further afield than the neighboring villages, demanded increased vigilance.[44] A decree was drawn up on 10 August 1789, in the wake of the Great Fear, according to which local officials were to compile a list of vagrants and disarm them, and after September 1793, any traveller who could not justify his existence with a paper document was liable to be arrested as a suspect.[45] Innkeepers were required to keep a register and to note the details of their guests,[46] and fairgrounds were often portrayed, in police and administrative documents, as potential hotbeds in which the presence of 'foreigners' might lead to the stirring up of new ideas and the spreading of sedition. During a series of grain riots in Paris in June 1793, the *conventionnel* Thuriot attributed the disorders, in part, to the influence of outsiders: 'there are some men, recently arrived from the Vendée, who seem to have no purpose other than to stir up trouble. In the guest houses, foreigners rail against the revolution of May 31st.'[47] Pierre Grelety, a teacher, was accused by the municipality of Bergerac of travelling from place to place, with the sole intention of 'disseminating his incendiary words everywhere.'[48] Pedlars and beggars were regarded with a wary eye, as transients of questionable means, and servants were invariably relegated to the edges of rural society, their employment with the wealthier members of the community both enviable and suspicious. The members of each of these marginalized groups attracted more than their due share of attention, as local authorities attempted to shift the blame for the seditious ideas circulating in the countryside away from their own communities.

Conspiracies real and imagined

In fact, so convinced were the deputies that the currents of seditious speech rippling through the countryside were the work of agents of the counterrevolution, they came to wonder if it might not be part of a greater conspiracy against the Republic.[49] Considering that the peasantry made up more than four-fifths of the population of France, they reasoned that any group able to sway its collective mind, winning its allegiance and the strength of its numbers, would be in a position to dictate policy and politics. In addition to the parish priests, whose role as communicators of political news and information in the village would have made them effective conduits of sedition, the authorities were particularly concerned about the activities of ex-nobles who continued to live out their existence in rural areas where they had previously commanded respect as knowledgeable, worldly individuals. St. Just, a defrocked priest living in the Lot-et-Garonne, was described as an 'apostle of discord;' all those of his caste, the indictment read, 'lay traps for citizens who are good-intentioned but weak and faint-hearted of conscience, in order to bring about trouble and division among the people and to destroy the principles of reason and republicanism . . .'[50] The indictment for conspiracy for Jean de Malet, an ex-noble, similarly notes that words like his were 'one of the maneuvers often used by enemies of the Republic to shake the courage and loyalty of soldiers and other citizens.'[51] Joseph Duthiers, finally, another ex-noble, was arrested for spreading false news and exaggerating the setbacks of the republican armies, reportedly in the hope of spreading discouragement about the viability of the new régime. The public prosecutor appears to have been convinced that Duthiers' words were part of a greater plot: he had chosen this part of the country in which to move about, the court was told, because it was here that he could be 'most useful to his party'.[52]

As the Revolution wore on, the number of issues causing dissent grew and the social spectrum of defendants widened accordingly. Increasingly, rural artisans, sharecroppers, day-laborers, and the like began to make up a noticeable proportion of the defendants in cases of seditious speech. Nevertheless, even when the prosecuting authorities could not avoid conceding that seditious statements had in fact been made by peasants, there is evidence of a marked reluctance to admit the possibility that they had done so independently or intentionally. As one public prosecutor pontificated,

> counterrevolutionary plots do not come from the hearts and minds of peaceful farmers; their devotion to their difficult tasks leaves them little time to acquire knowledge of political matters, and while they might for a moment be led astray, conspiracies against liberty and popular sovereignty simply cannot be imagined or planned by those imbued with the gentleness and the innocence of the bucolic life.[53]

Indeed, the only means of resolving the tension that had arisen between the myth of the 'good peasant' and the reality of increasingly large numbers of peasants expressing antirevolutionary points of view was to imagine yet another conspiracy. According to revolutionary authorities, the enemies of the nation had concocted a new plan: to use innocent rustics as spokespeople to spread their sedition and turn public opinion to their favor.

In fact, even a cursory glance at our total sample of seditious speech trials reveals that revolutionary prosecutors were loath to convict members of the rural majority for crimes of opinion. While it would be incorrect to say that rural laborers from the agricultural and artisanal sectors were never convicted on indictments for seditious expression, such convictions occurred in only a small percentage of cases. In the few instances in which peasants *were* convicted – and the very few in which they were executed – such a verdict appears to have been a last resort, used in cases where the intentions of the defendant were so blatant that they could not be ignored or explained away by 'extenuating circumstances,' a catch-all phrase that was a favorite with juries. An overwhelming number of cases, for example, were dismissed for cause of inebriation: defendants routinely escaped punishment with the excuse that they had been drunk (usually *'pris de vin,'* *'dans le vin,'* or, most evocatively, *'plein de vin'*) at the time, and had not meant to say the words of which they were accused. A typical example is that of Louis Dejean, a 33-year-old tailor who had loudly announced, in a tavern in the village of Ladignac, in the Lot-et-Garonne, 'that soon we would have a king.' Dejean was arrested as an 'instigator of monarchy,' but when interrogated, he insisted that he had been drinking and had no recollection of the incident. A similar situation involved Jean Casse, *dit* Lartigue, a 40-year-old farmer who was found decrying the Republican régime to the tune of several bottles of wine.[54] Although it turned out that Lartigue was quite genuinely upset, as several of his mules had been requisitioned by the Republic, he was easily acquitted. In cases in which the defendants did not actually pose a danger to the internal security of the state, the desire of both jury and village witnesses to keep zealous urban revolutionaries from interfering in local affairs invariably resulted in an acquittal.

Furthermore, if the antirevolutionary statements of a supposedly ignorant laborer could not be explained away by drunkenness or spite, they could be ascribed to someone else, whose animosity toward the Revolution was easier for the courts to swallow. As a result, investigating authorities often asked rural defendants to reveal the identity of the individual who had told them or even bribed them to speak in such a manner. In one case, for example, in which a group of young people was arrested for counterrevolutionary shouting and singing in a tavern in the Ariège, each young man was asked in turn whether anyone had attempted to turn him against the current government 'with gifts, promises, solicitations, invitations, generosity or lavishness, fears, [or] threats.' Indeed, such phrasing hearkens back to the idea that peasant revolts were led by the nobility, and to ancien régime injunctions to reveal the 'motivators, instigators and accomplices' of rural disturbances, a phrase which still occasionally turns up in investigations after 1789. In most instances, peasants who were prompted to name a guilty party refused to do so. One defiant artisan was told that it was only by revealing 'who had advised or otherwise incited him to speak out' that he would lessen the gravity of his own crime. As it turned out, he was, indeed, a spokesperson – but for a group of like-minded villagers who were too afraid to voice their own opinions.[55] In a few cases, however, defendants were acquitted when they 'confessed' to doing another's bidding. Benoît Lamarque, a youth of 16 from the Ariège, volunteered the names of local individuals who had paid him to sing counterrevolutionary songs and to insult the parish priest; he was subsequently released, although the investigating officer did pause to ask if the list of conspirators was complete.[56]

In this way, rural citizens were able to use the prejudices and assumptions of the authorities to their advantage, encouraging them to accept any explanation as more likely than the possibility of day-laborers and shepherds holding contentious political views. Yet it would serve us well to consider *which* authorities held these prejudices and assumptions, for local justices of the peace and village authorities were certainly not fooled by suggestions from their superiors that peasants were ignorant scapegoats of high-level conspirators. On the one hand, their instructions were clear: local counterrevolutionaries and conspirators were to be rooted out and brought to justice. On the other, in many cases village officers seem to have known that their friends and neighbors were simply letting off steam in a stressful time. Jeannet Begarrie, whom we met at the start of this chapter, was aided not only by 'witnesses' who refused to incriminate her, but also by officers of the local police who appear to have made the most cursory of searches in response to the arrest warrant issued by the district court.[57] Such a lack of cooperation might be attributed to the remote location of Jeannet's village, high in the Pyrénées, but a number of similar instances occurred in far more accessible regions of the south-west. The charge of 'royalist words' brought against landholder Antoine St Martin, known as 'Bronquet' in his village of Maurillac in the Lot-et-Garonne, was summarily dismissed by a jury, despite the criminal court's observations that he spoke 'deliberately and without provocation' and that 'he hadn't even been induced by a third party.'[58] And in the case against Pierre Barrot, a sharecropper charged with sedition for hindering the recruitment process, the local authorities of the defendant's home village of Bars (Dordogne) went to great expense to send nine of the original fourteen witnesses when revolutionaries in the nearby town had the case forwarded to the Revolutionary court in Paris.[59]

However, a closer look at the use of conspiracy rhetoric in rural trials reveals that the impetus to exaggerate the charges came from local individuals about as often as it came from the public prosecutor in the distant criminal court. Rural politics after 1789 were a more complex affair than the phrase 'old wine in new bottles' suggests, but long-standing conflicts certainly played a role, not the least of which was in denunciations which brought incidents of seditious speech to the attention of the authorities. Many of the accusations against parish priests in the early years of the Revolution appear related to local religious divisions, and there is at least one example of a widow exacting revenge on the individual responsible for her husband's beheading.[60] A further layer of nuance is added, moreover, when the sample trials are compared against a basic timeline, for the pressure felt by administrators both high and low to root out conspiracy was itself clearly linked to the different phases of the Revolution. In 1791, the large number of parish priests speaking out against the Civil Constitution led prosecutors to imagine a 'coalition of priests,' and the royalist uprising known as the 'Year VII Insurrection,' which wracked the countryside of the Haute-Garonne and the Ariège in the summer of 1799, produced renewed efforts to discover counter-revolutionary plots. However, the peak of indictments for sedition and conspiracy in the countryside undoubtedly came during the Terror: nearly two-thirds of those trials which explicitly mention the possibility of conspiracy – a subset representing 20 percent of the total sample – took place under the government of the National Convention. A crucible of extreme revolutionary values, the Terror has drawn the attention of countless historians, and the inflammatory, rhetorical nature of its speeches and decrees is well-known. As the paranoia of those in power increased, the exhortations to seek out and destroy sedition multiplied endlessly. The fanatical activity of local surveillance committees, and the pressure they placed upon their members to 'denounce or be denounced,' resulted in an ever-greater number of prosecutions for conspiracy.[61] Many of these were countered either from above – as cases referred to the revolutionary court in Paris were dismissed for lack of evidence – or from below, with municipal authorities producing character witnesses and 'certificates of civic standing.' As long as the trial was kept out of those courts which were authorized by representatives-on-mission to make 'revolutionary' judgments, juries continued to assert their right to acquit their rural neighbors of conspiracy charges.[62] However, the obsession with conspiracy which characterized these months, and the seriousness of the charge in wartime, combined to produce a conviction and execution rate much higher than average, even in the countryside: of the thirteen defendants in this sample who were guillotined for verbal sedition, six were accused of conspiracy, including three of the four peasants who were beheaded for not watching what they said.

Conclusion

Like those magistrates of more than two centuries ago, we are still fascinated today by the question of conspiracy. The tendency to search for an explanation other than the one readily presented, and to wonder if secrets are being withheld, is at least partially motivated by the fact that in some instances, conspiracies have, in fact, been proven to be real. Did the conspiracies imagined by provincial judges and prosecutors in the courts of revolutionary France truly exist? On the one hand, defendants rarely revealed their supposed coconspirators, despite repeated injunctions to do so. On the other, it is unlikely that the authorities were entirely wrong in their suspicions. The few trials in which there was some evidence of collusion have received plenty of attention from historians; such is the case, for example, with Bernard Layrix, a laborer from the community of Labastide de Garderenoux, in the Ariège, who was accused of plotting against the Republican state in 1793.[63] Another case occurred shortly before the royalist uprising in the Haute-Garonne, and concerned a peasant who had reportedly approached a man at the market in Toulouse and asked him to support the restoration of the monarchy.[64] Examples such as these show that the authorities' fears of conspiracy could be justified; Bernard Layrix was convicted, and in the latter instance, those caught in the uprising would, indeed, turn out to be rural day-laborers and artisans, led by local elites. Ironically, the departmental administration had dismissed the account as a wild accusation.

However, in the overwhelming majority of cases, 'seditious' statements from peasants appear to be simply expressions of personal opinion: royalist opinions, certainly, but with no clear connection to a greater conspiracy. As historians, we need to distinguish between counterrevolution among local elites, clergy, and perhaps, some peasantry, and the more basic *anti*revolutionary feelings of the wider population, who grumbled and protested about conditions brought on or aggravated by the upheaval, but whose hostility was not harnessed by conspirators. The fact that such statements paled in comparison to the plots imagined by authorities can be explained, at least in part, by revolutionary experience in the region upon which this study is based. The south-west was a relatively quiet sector of France during the Revolution; it was sheltered from waves of counterrevolution and federalism which plagued other extremities of the nation. As we have seen, legislation against seditious speech and conspiracy was most often enacted in response to real concerns elsewhere in France, and particularly in the western regions affected by civil war. As Claude Petitfrère has argued, Republican authorities preferred to explain peasant resistance by the existence of a plot involving ex-priests and nobles, rather than to accept the possibility that the 'People' had rejected the Revolution.[65] However, even in areas recognized at the time to have been devoutly Catholic and traditional – or recognized since by historians to have also been socially and economically inclined to counterrevolution – there was a reluctance to admit that the peasantry was responsible for its own political opinions.

Indeed, while it may be interesting to reflect on the 'what ifs' inspired by conspiracy fears in the Revolution, it is more revealing to consider what these fears tell us about contemporary attitudes toward peasant politicization. The myth that the People of France were essentially good, honest, and hard-working was extremely long-lived. From the Jacobin perspective, dissent and popular opposition had to come from outside of the People; in the tradition of the Social Contract, it was the particular will of the individual which was suspect.[66] The architects of the Revolution fervently desired to believe that *le bon peuple* wholeheartedly supported their masterpiece, and if they did not appear to do so, they must have been led astray by an enemy. Eighteenth-century administrators and police forces clearly recognized the power of words: Louis XV had employed spies to eavesdrop on conversations, and the officers of the *maréchaussée* were instructed to look for those who had instigated revolts. The

Revolution merely confirmed and magnified this fact, for never before had words threatened to turn so many people against the régime. Yet the tendency of revolutionary authorities to focus upon conspiracy as the explanation for dissent blinded them to what was actually happening in the countryside: the development of critical public opinion.

Notes

1 This chapter is based upon material first presented at the 49th annual meeting of the Society for French Historical Studies, 11–13 April 2002, Toronto, Canada. It has benefited from discussion at the Toronto conference, as well as from comments from Timothy Tackett, Thomas Kaiser, David Andress, Mike Rapport, Paul Cohen, Alan Forrest, Colin Jones, and Geoff Cubitt. All translations are my own.

2 Archives Départementales (henceforth A.D.) Hautes-Pyrénées, 2L (justice non-côtée), procès contre Jeannet Bégarrie, an VII. Jeannet's words were: 'Vive le roi, vive le roi dix-sept; vive l'intendant de Pau; merde pour la nation, merde pour la République'.

3 The phrase is that of G. Wood, in 'Conspiracy and the Paranoid Style: Causality and Deceit in the Eighteenth Century,' *William and Mary Quarterly*, 39 (1982), pp. 401–441.

4 This theme is discussed in B. Coward and J. Swann, eds, *Conspiracies and Conspiracy Theory in Early Modern Europe: From the Waldensians to the French Revolution* (Aldershot, 2004), pp. 1–2; and in Bercé, *Complots et Conjurations*, p. 4. Interestingly, Wood, in 'Conspiracy and the Paranoid Style,' p. 410, argues that in the Anglo-American example, the involvement of a greater number of people resulted in a depersonalization of politics and greater conspiracy fears.

5 On the discussion of politics in the countryside, see my 'Of News and Networks: the Communication of Political Information in the Rural South-West during the French Revolution,' *French History*, 15 (2001), pp. 273–306, as well as R. Dupuy, *La Politique du peuple: Racines, permanences, et ambiguïtés du populisme* (Paris, 2002).

6 S. Kaplan, *Bread, Politics and the Political Economy in the Reign of Louis XV* (The Hague, 1976), 1, pp. 390–406; *The Famine Plot Persuasion in Eighteenth-Century France* (Philadelphia, 1982).

7 G. Lefebvre, *La Grande Peur de 1789* (Paris, 1932), especially pp. 107–117; T. Tackett, 'La Grande Peur et le complot aristocratique sous la Révolution française,' *Annales historiques de la Révolution française*, 335 (2004), pp. 1–17.

8 See for example J. Samaha, 'Gleanings from Local Criminal-Court Records: Sedition amongst the "inarticulate" in Elizabethan Essex,' *Journal of Social History*, 8 (1975), pp. 61–75, and B. Sharp, 'Popular Political Opinion in England, 1660–1685,' *History of European Ideas*, 10 (1989), pp. 13–29.

9   A. Farge, *Subversive Words: Public Opinion in Eighteenth-Century France*, trans. Rosemary Morris (Cambridge, UK, 1994); R. Darnton, 'An Early Information Society: News and the Media in Eighteenth-Century Paris,' *American Historical Review*, 105 (2000), pp. 1–35, and L. J. Graham, *If the King Only Knew: Seditious Speech in the Reign of Louis XV* (Charlottesville, 2000).

10 J. M. Walshaw, 'Controlling Public Opinion in the Old Regime: Did the King Care what the Peasants Thought?' to appear in the *Proceedings of the Annual Meeting of the Western Society for French History*, 33, 2006.

11 G. Kelly, 'From *lèse-majesté* to *lèse-nation*: Treason in Eighteenth-Century France,' *Journal of the History of Ideas*, 42 (1981), pp. 269–286; J. Merrick, *The Desacralization of the French Monarchy in the Eighteenth Century* (Baton Rouge, 1990); and Darnton, 'An Early Information Society,' pp. 14–15.

12 C. Jones, *The Longman Companion to the French Revolution* (London, 1988), p. 93; P. Caillet, ed., *Comité des recherches de l'Assemblée nationale, 1789–1791: inventaire analytique de la sous-série D XXIXbis* (Paris, 1993); introduction, pp. 9–26. See also M. Eude, 'Le Comité de surveillance de l'Assemblée législative, 1791–1792,' *Annales historiques de la Révolution française*, 36 (1964), pp. 129–148, and A. Troux, 'La Police politique pendant la Révolution française,' *Information historique*, 14 (1952), pp. 1–14 and 127–135.

13 J. Godechot, *Les Institutions de la France sous la Révolution et l'Empire* (Paris, 1951), p. 145; J.-P. Royer, *Histoire de la justice en France: De la monarchie absolue à la République* (Paris, 2001), p. 300. See too Charles Walton's recent treatment of the *Haute Cour Nationale*, in 'Policing Public Opinion in the French Revolution,' unpublished Ph.D. dissertation (Princeton University, 2003), chapter 5.

14 D. Greer, in his seminal work *The Incidence of the Terror during the French Revolution* (Cambridge MA, 1935), pointed out that 'the courts of the Terror used the term [conspiracy] quite indiscriminately to denote every crime in the revolutionary calendar from the improper use of trees of liberty to assassination,' p. 73ff.

15 Archives Nationales (henceforth A.N.) BB³ 19, letter from L. Debuc to the president of the National Assembly, 21 April 1791. Debuc's argument is an exact parallel of that of both Louis de Jaucourt, in his article in the *Encyclopédie*, where the latter writes, 'In the end, labeling other offences «lèse-majesty» only serves to diminsh the horror of the crime.'

16 *Réimpression de l'Ancien Moniteur* 6, 26 novembre 1790, pp. 480–484.

17 Ibid., pp. 498–500.

18 The entire penal code, promulgated on 6 October 1791, is printed in the *Archives Parlementaires* (henceforth *AP*) 31, pp. 326–339.

19 *AP* 31, p. 330: Seconde partie, Titre 1ʳᵉ, Section 1ʳᵉ, Article 4.

20 On the use of the *Code pénal* to prosecute cases of political justice, see P. Lascoumes *et al.*, *Au nom de l'ordre: Une histoire politique du code pénal* (Paris, 1989), pp. 85–87, 251–252.

21 *AP* 54, 4 décembre 1792, pp. 350–351.

22 Decree of 4 décembre 1792, cited in *AP* 54, p. 351. My emphasis.

23 *AP* 61, pp. 397–398 and 500–503.

24 *AP* 74, 17 septembre 1793, pp. 303–305. See also Royer, *Histoire de la justice*, pp. 394–395, and T. Tackett, *When the King Took Flight* (Cambridge, MA, 2003), p. 172.

25 See, for this era, J. Bourdon, 'Le mécontentement public et les craintes des dirigeants sous le Directoire,' *Annales historiques de la Révolution française* 18 (1946), pp. 218–237.

26 Jones, *Longman Companion*, pp. 145–146; A. Forrest, *Conscripts and Deserters: The Army and French Society during the Revolution and Empire* (New York, 1989), chapters 5 and 7.

27 A.D. Ariège, 1L134, Police, loi du 27 germinal IV, article premier.

28 L. Vardi, 'Imagining the Harvest in Early Modern Europe,' *American Historical Review*, 101 (1996), pp. 1357–1397.

29 L. de Jaucourt, Article 'Peuple,' *Encyclopédie, ou dictionnaire raisonné des sciences, arts et métiers* ... (Neufchastel, 1765), 12, pp. 475–477; Baron d'Holbach, *La Morale Universelle*, 3 vols (Amsterdam, 1776), 2, pp. 250–251.

30 H. Payne, *The Philosophes and the People* (New Haven, 1976), pp. 1–17; Vardi, 'Imagining the Harvest.'

31 See Payne, *The Philosophes*, and H. Chisick, *The Limits of Reform in the Enlightenment: Attitudes toward the Education of the Lower Classes in Eighteenth-century France* (Princeton, 1981).

32 Such assumptions were part and parcel of contemporary discourses surrounding peasant uprisings. See for example J. Nicolas, *La Rébellion française: Mouvements populaires et conscience sociale, 1661–1789* (Paris, 2002), pp. 91–113, 271–273.

33 A.N., AD+1089, 14 août 1789.

34 Décret qui établit une loi martiale contre les attroupements, 21 octobre–3 novembre 1789. *Recueil général annoté des lois, décrets, ordonnances, etc* (Paris, 1834), t. 1, pp. 22–23.

35 *AP* 16, 2 juin 1790, p. 41.

36 A.N. D XXIX 37, Petition from the municipality of Estampures to the Comité des Rapports, 14 juillet 1790.

37 See, for example, the contributions of Louis-François François, *cultivateur* and deputy of the Pas-de-Calais, and of the departmental administration of the Ariège, in *AP* 35, 18 novembre 1791, pp. 140–146.

38 *AP* 54, 4 décembre 1792, pp. 350–351.

39 *AP* 60, 19 mars 1793, article 6, pp. 331–332.

40 A.D. Ariège, 1L134.

41 A.D. Lot-et-Garonne, 2L98–49 and 2L105–3, procès contre Suzanne Guérineau, an II.

42 *Tribunal criminel et révolutionnaire de la Dordogne sous la Terreur* (2 vols, Périgueux, 1880), procès contre Jean Ganivet, an II.

43 A.D. Dordogne, 24L37, procès contre Gauthier *dit* Viroulet, an II.

44 On this topic see M. Rapport, *Nationality and Citizenship in Revolutionary France: The Treatment of Foreigners, 1789–1799* (Oxford, 2000).

45 Loi des suspects, article II; *AP* 74, 17 septembre 1793, p. 304. The denomination of 'gens suspects' had, in fact, existed since the *Code de police municipale et de police correctionnelle*, decreed on 19 July 1791; those who were unemployed but not unable to work would be considered 'gens sans aveu;' those who refused to make a declaration were 'gens suspects,' and those who were convicted of having made a false declaration were 'gens malintentionnés.' *AP* 28, pp. 425–433.

46 While this law dates back to the medieval period, it was not often enforced except in times of uncertainty; inns which were not on main roads generally escaped notice, particularly since most innkeepers were illiterate. During the Revolution, the law was resurrected as part of a general increase in surveillance of movement (*AP*, 28, p. 426).

47 *AP* 67, 27 juin 1793, p. 544.

48 A.D. Dordogne, 24L57–489, procès contre Grelety, an VII.

49 Cf. H. Wallon, *Histoire du tribunal révolutionnaire à Paris avec le journal de ses actes*, 2 vols (Paris, 1880), 1, pp. 130–145.

50 A.D. Lot-et-Garonne, 2L105–11, procès contre Joseph St. Just, an II.

51 *Tribunal criminel et révolutionnaire de la Dordogne*, procès contre Jean de Malet, an II, 1, pp. 265–280.

52 A.D. Lot-et-Garonne, 2L98–28, procès contre Duthiers, an II.

53 A.D. Lot-et-Garonne, 2L98–35, procès contre Dasti, an II.

54 A.D. Ariège, 13L24–8, procès contre Casse, *dit* Lartigue, an IV.

55 A.D. Dordogne, 24L45–260, procès contre Bordas, an IV.

56 A.D. Ariège, 8L36–14, procès contre Lamarque, 1793.

57 A.D. Hautes-Pyrénées, 2L (justice non-côtée), procès contre Begarrie, an VII.

58 A.D. Lot-et-Garonne, 2L51–5, procès contre Antoine St. Martin, *dit* Bronquet, an IV.

59 A.N. W347–686, *Tribunal révolutionnaire de Paris*, and *Tribunal criminel et révolutionnaire de la Dordogne* 1, pp. 325–328, procès contre Pierre Barrot et Guillaume Chaveroche, an II.

60 A.D. Dordogne, 24L42, procès contre Jean Bernard, *dit* Biotte, an II; denunciation of Cécile Desages. Biotte was acquitted.

61 R. Cobb, *The People's Armies. The armées révolutionnaires: Instrument of the Terror in the Departments, April 1793 to Floréal Year II* (New Haven, 1987), pp. 420–429; G. Cubitt, 'Denouncing Conspiracy in the French Revolution,' *Renaissance and Modern Studies*, 33 (1989), pp. 144–158; C. Lucas, *The Structure of the Terror: The Example of Javogues and the Loire* (Oxford, 1973), chapter 5, and 'The Theory and Practice of Denunciation in the French Revolution,' in S. Fitzpatrick and R. Gellately, eds, *Accusatory Practices: Denunciation in Modern European History, 1789–1799* (Chicago, 1996), pp. 22–39.

62 See Walshaw, 'Of News and Networks'; R. Allen, 'Political Trials by Jury in the Côte-d'Or, 1792–1800,' *Proceedings of the Annual Meeting of the W.S.F.H.* 18 (1991), pp. 222–232.

63 AD Ariège, 8L35–2, procès contre Bernard Layrix et d'autres, 1793. The trial is also discussed at length in P. Marty, *Trois localités de l'Ariège: la-Bastide-de-Lordat, Le Carbaret, Trémoulet et la région située à l'orient de Pamiers* (Foix, 1909), pp. 212–235.

64 This example is taken from D. Higgs, *Ultraroyalism in Toulouse from its Origins to the Revolution of 1830* (Baltimore, 1973), pp. 44–45.

65 C. Petitfrère, 'Le Peuple contre la Révolution française,' *L'Histoire*, 53 (1983), pp. 34–43.

66 J. L. Talmon, *The Origins of Totalitarian Democracy* (London, 1952), p. 41; F. Furet, *Interpreting the French Revolution* (Cambridge, 1981), pp. 53–54. See also P. Higonnet, 'The Harmonization of the Spheres: Goodness and Dysfunction in the Provincial Clubs,' in K. M. Baker, ed., *The French Revolution and the Creation of Modern Political Culture*, pp. 117–138; Lucas, 'The Theory and Practice of Denunciation,' p. 23; and Tackett, 'Conspiracy Obsession,' p. 694.

6

'Do you believe that we're conspirators?': conspiracies real and imagined in Jacobin politics, 1793–94

Marisa Linton

Introduction

We have seen elsewhere in this book that belief in the existence of conspiracies was prevalent throughout the Revolution. It could be found at every stage and among every group. But nowhere did the propensity to characterize opposition in terms of conspiracy play such a critical role as it did for the Jacobins. Before we come to look this subject, however, it is necessary first to define the 'Jacobins,' for the word itself is problematic. At its widest this term came to be used to describe any radical revolutionary. More specifically, it was a term for the members of the Jacobin Club in Paris and its provincial affiliates. But its meaning, and the composition of its membership, changed over the course of the Revolution, becoming ever more radical. Thus, Brissot and some of the other members of what later became known as the Girondin group had attended the Jacobin Club up until the autumn of 1792 when they were expelled from it. For the purposes of this chapter I am using the term 'Jacobin' to denote those who attended the Jacobin Club after the expulsion of the Girondins and up until the fall of Robespierre in July 1794. Leading Jacobins in the Convention (also known as Montagnards) came to dominate the revolutionary government in the summer of 1793 and thus played a key role in directing the Terror, though not all the members of the ruling Committees were members of the Jacobin Club.

Jacobin rule operated by means of the resort to an official and legalized policy of Terror. Historians have been struck by the links between the language of conspiracy and the practise of Terror, though they have accounted for it in different ways. For Furet, conspiracy theory was an integral and specific organizing principle of Jacobin ideology.[1] More recently, Gueniffey has built on Furet's approach in addressing Jacobin fear of conspiracy specifically in terms of its abstract intellectualized function. He depicts the ideological function of conspiracy theory as providing an intellectual basis for the unity of the nation in opposition to illusory plots.[2] Hunt, however, has pursued a different line of argument in pointing to the links between belief in conspiracy and the revolutionaries' obsession with the need for 'transparency.' This was the idea that the thoughts and motivation of all political participants should be open to the sight and scrutiny of others. Political participants should be devoted to the public good, rather than to self-interest or the interest of particular groups. The formation of political factions was thus seen as inimical to transparency. Factions were considered to be inherently furtive, self-interested, and – possibly – conspiratorial.[3]

Fear of conspiracy played a central part in Jacobin political rhetoric. But this fear was neither unique to Jacobinism, nor entirely an intellectualized abstraction. First, many features of the Jacobin notion of political conspiracy were not exclusive to Jacobins or even to revolutionary ideology as a whole. The Jacobin brand of conspiracy theory, with its fear of factionalism, corruption, and the exploitation of public posts to serve private interests, drew significantly on political conceptions familiar from ancien régime rhetoric.[4] Secondly, although much of the Jacobins' rhetoric of conspiracy seems to have been directed against illusory enemies, we should not forget that they were also confronted by genuine conspiracies. The political context of war and civil war meant that the Jacobins had genuine reasons to fear conspiracies. The Jacobins had many enemies among the foreign powers, *émigrés*, and their sympathizers within France, and so could not know from which direction a threat might come. It can be hard even for historians today, with access to all the available documentation, including private papers of the accused, and secret negotiations between foreign powers arrayed against France in the Year II, to distinguish between genuine and imagined conspiracies. Many of the original documents are missing or destroyed. In cases of genuine secrets and plots, many people had a vested interest in ensuring that incriminating material disappeared. It is hard to pick one's way through this minefield of imagined enemies and genuine ones: there are few certainties, and many questions that remain – and probably will always now remain – unanswered. This makes it all the more necessary to avoid the temptation to examine Jacobin ideology as though it existed in an intellectualized vacuum, divorced from its context.

Jacobin fears of conspiracy drew on three themes in particular that were familiar to eighteenth-century thought. The first of these derived from ancien régime political theorists, who characterized the factional politics of the court in terms of duplicitous individuals who grouped together using clandestine tactics to pursue their own self-interest and self-advancement at the expense of the state and good government. The second theme was drawn from the classical republican model of politics that was steeped in allusions to the dangers of conspiracy. The archetypal example of this was Catiline's conspiracy. The classical authors saw public denunciation as a public duty and a sign of virtue. Cicero's polemics served as a model of this kind of patriotic denunciation.[5] The third theme was the popular preoccupation with the 'famine plot.' During the Revolution this extended into fears of hoarding and price-fixing by unscrupulous merchants and counterrevolutionaries. This rhetoric was associated with the urban lower orders, the social group who were the most likely to suffer directly from food shortages, but the Jacobins also adopted it, partly to increase their own appeal to the *sans-culottes*.[6]

But the circumstances of 1793 overshadowed all else, and led to a hardening of attitudes toward anyone accused of conspiracy. The critical factors were the foreign war, the civil war, federalist revolts, and finally, demagogic pressure from below. The war with Austria that began in April 1792, and shortly included the German states, escalated further in February 1793 to include Britain, Holland, and (in March) Spain. France was thus threatened on all sides. In the early months of 1793 the war went badly for the French, culminating in their defeat by the Austrians at Neerwinden in March 1793, which forced the French out of Belgium and put them once more on the defensive. France also suffered betrayals and defeats through its own generals Lafayette, Custine and, most seriously, Dumouriez who, in April 1793, attempted to lead his French armies against the Convention in Paris. At the same time a series of internal revolts led by counterrevolutionaries culminated with the devastating civil war in the Vendée in western France which was at its height from March to August 1793. The foreign wars led to a reversal of the earlier policy of openness toward foreigners who supported the French Revolution.[7] In Paris there were a number of these foreigners, including the Englishman Tom Paine, the German noble Anacharsis Clootz, the Spaniard Guzman, the Austrian Proli and others. Now these men came under suspicion as possible spies for their countries of origin. Several would be denounced as conspiracy suspects, mostly with little justification. The fear of a foreign conspiracy, to be characterized later as 'the Foreign Plot,' became a defining characteristic of the revolutionary mentality.[8]

But the effect of the civil war and counterrevolution meant that fears of conspiracy were not confined to foreign agents: the revolutionaries also distrusted their fellow Frenchmen and women. This raised the problem of how you identified enemies when they spoke your own language and appeared to be 'people like us.' For the Jacobins, counterrevolutionaries were not an economic or social class (it was never illegal to have been a former noble): rather, counterrevolutionaries were those who had made a political choice to oppose the Revolution. For the demagogues on the Paris streets, the *sans-culottes*, there was more of an economic component in identifying opposition and they exerted pressure on the Jacobins to identify enemies in those terms also. The *sans-culottes* wanted heads: they wanted 'aristocrats' (by which they meant counterrevolutionaries) to pay for opposing the will of the people (by which they meant primarily the will of the *sans-culottes*). The Jacobins undertook to do this on their behalf, transmuting the anarchic terror of the *sans-culottes* into a formalized and legalized terror. In June 1793 the *sans-culottes* forcibly purged the Convention of the Girondin deputies. From that time on the Montagnards (that is, Jacobin deputies in the Convention) dominated the new government, but they were constantly under pressure to confirm to the will of the *sans-culottes* who had put them there. A key part of the Jacobins' policy of legalized terror was the extending of legal powers. Political cases were heard before specially constituted revolutionary law courts, above all by the Revolutionary Tribunal in Paris. In these courts accusations of conspiracy were difficult if not impossible to combat. This nebulous charge could be used to link together people who often had few connections, or were linked by ties of personal friendship rather than politics. Conspiracy against the revolutionary government was deemed tantamount to treason (*lèse-nation*), and hence subject to the death penalty.

This chapter will investigate the significance of conspiracy for the Jacobins and the part that conspiracy allegations played in their politics. It will approach this subject through an examination of some of the most traumatic and divisive uses of conspiracy allegations – those made not against overt opponents of the Revolution but against former comrades and fellow revolutionaries. It will look first at the case made against the Girondins; then at the politics of the 'Foreign Plot' (which included the trials of the Hébertist and Dantonist factions); and in conclusion briefly ahead to the summer of 1794 and the part played by belief in conspiracy in the discrediting of Jacobinism and the overthrow of Robespierre.

The Girondins

The process by which attacks on the Girondins escalated into conspiracy allegations went through several stages. Hostilities had first been aroused during the bitter campaign in the Jacobin Club over Brissot's pro-war policy. Behind Robespierre's dogged opposition to the war policy was an underlying concern over the conduct of power under the so-called 'Girondin ministry' and the fear that Brissot, Roland and others either were in league with the court or were its dupes.[9] The group of revolutionaries who gathered around Brissot was only loosely connected. Indeed it is debatable at what stage, if at all, the Girondins became a distinctive group. Part of the difficulty lies in the fact that their opponents at the Jacobin Club began to refer to a faction of 'Brissotins' (or later 'Girondins') the more easily to attack them as a group by making them appear a united faction. Sydenham went so far as argue that it was the Jacobins who constructed the 'Girondins' as a focus for opposition, though the meticulous work by Alison Patrick demonstrated the existence of numerous identifiable 'Girondins.'[10] The very accusation that the Girondins constituted a faction was itself used as evidence against them, factions being seen as inimical to the revolutionary project.[11] If the Girondins had a coherent identity it was as the group around Brissot himself. Insofar as the Girondins had a political leader at all, it was he, and it was against Brissot that the strongest criticism was made.

The Girondin leaders such as Brissot and Vergniaud were very far from being the politically idealistic, high-minded revolutionaries that some historians (in a tradition beginning with the romantic poet Lamartine) liked to portray them. The idealized image was used to contrast them favorably with the more hard-line terrorist Jacobins. But the Girondins themselves bear much responsibility for the escalation of violence in 1792 and early 1793 through their deliberate manipulation of the Revolution for their own ends, a policy that laid the foundations of the Terror. Most crucial of all was the role played by Brissot and others in leading the clamor for war in the winter of 1791/92. In pushing for war they aimed to break the Constitution of 1791 and overthrow the monarchy, or at least to bring the monarchy under their own control – a policy certain to push France into renewed turmoil. They showed themselves more than willing to encourage the demagogic militancy of the Parisian crowd in order to intimidate the Legislative Assembly. They also made liberal use of the language of conspiracy to denounce political opponents such as de Lessart. It was they who instigated the fears of a Foreign Plot that were to dominate the later history of the Revolution, by their denunciation of a secret 'Austrian Committee,' a strategic tactic to bolster their demands for a war with Austria. The Jacobins learned from these tactics. The Girondins started the war, and all that came with it, but then proved incapable of finishing it. The Jacobins would be more ruthlessly effective. And some of the first casualties of that ruthlessness were to be the Girondins themselves.

One of the earliest, most comprehensive and damagingly articulate of the attacks on the integrity of the Girondins was Camille Desmoulins' pamphlet, *Jean-Pierre Brissot démasqué* (February 1792). Desmoulins wrote in response to an article in *Le Patriote français* (a journal effectively controlled by Brissot), which attacked him as an unworthy patriot for his defense of people's rights to engage in gambling. Desmoulins proceeded to take his revenge by calling into question Brissot's integrity since the beginning of the Revolution. Desmoulins stated, 'you have been in the worst faith, a real Tartuffe of patriotism and a traitor to the patrie . . .,' though he qualified this by adding 'in the sense of a man who thinks otherwise than how he speaks.'[12] Even Brissot's republicanism was depicted as a sign of his bad faith. Desmoulins accused him of having affected a republicanism that could only further destabilize an already volatile situation in the days prior to the Champ de Mars massacre, and of having been behind the petition that led to it.[13] The pamphlet stopped short of declaring Brissot to be a counterrevolutionary, nor was it directed against anyone other than himself. But it made a great stir and injured Brissot's reputation by making him look a fool, if not worse. He made no effective attempt to respond to the allegations.[14]

Fifteen months later Desmoulins launched a much more comprehensive attack in his *Fragment de l'histoire secrète de la Révolution* (May 1793, later known as *L'Histoire des Brissotins*). This time Desmoulins' target went beyond Brissot himself, to include the network of Brissotins as implicated in what Desmoulins now openly called a conspiracy. In the space of the fifteen months between the two pamphlets much had changed to make the implications of such a denunciation far more dangerous. The war, which Brissot had done so much to precipitate, had not resulted in the successes he had expected, but in military reverses, political instability, surging patriotism, and a second revolution which had overthrown the constitutional monarchy. The first months of the new political assembly, the National Convention, had been dogged by rivalries between two emerging groups: the Girondins and the more radical Jacobins. Brissot himself had been formally expelled from the Jacobin Club in the previous October. Within the Convention, Girondins and Jacobins had fought over a number of issues: over the fate of the king; over the political role of the *sans-culottes*; over the need for a concerted war policy; and over the right of Paris (in the shape of the Paris Commune) to impose its will upon the rest of France (in the persons of the nation's deputies). In this volatile context, Desmoulins accused the Brissotins of being behind a conspiracy to destroy the gains of the Revolution. Brissot would deny it, but as Brissot himself had said when he made his claims about the existence of the Austrian conspiracy: 'It is absurd to ask for hard evidence and judicial proofs that one has never had. Not even in the conspiracy of Catiline, for conspirators have never been in the habit of letting evidence against themselves be open to discovery.'[15] Desmoulins accused the Brissotins collectively of being in league with Lafayette and the Orléanist faction. Worse still, he claimed that they were working for Pitt – and therefore in cahoots with the enemies of France: '. . . never in history has there been a conspiracy for which there is more evidence . . . than this Conspiracy, which I call that of the Brissotins because Brissot has been at the heart of it.[16]

To give substance to his claims, Desmoulins went back over the history of the whole Revolution. Past events were put under review, and their meaning reinterpreted to paint the actions of the Brissotins in the darkest light. No one was better placed than Desmoulins to give the 'inside story' of Brissot and other former fellow revolutionaries, now his enemies, for they had worked closely together, shared the same political experiences, and even attended the same private dinners. Some of these took place at the home of Sillery, in the salon of Apollo, which Desmoulins now depicted as a den of Orléanist intrigue.[17] Curiously, while Desmoulins included Sillery, his wife (Madame de Genlis), and Laclos as members of the conspiratorial Orléanist faction, he speculated that d'Orléans himself (who until his arrest the previous month had sat with the Jacobins) might not have been part of it. According to Desmoulins, the former duke was so idle, and so hopeless at politics that he might have been a pawn of his own faction: 'the thing is not impossible.'[18] The subsequent charges made against the Girondins when they were eventually brought before the Revolutionary Tribunal were to owe much to Desmoulins' account of their conspiracy. According to Villate, a witness at their trial, Desmoulins collapsed on hearing the verdict, crying: 'It is my 'Brissot Unmasked' that is killing them!'[19] While the principal charges of conspiracy against the Girondins remained largely the same, there would be two significant new allegations, as well as a considerable extension of the numbers of accused, and in the degree of guilt attributed to them.

The insurrection of 31 May to 2 June led to the arrest of twenty-nine Girondin deputies and two ministers, Clavière and Lebrun. The Jacobins came to power with the support of the *sans-culottes* who had used the threat of violence to coerce the Convention. The Girondins were placed under loose house arrest. At that stage there seemed good reason to hope that the Girondins would eventually be readmitted to the Convention.[20] But the flight of nine deputies, and the involvement of several of them in an armed revolt against the Convention made any compromise highly unlikely. The initial report on their arrest, given by Barère on 6 June on behalf of the Committee of Public Safety, was relatively moderate, deliberately vague, and judicious. The culpability of the men arrested 'was still uncertain,' he said, and it was not for the 'men of the Mountain' to put themselves above the truth, and pass premature judgement on the accused. 'It is for France, it is for the entire republic, to judge their case.'[21] This was followed by a more comprehensive report by Saint-Just on 8 July. His report accepted the idea of conspiracy, but was still relatively judicious in that it made an attempt to prove the chargers. It was also selective in the numbers of men accused of conspiracy. Only the men who had fled from arrest to become involved in revolt should be accused. He said: 'You must distinguish between those detained: most were misled; and who among us can flatter himself that he has never been deceived? The true culprits are those who fled . . .'[22] The final advice to the Convention was notably pragmatic and emphasized culpable actions, not culpable opinions: 'Proscribe them, not for what they said but for what they did; pass judgment on the others and pardon the greater number.'[23]

But when Billaud-Varenne spoke on 15 July his account of the Girondin conspiracy was much more sinister in tone. He employed the language of revolutionary denunciation; presented the idea of a concerted, active, and long-standing conspiracy; and included the names of more suspects. He traced 'the plan of a conspiracy which appears to embrace the whole republic.' He conceded that there were few formal proofs since 'conspirators work in the shadows' but their plots could be uncovered by means of 'a simple moral conviction,' and by observing how far their plans were in conformity with those of other conspirators.[24] As Sydenham observed, 'within a week the policy of compromise was jettisoned.'[25] What had happened to change the attitude of the Jacobins, who had seemed capable up till then of differentiating between those who had engaged in armed revolt and those who had not? The murder of Marat two days before had clearly unnerved the Jacobin leaders, making them fearful for their own lives. More important still, the federalist revolt was having serious implications. On 13 July the Girondin insurgents at Caen had been defeated with relative ease. But federalist protests were spreading to other parts of the country, and in some areas – most notably Lyons, Marseilles, and Toulon – were shading into outright counterrevolution.[26] At one point a majority of the departments were protesting against the centralization of power in Paris, and the coup to exclude the Girondins. The fact that escaped Girondins were doing their best to encourage the revolt appeared to Jacobins, at a time of war and civil war, to be an act of treason. This explains their hard-line attitude toward the leaders of the revolt, including Pétion, Barbaroux, and Buzot, though not their decision to include on the list of the accused many deputies, including Vergniaud and Gensonné, who had not fled. In the case of Deperret and of Fauchet, they were implicated through Corday who had sought their help when she arrived in Paris to pursue her plan to assassinate Marat. Though neither man, nor indeed Barbaroux who had recommended her from Caen, seems to have had any idea of what Corday intended, to the Jacobins it seemed that a plot was afoot to assassinate them. Deperret and Fauchet denied involvement, but their pleas were ignored.[27] Thus two new allegations, of federalist revolt and assassination plots, were added to the other claims about conspiracy.

Amar's speech on 3 October on behalf of the Committee of General Security proved the culmination of this conspiracy discourse. This was the formal *acte d'accusation*, which formed the basis of the legal case made against the Girondins at their trial: it was a sledgehammer of a document. The key charges against the Girondins were that they had secretly tried to save the monarchy; that they had made a catastrophic mess of the war which they themselves had brought into being (and here their association with Dumouriez added to suspicions against them); and lastly (and most crucially) they had taken up arms in the federalist revolt.[28] The charges against the Girondin leaders of recklessness and even criminal incompetence in wartime were serious ones. In the matter of the federalist revolt there was a case for saying that the actions of the participants had been treasonous. But the Jacobins went further than this: they depicted the Girondins collectively and systematically as conspirators. They had always been against the true Revolution and the true patriots.[29] Amar stressed their unity: 'they are all part of the conspiracy.'[30] Yet there were now thirty-six more men implicated than in Saint-Just's original report. These additional names were of men who had not been involved in the federalist revolt, and who were only marginally associated with the Girondins' inner network. They were accused of being agents in the service of Pitt. Amar listed ways in which Girondin politics corresponded with Pitt's aim to destroy France. The ills of the present war and political disasters were attributed to malevolent machinations of the Girondins, including the declaration of war against the leading powers of Europe, the scourge of civil war, the putting in place of treacherous generals at the head of the armies, the loss of French colonies, and the assassination of the leading Jacobins, Marat and Lepeletier.[31]

It was a defining moment of choice for the Jacobins: through it, the mind-set behind the Terror began to fall into place. Still, there was some limitation of the number of victims. At this same meeting of the Convention Robespierre opposed Billaud-Varenne's motion to force the deputies to choose sides in a vote by *appel nominel* on the fate of the Girondins. Robespierre argued that such a vote would polarize the Convention into those for and those against conspiracy. He also defended the seventy-five deputies who signed a protest at the arrests, saying that the Convention should not seek to multiply the numbers of the guilty. Though the protestors were arrested, they were not put on trial.[32]

Rather than focus on the more plausible charge that the Girondin leaders had acted with incompetence and recklessness while in a position of power during a time of war, the Jacobins chose to present them in terms of their immorality, as evil conspirators against virtue and the republic. Did the Jacobins really believe the arguments about a conspiracy? This is hard to judge. Many people do seem to have given it credence, especially among the *sans-culottes* – whose rhetoric, in large part, it was. But others were undoubtedly more cynical in manipulating the evidence. The point of the trial, in the end, was not to prove the guilt of the Girondins, but to bring about their deaths, and to make the case look vaguely credible. It was true that the actions of the Girondins had helped to imperil the republic, but this was an inadvertent consequence of their mismanagement of their authority. The intense fears and pressures aroused by military disasters and social and political turmoil contributed enormously to the brutal treatment of the Girondins and the decision to destroy them. And possibly it was easier for the Jacobins to cling to the belief that they owed France's military disasters to an internal conspiracy, as this helped them give a name and substance to their enemies and thus feel in control of a situation that was outside their experience and of a magnitude hard to comprehend. The judgment of the Jacobin Levasseur, thirty years after these events, when most of the protagonists had gone to their graves, offers a more dispassionate insight. He deplored the trial and stated that most of the Girondins had been sincere republicans. But he also sought to exonerate his old Jacobin colleagues who, he said, had been driven by circumstances to take this fatal step.[33] The Girondins had brought their fate on themselves by stirring up revolt and civil war. He said that the accusation against them that they were secret royalists was untrue, but it was true that their reckless actions lent support to the royalists: 'the Girondins were not cut out to be conspirators: they were simply elegant sophists, marked by a radical nonentity.' Their 'lack of political skills' and their 'errors, in the course of discussions on matters of the gravest national interest, gave the appearance of concerted treachery.'[34]

The Foreign Plot

During the winter that followed, Jacobins began to warn of the dangers of another conspiracy: the so-called 'Foreign Plot.' The rhetoric around this plot became the very apogee of revolutionary conspiracy theory. It hinged upon the idea that certain leading revolutionaries, members of the

Jacobin and Cordelier Clubs, were secretly in league with the hostile foreign powers, particularly the British and the Austrians, to bring down the Jacobin government. The two factions on which suspicion chiefly focused were both, for different reasons, in political opposition to the rule of the Committees. The Hébertists, led by the journalist Hébert, were self-appointed spokesmen of the *sans-culottes*. Their political power was centered on the Paris Commune and the Cordelier Club. They also dominated a number of administrative positions, particularly within the war ministry.[35] Their calls for an intensification of the Terror, action against counterrevolutionaries, support for *sans-culotte* measures, and policy of forcible de-Christianization, placed them on the extreme radical edge of the Revolution. From this position they threatened to undermine the Jacobin leadership. From a very different perspective, the Dantonists (or Indulgents) also threatened the rule of the Committees. Led by Danton, these were leading revolutionaries who now called for a policy of clemency and amnesty toward counterrevolutionaries. These two groups were opposed to each other, even more than they were to the Committees. The motives of Danton and others were somewhat shadowy, as the taint of financial and even political corruption hung over him, as it did over many others. On the question of how far his venality had extended to political corruption – particularly to taking bribes on behalf of the court – the evidence is less irrefutable, though still very suggestive.[36] The 'Foreign Plot' became linked to the East India Company affair. This was a scandal involving profiteering from the sale of shares, which implicated a number of Jacobins, not least Danton's close friend Fabre d'Eglantine.

It was in an effort to clear himself and divert attention from this financial scandal and onto other revolutionaries that Fabre told the Committees about the existence of the Foreign Plot. One of the chief figures implicated by Fabre was Chabot. He too, in an effort to save himself, 'coughed.' He went to Robespierre's home early on the morning of 14 November, and revealed a tale of a vast conspiracy by counter-revolutionaries to financially – and politically – corrupt leading Jacobins. He said that counterrevolutionaries including Benoît d'Angers were involved: '[T]heir goal is the dissolution of the Convention. And all those who work to undermine it, to corrupt it or to defame its members who have given service to the Republic are involved in this plot.'[37] Most of the evidence for the subsequent trials of those accused of participating in the Foreign Plot stemmed from the denunciations of Fabre and Chabot. Their separate testimonies, entangled as they were, implicated the Hébertists and the Dantonists in complicated allegations of a vast plot involving financial speculation, duplicitous foreigners, de-Christianizers, British secret agents, and French royalists. Sinister figures such as Pitt himself and the Gascon adventurer the baron de Batz were described as puppeteers who pulled the strings of the corrupted Jacobins.

One of the chief questions asked by historians is whether there was any substance to the allegations. This is a question that is unlikely ever to have a definitive answer. Undercover espionage leaves few written sources, either for people at the time or for subsequent investigators. Nevertheless, historians have found indications of the existence of some kind of political plot.[38] With regard to genuine spies, Proli in particular seems to have been an Austrian agent, although purportedly an Hébertist. Batz, for his part, appears to have been involved in attempts to corrupt certain Jacobins.[39] How far any Jacobins themselves were party to a political plot is much more difficult to ascertain, then as now. There is a degree of circumstantial evidence about the financial corruption of Danton, Fabre, Basire, and members of the group around them. There were also suspicious circumstances surrounding Hébert. There is considerable evidence of financial corruption regarding Chabot through his link to the Frey brothers, whose sister he had recently married for an implausibly large dowry of 200,000 livres – that looks to the present-day observer very much like some form of money laundering.[40] But did financial corruption lead to political corruption? It seems likely that certain Jacobins were not averse to accepting bribes, particularly to save eminent prisoners such as the queen and Madame du Barry. In the matter of the queen, there is some evidence to suspect both Hébert and Danton. But beyond this, there is little indication that there was a concerted plot, still less that the Hébertists and Dantonists (who were implacably opposed to one another) would be secretly in collusion.

The politics around the Foreign Plot were about much more than simple paranoia. Nor were they simply a cynical way of disposing of political rivals, though it is true that there was a new degree of ruthlessness about the Jacobins' resort to the Terror as a means of eliminating real or perceived enemies. Whatever the truth of the details of the Foreign Plot, it seems clear that many leading Jacobins (not just Robespierre, who was prone to see conspiracy everywhere) felt under threat and gave some credence to the allegations. So as an insight into Jacobin thinking, these conspiracy fears are highly significant. Most importantly, much of Jacobin politics from the autumn of 1793 to April 1794 has to be understood in relation to conspiracy – both real and imagined.

A key characteristic of conspiracy theory in the minds of the Jacobins was the connection they made between financial and political corruption. Venality for them was a hallmark of ancien régime politics and indicative of a corrupt government. It could corrupt the integrity of the Jacobins unless they stood firm against it. And a man who had lost his financial integrity could also lose his political integrity (his virtue) and could be 'bought' by foreign agents. This connection is seen in the confrontation between the two factions, Hébertists and Dantonists, over the winter of 1793/94 which was characterized by mutual recriminations over financial corruption and suspect political allegiances. These mutual allegations of conspiracy featured strongly in Hébert's journal the *Père Duchesne* and in Desmoulins' new journal, *Le Vieux Cordelier*, where each of them accused the other of financial corruption and of collusion with Pitt.[41]

At first Robespierre had given Desmoulins qualified support. He had read the first two issues of *Le Vieux Cordelier* in proof and approved their contents insofar as they constituted an attack on the ultrarevolutionaries. But when Danton and Desmoulins became more outspoken in their criticism of the policies of the Committee of Public Safety itself, Robespierre made a fateful decision to side with his fellow Committee members as they worked to bring about the destruction of both the Hébertist and Dantonist factions on charges of conspiracy and involvement in the Foreign Plot.

The Hébertists were arrested first. From the springboard of the Cordeliers they had called for a *sans-culotte* insurrection against the Convention. That sealed their fate. The rhetoric employed to denounce them reverberated with the Jacobin fear of the universal plot. There was intense anxiety over the fact that these men were known revolutionaries, and in many cases had been so since 1789. How then could 'genuine patriots' and 'conspirators' be told apart? A panoply of exterior signs was invoked to identify conspirators, including their private friendships, suspicious gestures, and overacting.[42] But the problem, as Robespierre saw it, was that in practise these men were virtually indistinguishable from the 'genuine' revolutionaries: 'they mingle with the defenders of the patrie; they imitate our language; they flatter our love of liberty; they appear at times to surpass it; they adopt all the exterior signs of the Revolution, they even think up new ones; they do not simply participate in our Popular Societies, they preside over them, they direct them.'[43]

Saint-Just delivered the official accusation of 'the foreign faction' on 23 ventôse (13 March 1794). The picture he painted of this conspiracy was very different from his much more measured description of the Girondins' plot the previous summer. This was a kind of super-conspiracy: '[T]here is in the Republic a conspiracy organized by the foreigner, which prepares for the people famine and new chains. A large number of people appear to serve this conspiracy.'[44] It sought to undermine the republic by attacking virtue. It was founded on dissimulation. The conspirators imitated true patriots, the better to bring about their downfall.[45] Now there was no acceptable form of faction. 'Every faction is therefore

criminal, because it tends to divide the citizens; every faction is therefore criminal, because it neutralises the power of public virtue.'[46]

The Jacobin leadership was using a rhetoric of conspiracy – encom-
passing aristocratic plots against the people – that was already familiar to
the urban populace through the denunciations of men like Marat and
Hébert himself. Now that language was being turned against the very men
who had employed it as spokesmen for the cause of the *sans-culottes*. The
reaction of the popular classes to the arrest and trial of the 'Père Duchesne'
was one of confusion, which mirrored their reaction the previous autumn
after the fall of the *enragés*. After the initial shock, the sections chose to
profess loyalty to the Convention. But the *sans-culottes* were unsure of
whom to believe and increasingly doubtful about the trustworthiness
of any of the Revolution's professed leaders.[47] The rhetoric of conspiracy
when used against revolutionaries had the effect of undermining all
confidence in the Revolution itself.

But the rhetoric of conspiracy was not just an attempt on the part of the
Jacobin leaders to win the compliance of the *sans-culottes*. A number of
Jacobins, particularly those closest to Robespierre, genuinely felt that the
Revolution was being taken over by men acting from their own interests
and from motives of self-advancement. They were particularly concerned
about a rising tide of bureaucrats who exploited revolutionary government.[48] Much of the language, and indeed the repressive actions, of the
Jacobin leadership were thus directed against their own people, for they
feared that the Revolution was being brought down from within. At the
heart of Jacobin ideology there was a conflict between using an official
position as an opportunity for self-advancement and for that of one's
friends and family, and the new ideal of revolutionary 'transparency'.
This concern lay behind much of the impetus to establish a 'republic of
virtue,' for a 'man of virtue' would be dedicated to the public good, and
would not accept bribes or act from motives of self-interest and self-
advancement.

It appears that corrupt practices had penetrated into the heart of the
institutions of Jacobinism. One place where it seems to have been rife was
in the Committee of General Security and among its agents. As the police
Committee, responsible for arrests and the prisons, there were many
opportunities for its agents to exploit their power in a way that had
political implications. Most notoriously Dossonville, a key agent, worked
closely with a prison informer, Armand, who denounced fellow prisoners
in the hope of remission for himself. Together these two constituted the
principal source of the accusations against the 54 people executed in
red shirts (as parricides) on 17 June 1794 as alleged participants in the
'Foreign Plot.'[49]

Even the integrity of members of the Committee of General Security could not be relied upon. There is evidence that Amar was involved in profiting from the East India Company corruption scandal.[50] Yet the previous July he had been charged with investigating the Company's accounts and had declared that they were in order. He was also in charge of the interrogation of Chabot – about which Chabot complained repeatedly. The text of this interrogation disappeared mysteriously in 1795.[51] It was Amar, too, who finally presented the report on Chabot, Basire, Fabre, and the others and their involvement in the East India Company on 26 ventôse (16 March) in which he focused exclusively on the financial corruption of these deputies, and failed to connect it to political corruption. Amar's motives remain obscure: perhaps he was trying to keep the men away from the Revolutionary Tribunal (which meant the death penalty) and before the ordinary criminal courts. But Robespierre and Billaud-Varenne would have none of it. An odd scene followed in which the two members of the Committee of Public Safety publicly rebuked Amar for leaving out the political dimension of corruption and he accepted their criticism, saying he had only been doing his duty.[52] It seems that Robespierre was genuinely shocked by the extent of corruption among the Jacobins as revealed by Fabre and Chabot, but he delayed acting, possibly because he was trying to defend the honor of the Jacobins. It was only when he became convinced that political conspiracy was accompanying financial corruption that he acted, and even then, some of the evidence against Chabot and Hébert may have been suppressed because it reflected so badly on the Jacobins.[53]

The Dantonists

The second part of the 'Foreign Plot' tragedy concerned the trial of the Dantonists. It was a pivotal moment for the Revolution, not least because of the powerful contrast it provided between Robespierre and Danton who between them epitomized very different perspectives of what the Revolution was, and what it was meant to achieve. For five years these men had been on the same side. What now separated them? One thing on which they differed was the issue of venality for which, as we have seen, there is considerable circumstantial evidence against Danton. But this is not why he was arrested, and little was made of his financial corruption at his trial. The reason that Danton was brought down was political: his opposition to the policy of Terror conducted by the ruling Committees. Had he succeeded, the government would have lost power, and possibly even their own lives, and the Revolution (at least as they understood it) would have been fatally weakened. The dilemma of Robespierre seems to have been particularly severe, not simply because he was the personal friend of Desmoulins and had formerly been friendly with Danton, but because to some extent he seems to have sympathized with their aim of winding down the Terror. Yet for some reason he changed his mind and sided with the Committees. It may be because Danton had refused to moderate his views, and had rejected a compromise, that Robespierre threw in his weight against him – because he knew Danton was unlikely to win.[54] But whatever his motives for joining them, once the Committees had decided on the proscription of the Dantonists there could be no going back. They were driven by their own fear: the losers of the struggle would face the death penalty. This time the Committees took the precaution of having the accused arrested before their denunciation, giving them no chance to speak in their own defense. Robespierre had some initial qualms about this, but as Vadier put the choice somewhat pithily to him: 'If we do not guillotine them, they will guillotine us.'[55]

Once again Saint-Just, the rottweiler of the Committee of Public Safety, was charged with the task of making the official accusation of conspiracy against another faction. The allegations followed a similar pattern to those used on previous occasions. Saint-Just linked the Dantonists to the chain of earlier conspiracies: to the Orléanists, the Girondins, and the Hébertists. It seemed that the history of the Revolution had been dogged by conspiracies since its very inception, and all the ills that had beset it could be traced to conspiracy. There were few specific charges against Danton and the others – the accusations were at once vague and all embracing. There was much emphasis on signs and indications whereby conspirators disclosed their 'true' natures.[56] None of the accused had ever, it seems, been a genuine patriot.

> Those people, who for four years have conspired under the veil of patriotism, now that justice is closing in on them repeat the words of Vergniaud: *The Revolution is like Saturn, it will devour its own children.* Hébert repeated these words during his trial; they are repeated by all those who tremble as they see themselves unmasked. No. The Revolution will not devour its children, but its enemies; no matter with what impenetrable mask they have concealed themselves. Were the conspirators who perished the children of liberty because for a moment they resembled them?[57]

Saint-Just was heard in fearful silence: there was no further dissent within the Convention.

For the trial itself the Committees brought together disparate groups of men. Alongside the Dantonists whose offenses were chiefly political were a number of others, including Chabot, Delaunay, Basire, and Fabre, who had been involved in the East India Company scandal. Several 'foreign agents' were also included to add substance to the idea of the foreign plot, including Guzman and the brothers Frey. There was little to suggest a common thread uniting some of these men except in the minds of their accusers, as the Jacobins well knew. Indeed, some had denounced one another: Chabot had denounced Fabre, and Fabre had denounced Chabot. Fabre had also denounced the former member of the Committee of Public Safety, Hérault, for selling the Committee's secrets to the foreign powers. Now Hérault and Fabre stood together designated as fellow conspirators. As before, the point of the trial was to secure convictions and to kill. The language of conspiracy was applied liberally to taint the accused. This process of deliberate manipulation and inversion of revolutionary rhetoric was clear to the accused. Danton mocked the notion that Barère was now a 'patriot' and he himself an 'aristocrat.' And he addressed his fellow Montagnard, Cambon, whom he had spotted among the witnesses, challenging him to say the truth. 'Do you believe that we're conspirators? Look, he's laughing! He doesn't believe it. Write down that he laughed.'[58]

The spirited defense of the Dantonists looked for a moment as though it might turn the tide of opinion. In desperation, the Committees acted. Saint-Just and Billaud-Varenne announced to the Convention that yet another conspiracy had been detected. This time it was in the prisons, incited by general Dillon and the wife of Desmoulins, to free the prisoners and assassinate members of the Committee of Public Safety and the Revolutionary Tribunal. The far-fetched account of the prison plot was bolstered by flimsy evidence: a letter from the police administration based on the dubious evidence of one prisoner, Laflotte, that Dillon had sought to win him over to the plot.[59] But it seems to have been sufficient to stir among the deputies fears of vengeful aristocrats and assassinations. The Convention voted a decree which stated that 'anyone accused of conspiracy who resists or insults national justice will be excluded immediately from the court.' It was the end of even a notional form of defense against a charge of conspiracy.[60]

The Robespierrists and the last Jacobin conspiracy

Over the course of the year of Jacobin rule, we have seen the intensification of the language of conspiracy as all traces of the moderation of judgment that had featured in the earliest indictments of the Girondins were swept away by an overwhelming tide of conspiracy theory. Arguably, this clutching at conspiracy to explain the events of the Revolution was motivated by fear and by the relative weakness of the ruling Jacobins. As Kaiser argues in the conclusion to this work, the revolutionaries were beset by two contradictory ideas. One was that the Revolution presented the inevitable triumph of progress and reason. The other, which gained ground considerably in the tense atmosphere of the Year II, was that virtuous republics were inherently doomed to failure. Increasingly it was seen as inevitable that counterrevolutionaries would conspire to overthrow the republic.

True to their classical education, the Jacobins tended to see the Revolution in moral terms, as a struggle between virtuous men and those of wicked intent. The idea that virtue was the mainspring of a republican government (a theory originally derived from classical antiquity, but adapted and made familiar largely by Montesquieu) was well known to the Jacobins.[61] They followed Montesquieu, too, in believing that selfless virtue was ultimately unsustainable. Human nature being what it was (or at least as it had been corrupted by the ancien régime), political virtue would always tend to be undermined by vice, corruption, and self-interest. Robespierre, for one, had been reluctant to call for the founding of a republic, even after the king's flight to Varennes, precisely for this reason.[62] When the republic was established, many Jacobins assumed, in line with this model of political thought, both that the French republic's basis must be virtue, and that such virtue would constantly be undermined by conspirators motivated by their self-interest. It was a way of seeing politics that was – ironically for revolutionaries – deeply pessimistic.[63] The only way through this bind was through projects for education, and the establishment of social institutions that would regenerate French society – but such undertakings, even if viable, would take rather more time than the Jacobins were likely to have in power. Ultimately, they themselves suspected that the republic of virtue was bound to be overwhelmed, and the conspirators to succeed.

No one was more haunted by this conviction than Robespierre.[64] By July 1794, however, this Manichean political approach was evidently becoming redundant, outflanked by a series of events, including the victory at Fleurus, which made Terror unnecessary as a force to sustain the government. Possibly Robespierre would have wished to disengage himself from the Terror, and repudiate it, but his faith in the ideology of moral virtue, and his belief in conspiracy, made a tactical withdrawal unlikely. So he was left clinging to the mast of the Terror in Thermidor. Ironically, Thermidor showed that up to a point the Jacobins were right to fear conspiracy. Their government had only held on by a thread, kept there by the circumstances of the war, and by the use of the Terror. The ease with which the Robespierrists were overthrown shows how fragile was their hold on power. When Robespierre on the 8th Thermidor declared that a conspiracy existed in the heart of revolutionary govern-ment, he had this time identified a genuine plot, one that was about to result in his own overthrow. 'Let us say then that there is conspiracy against public liberty; that it derives its force from a criminal coalition which plots within the Convention itself; that this coalition has accomplices in the Committee of General Security and in this Committee's offices which they control . . . that members of the Committee of Public Safety are also in this plot.'[65] In a private notebook he was more open, denouncing the corruption of clerks for the Committee of General Security, under the patronage of Amar and Jagot, who were also in league with members of the Committee of Public Safety and with the enemies of republican government or public morality 'because they are one and the same.'[66]

The actual plot to overthrow him was indeed, as he had surmised, mounted by his fellow Jacobins, including a number of Robespierre's own colleagues on the Committees. To some extent Robespierre's own fears had been instrumental in bringing this conspiracy into existence, for it was led by men who banded together in fear of their lives to protect themselves against Robespierre's desire to purge the Convention. Their intention was to save themselves, not to end the Terror or Jacobin rule. Ironically, but hardly surprisingly, the coup of Thermidor was followed by a systematic attempt to depict Robespierre himself as having been the archconspirator against the Revolution. Even this most dedicated of revolutionaries, it seems, had plotted against it. In the event Robespierre was proved right: the conspiracy to overthrow him also resulted in the fall of Jacobinism.

On 10 Thermidor an associate of Saint-Just, Gatteau, who had protested against the arrest of the Robespierrists, was thrown into prison where he spent many miserable months without any appreciable effect on his Jacobin convictions. This period of enforced reflection did, however, make him reconsider the role of conspiracy in the cause of the Revolution. A year after Thermidor he was finally given a reason for his arrest, in the shape of a single phrase: 'friend of the conspirator Saint-Just.' This so incensed him that he wrote defiantly to his captors that the Robespierrists had fallen precisely because they had *not* been conspirators. In words which echoed the conclusions of Babeuf and many subsequent revolutionaries of the nineteenth century, he claimed that it would have been better had the Robespierrists launched a 'holy conspiracy' to defend the Revolution. Had they been conspirators they 'would be powerful still, and you would be dead.' Against those who 'plotted the ruin of liberty,' a 'holy conspiracy' could be justified.[67]

In conclusion, we have seen some of the tortuous and traumatic paths down which the Jacobin version of conspiracy theory led. Their motivation for following this route remains complex and hard to pronounce upon. But it seems to have been a combination of several factors: pragmatism (kill or be killed); political conviction (the belief to which they clung that they were in the moral right); and intense anxiety and fear. Not all of these fears were misplaced, for there were genuine conspiracies, and the context was one of war, civil war, and profound social instability. Not least, the Jacobins feared the *sans-culottes*, the very people who had put them in power, and whose rhetoric they used. This seems to bear out the psychological argument that to see politics in terms of conspiracies is a way of trying to alleviate stress and anxiety, because it provides a way of mastering a situation that is spiralling outside one's understanding and control.[68] In these circumstances the Jacobin leaders made a fateful decision to abandon the more moderate treatment of political opponents that they had displayed on first coming to power, and adopted the rhetoric of conspiracy wholesale. This rhetoric was a drink they would drain to the bitter dregs, and it would eventually prove as lethal to many of themselves as it was to their rivals: Saturn's children indeed!

Notes

1 F. Furet, *Penser la Révolution* (Paris, 1978), pp. 78–79.
2 See P. Gueniffey, 'La Terreur: circonstances exceptionnelles, idéologie et dynamique révolutionnaire,' *Historical Reflections/Réflexions Historiques*, 29(3) (2003), pp. 433–450.
3 L. Hunt, *Politics, Culture and Class in the French Revolution* (Berkeley, 1984), pp. 39–44. On political transparency see also the classic study by J. Starobinski, *Jean-Jacques Rousseau: La Transparence et l'obstacle* (Paris, 1957).
4 Ancien régime concepts of conspiracy are discussed by Campbell in Chapter 1 of this present work. J. M. Burney, 'The Fear of the Executive and the Threat of Conspiracy: Billaud-Varenne's Terrorist Rhetoric in the French Revolution, 1788–1794,' *French History*, 5(2) (1991), pp. 143–163, shows the ancien régime origins of Billaud-Varenne's conspiracy ideas.
5 On the revolutionary rhetoric of denunciation as a civic virtue and its links to classical Rome, see C. Lucas, 'The Theory and Practice of Denunciation in the French Revolution,' *Journal of Modern History*, 68(4) (1996), pp. 768–785.
6 On the *sans-culotte* language of conspiracy see David Andress in Chapter 4 of the present volume.
7 On the treatment of foreigners, which generally remained pragmatically positive, except for those who incurred suspicion as a consequence of the war, see M. Rapport, *Nationality and Citizenship in Revolutionary France: The Treatment of Foreigners, 1789–1799* (Oxford, 2000).
8 On this fear of the Foreign Plot as a meta-text for the Terror, see T. E. Kaiser, 'From the Austrian Committee to the Foreign Plot: Marie-Antoinette,

Austrophobia, and the Terror,' *French Historical Studies*, 26(4) (2003), pp. 579–617.

9   The classic account of Robespierre's opposition to the war is G. Michon, *Robespierre et la guerre révolutionnaire, 1791–1792* (Paris, 1937).

10 See M. Sydenham, *The Girondins* (London, 1961); and A. Patrick, *The Men of the First French Republic* (Baltimore, 1972).

11 According to De Luna the first references to the 'Girondins' as a faction began with the meeting of the Convention in September 1792. F. A. De Luna, ' "The Girondins" Were Girondins, After All,' *French Historical Studies*, 15(3) (1988), pp. 506–518. This volume contains a special debate on the Girondins with other contributions of interest.

12 C. Desmoulins, *Jean-Pierre Brissot démasqué*, in *Œuvres de Camille Desmoulins*, ed. J. Claretie, 3 vols (Paris, 1874) 1, p. 268.

13 Ibid., p. 281.

14 E. Ellery, *Brissot de Warville* (Boston, 1915), p. 242.

15 Desmoulins, *Fragment de l'histoire secrète de la Révolution*, in *Œuvres de Camille Desmoulins*, p. 305.

16 Ibid., p. 306.

17 Ibid., p. 309.

18 Ibid., pp. 320–321.

19 H. Wallon, *Histoire du Tribunal révolutionnaire*, 6 vols (Paris 1880–81), 1, p. 418.

20 L. Whaley, *Radicals: Politics and Republicanism in the French Revolution* (Stroud, 2000), p. 157.

21 Barère's report on the Girondins, *Le Moniteur* 16, 6 June 1793, p. 585.

22 Saint-Just, *Œuvres complètes de Saint-Just*, ed. C. Vellay, 2 vols (Paris, 1908), 2, p. 28.

23 Ibid., p. 29.

24 Billaud-Varenne's report 'sur les trente-deux membres décrétés d'arrestation dans la journée du 2 juin,' *Le Moniteur* 17, 15 July 1793, pp. 198–199.

25 See Sydenham, *The Girondins*, pp. 20–25.

26 On the aims of the federalists, and the political threat that they posed, see A. Forrest, 'Federalism,' republished in P. Jones, ed., *The French Revolution in Social and Political Perspective* (London, 1996), especially pp. 363–364.

27 See S. Wahnich, *La Liberté ou la Mort: essai sur la Terreur et le terrorisme* (Paris, 2003). Fauchet vehemently denied having even met Corday, but his protestations were ignored. See his letter to the Convention, in E. B. Courtois, *Papiers inédits trouvés chez Robespierre, Saint-Just, etc., supprimés ou omis par Courtois*, 3 vols (Paris, 1828), 3, pp. 255–257.

28 *Archives parlementaires* 75, 3 October 1793, p. 532.

29 See Sydenham, *The Girondins*, pp. 25–28.

30 *Archives parlementaires* 75, 3 October 1793, p. 534.

31 Ibid., p. 533.

32 Ibid., pp. 535–537.

33 R. Levasseur, *Mémoires de R. Levasseur (de la Sarthe) ex-conventionnel* (first published 1829–31; this edn Paris, 1989), pp. 339–345.

34 Ibid., pp. 341–342.
35 On the Hébertists see M. Slavin, *The Hébertistes to the Guillotine: Anatomy of a 'Conspiracy' in Revolutionary France* (Baton Rouge, 1994).
36 On the financial and political corruption of Danton see A. Mathiez, *Etudes Robespierristes* (Paris, 1917). This work, especially the chapter on 'La Corruption parlementaire sous la Terreur,' is a detailed study of financial corruption, particularly that of Danton. Also N. Hampson, *Danton* (London, 1978), especially pp. 55–66; and Hampson, 'François Chabot and his Plot,' in *Transactions of the Royal Historical Society*, 5th Ser., 26 (1976), pp. 1–14. See also O. Blanc, *La Corruption sous la Terreur (1792–1794)* (Paris, 1992), pp. 28–30.
37 Cited in A. de Lestapis, *La 'Conspiration de Batz' (1793–1794)* (Paris, 1969), pp. 28–29.
38 Mathiez wrote on this subject on several occasions: most importantly, A. Mathiez, *La Conspiration de l'étranger* (Paris, 1918); and *L'Affaire de la compagnie des Indes: un procès de corruption sous la Terreur* (Paris, 1920). Other significant discussions include N. Hampson, *The Life and Opinions of Maximilien Robespierre* (London, 1974), pp. 201–223; and Hampson, 'François Chabot and his Plot.' More recently, Kaiser has argued convincingly that there was probably some substance to the idea of a 'Foreign Plot': Kaiser, 'From the Austrian Committee to the Foreign Plot.'
39 On Batz's role see M. Price, 'The "Foreign Plot" and the French Revolution: A Reappraisal,' in B. Coward and J. Swann, eds, *Conspiracies and Conspiracy Theory in Early Modern Europe: From the Waldensians to the French Revolution* (Aldershot, 2004), pp. 255–268.
40 Mathiez, 'La Corruption parlementaire sous la Terreur.'
41 See for example C. Desmoulins, *Le Vieux Cordelier*, eds A. Mathiez and H. Calvet (Paris, 1936), Issue 5, pp. 154, 155–156, 159; *Père Duchesne*, no. 332, pp. 5–6; and *J.R. Hébert, auteur du Père Duchesne, à Camille Desmoulins et Compagnie*, pp. 8–9. On the quarrel and on the reaction of *sans-culottes* to it, according to police spies, see Slavin, *The Hébertistes*, pp. 22–25.
42 Regarding the Jacobins' obsession with external signs of conspiracy and their anxieties regarding theatrical dissimulation, see M. Linton, 'The Tartuffes of Patriotism': Fears of Conspiracy in the Political Language of Revolutionary Government, France 1793–94,' in Coward and Swann, *Conspiracies and Conspiracy Theory*, pp. 235–254. On the revolutionary fear of masks and disguise, see J. H. Johnson, 'Versailles, Meet Les Halles: Masks, Carnival, and the French Revolution,' *Representations*, 73 (2001), pp. 89–116.
43 Robespierre, 'Discours non prononcé sur les factions,' in *Œuvres*, 10, p. 400.
44 Saint-Just, *Œuvres*, 2, p. 259.
45 Ibid., pp. 261–264.
46 Ibid., p. 273.
47 Slavin, *The Hébertistes*, chapter 6.
48 See Saint-Just, *Œuvres*, 2, p. 270, in the 'Rapport sur les factions de l'Etranger,' he said: '[la cité] est presque usurpée par les fonctionnaires.'

49 See A. Goodwin, 'The Underworld of the French Revolutionary Terror,' in *Memoirs and Proceedings of the Manchester Literary and Philosophical Society*, 38–56 (Manchester, 1954–55), pp. 38–56.

50 On Amar's involvement, see Hampson, 'François Chabot and his Plot,' pp. 1–14, especially. pp. 6–7, 10–11.

51 Hampson, *The Life and Opinions of Maximilien Robespierre*, pp. 207–208, 219, 52.

52 *Archives parlementaires* 86, 26 ventôse an II, 16 March 1794, pp. 553–557.

53 See Lestapis, *La 'Conspiration de Batz,'* pp. 236–247; 256–257.

54 This is the view of Hampson, *Robespierre*, pp. 254–261.

55 Thompson, *Robespierre*, p. 470.

56 For an account of the signs of conspiracy employed in Saint-Just's speech, and its relationship to the notes provided by Robespierre, see Linton, 'The Tartuffes of Patriotism.'

57 'Rapport sur la conjuration ourdie pour obtenir un changement de dynastie, et contre Danton . . .', delivered before the Convention,11 Germinal an II, 31 March 1794. In Saint-Just, *Œuvres*, 2, p. 329.

58 Wallon, *Histoire du Tribunal révolutionnaire*, 3, p. 173.

59 Laflotte was soon afterward convicted of perjury for manufacturing evidence in another case; see Hampson, *Danton*, p. 172.

60 15 Germinal (4 April 1794), in B. J. B. Buchez and P. C. Roux, eds, *Histoire parlementaire de la Révolution française*, 40 vols (Paris, 1834–38), 32, pp. 183–192.

61 On the traditions of virtue in political life, see M. Linton, *The Politics of Virtue in Enlightenment France* (Basingstoke, 2001).

62 On Robespierre's conception of a virtuous republic, see M. Linton, 'Robespierre's Political Principles,' in C. Haydon and W. Doyle, eds, *Robespierre* (Cambridge, UK, 1999), especially pp. 45–46.

63 On the increasing pessimism of the Jacobin leaders about the future of the republic, see M. Linton, 'Ideas of the Future in the French Revolution,' in M. Crook, W. Doyle and A. Forrest, eds, *Enlightenment and Revolution: Essays in Honour of Norman Hampson* (Aldershot, 2004), pp. 153–168.

64 See G. Cubitt, 'Robespierre and Conspiracy Theories,' in Haydon and Doyle *Robespierre*, pp. 75–91.

65 Robespierre, *Œuvres*, 10, p. 576.

66 Ibid., pp. 551–552, footnote 2.

67 Gatteau's defense is reproduced in Saint-Just, *Œuvres*, 1, introduction, pp. vii–xiv. On Babeuf's defence of the 'holy conspiracy,' see Laura Mason's discussion in Chapter 8 of this volume.

68 This argument is made by D. Groh, 'La Tentation des théories de conspiration,' *Storia Della Storiografia*, 14 (1988), pp. 96–118. He claims this is a reason why fears of conspiracy can be found in every historical period and among every social group, and every political ideology, pp. 105–106.

7

The *émigrés* and conspiracy in the French Revolution, 1789–99

Simon Burrows

The spectre of the *émigré* conspirator, the most implaccable enemy of the Revolution, stalked the revolutionary imagination throughout the 1790s and beyond. In many ways this was natural. The *émigré* conspiracy represented the antithesis of the revolution's transparent, public politics. It was also the linear descendant of the despised court cabal, the hidden motive force of a secret, factional politics conducted behind closed doors of Versailles. While the legitimacy and triumph of the Revolution was based upon popular sovereignty, *émigré* conspirators seemed intent on ushering in a counterrevolutionary régime by the machinations of a self-interested few. The *émigré* conspirator was all the more chilling and ambiguous because he could not succeed in isolation. He needed assistance from foreign powers and/or influential collaborators inside France to achieve his ends, and this in turn implied the existence of sinister networks of agents to link conspirators abroad to activist cells inside the country. Thus, by his very existence, the *émigré* conspirator fed fears of enemies within and without France, and promoted suspicion, paranoia, and political instability.

Emigré malevolence seemed evident almost from the moment the king's youngest brother, the comte d'Artois, fled abroad with his mistress and cronies in July 1789.[1] Over the next three years he attempted to negotiate foreign intervention and gathered an army in the Rhineland. In 1792, this army invaded France with Prussian and Austrian forces, although allied generals kept it carefully in the rear fearing that *émigré* forces would prove unreliable, ill-disciplined, and vengeful. Moreover, *émigrés* were implicated in almost all the counterrevolutionary plots that punctuated the Revolution. Hence, at critical junctures, fear that *émigré* conspiracies would undermine the new régime and spill rivers of republican blood justified the revolution's lurches to the left and the imposition of emergency measures that violated the Declaration of the Rights of Man, including the Law of Suspects, Law of Hostages, and the Terror.

Revolutionary orators and government reports drew explicit links between *émigré* agents and alleged internal 'conspiracies.' *Emigré* involvement in the Foreign Plot of 1793–94, the 1796 Pichegru conspiracy, and the 1797 Brotier conspiracy helped to militate opinion behind the government and consolidate successive revolutionary régimes. Moreover, *émigré* conspiracies continued under the Napoleonic Consulate: the Opera bomb plot of 1800 and the Cadoudal conspiracy of 1804 in particular played a key role in the consolidation of the régime, and the latter resulted in the judicial murder of a Bourbon prince of the Blood, the Duc d'Enghien, and Napoleon's assumption of the Imperial title.

Nevertheless, historians have tended to play down the reality of the *émigré* threat, in part because *émigré*-orchestrated risings and plots to assassinate or corrupt revolutionary leaders or to rescue the King and Queen invariably failed to achieve their primary objectives and generally came to little, while other notorious plots have been judged chimerical or exaggerated. For example, Albert Mathiez and more recently Morris Slavin have found the prosecution's evidence to support charges that the Hébertists were involved in an immense 'foreign plot' involving the allies and *émigrés* devoid of foundation, although, as we shall see, several people on the fringes of the group may have been more culpable.[2] Likewise, the *émigré* army is not viewed as a serious threat. Other forms of direct subversion – including the propaganda efforts castigated by Edmund Burke – have also been seen as largely ineffectual.[3] In addition, several studies have stressed the huge ideological gulf and communications problems dividing *émigré* activists from internal forces of opposition.[4] Hence it is tempting to see alleged of conspiracies as the result of the revolutionaries' own phobias or political opportunism, or desperate tactics adopted by the *émigrés* in consequence of their own weakness. Yet contemporaries believed the threat was very real. Such a conviction, this chapter will argue, was far more than a result of the revolutionaries' own fantasies. Nevertheless, the *émigré* leadership's sponsorship of conspiracy was ultimately based largely on self-delusion and thus proved self-defeating.

Reliance on conspiracy, both among the *émigré* leadership and freelance activists was not due primarily to desperation. Instead, it stemmed from a belief that the Revolution was also the result of a conspiracy, and the natural consequences of this conviction. Conspiratorial modes of explanation were almost universal among the *émigrés* and counter-revolutionaries.[5] Such theories emerged early in the Revolution. One of the earliest hypotheses saw the Revolution as the outcome of a conspiracy by the duc d'Orléans to place himself on the throne at the expense of his cousin, Louis XVI. Given that d'Orléans had played a leading role in opposing the royal will, mixed freely with revolutionary politicians, and owned the Palais Royal, birthplace of so many revolutionary disturbances, this was an attactive theory. Among its first exponents was the pamphleteer Jean-Gabriel Peltier, a former Palais Royal demagogue who turned against the Revolution following the October days, when he published *Le Coup d'equinoxe d'Octobre 1789. Lettre de M. P. . . de Paris à M. M . . . son ami négociant à Nantes.* This proved to be the first of his many virulent denunciations of d'Orléans.[6] By the early 1790s, other variants of conspiracy theory were beginning to circulate in print, including the comte de Ferrand's *Les Conspirateurs démasqués*, first published in 1790, which saw Necker's revenge and the ambition of d'Orléans, Lafayette, and several others as the motive force behind the Revolution.[7]

However, the most famous conspiracy theory associated with the *émigrés* is found in the abbé Augustin de Barruel's *Mémoires pour servir à l'histoire du jacobinisme françois*, published in 1797–98. Barruel believed that the Revolution was the outcome of a concerted plot by freemasons and *philosophes* to overturn Church and state. His work enjoyed an enormous vogue, among both the *émigrés* and European elites, not least because the ideas it contained were already familiar to his readers. For, as Darrin MacMahon has shown, the idea of a *philosophe* conspiracy against religion and order actually predated the Revolution, and could be found in the work of a dedicated band of prerevolutionary Christian apologist pamphleteers, including Barruel himself.[8] Nor was the idea of the Masonic involvement new. It had been expounded in several previous works, notably Louis Cadet de Gassicourt's anonymous *Le Tombeau de Jacques Molai, ou le secret des conspirateurs*, which argued that freemasonry could trace its origins back to the Order of the Knights Templar, and was the instrument of the Templars' revenge on the French monarchy for suppressing them and executing the last Grand Master of the Order in 1314.[9] However, the earliest denunciations of the role of Masonic principles and leadership appeared five years before Gassicourt's pamphlet, in works such as the abbé Lefranc's *Le voile levé pour les curieux* and right-wing newspapers, notably Montjoie's *Ami du Roi*, Du Rozoi's *Gazette de Paris* and the *Journal à deux liards*. The latter even noted that the Grand Master of the Masonic order in France was none other than the duc d'Orléans, the suspected chief conspirator.[10]

Others besides extremist *émigrés* desperate to uncover the hidden key to the Revolution admired the work of Barruel and saw in it an antidote to the mania of revolution. Among them were foreign politicians, including the British minister Lord Liverpool.[11] In a letter to the militant anti-Jacobin John Reeves, Liverpool opined:

> The Abbé Barruel is certainly an excellent writer, particularly on all religious subjects, which is become at present so much allied to Political subjects, that they are in many respects the same – The Abbé Barruel's reputation stands high, at least in this country, and I believe in foreign countries; and he appears evidently disposed to treat religious subjects on the idea of supporting Christianity generally, without any reference to the distinctions of sects, into which Christianity is divided.[12]

Liverpool was so impressed with Barruel's work that he recommended a bizarre journalistic collaboration between Barruel and the veteran Genevan political commentator Jacques Mallet Du Pan. Mallet – who although a foreigner was technically an *émigré* because his name appeared (illegally) on the Parisian *émigré* lists – disdained the proposal, perhaps in part due to his reservations about the concept of a 'philosophic conspiracy.'[13]

A few months later Mallet revealed his position in a powerful refutation of Barruel. His essay 'Of the degree of influence which the French Philosophy has had upon the Revolution' offered a passionate defense of Voltaire, suggesting that although he attacked religion in works aimed at the elite, he had no desire to subvert society.[14] Mallet insisted that the *philosophes* were too divided to be considered a single sect and that 'no prior concert of doctrine or of measures, no common intelligence, no uniform wish in the generality of men of letters, disgraced by the nickname of *philosophy*, preceded that monstrous assemblage of events unforeseen and beyond the reach of all foresight, which have plunged France into barbarism.'[15] Yet at the same time he identified Diderot and Condorcet as 'the real heads of the revolutionary school.' It was Diderot who 'proclaimed equality before *Marat*, the rights of man before *Sieyes*, the sacredness of insurrection before *Mirabeau* and *La Fayette*, and the massacre of Priests before the Septembrists.'[16] Although Diderot died in 1784, he left Condorcet to lead the 'frantic scholars who, seizing the pen, have since the year 1788 pushed on the bloody car [sic] of anarchism and atheism.'[17] Hence Mallet refused to abandon the idea of conspiracy altogether, as he made clear in his concluding remark: 'It is therefore a mistake to impute to the whole of the *Philosophers*, the whole of the plots, maxims, and crimes which have invaded France for ten years past.'[18] Mallet's ambivalence towards the idea of a *philosophe* plot is significant, because he is generally considered the most judicious and clear-sighted of the *émigrés*.[19] If even he was unable to dispense entirely with the idea, it is hardly surprising that it had a powerful hold on other, less perspicacious and less well-informed *émigrés*.

The conviction that the Revolution was the outcome of a conspiracy was enormously attractive psychologically. Such 'wishful thinking' allowed for a simple all-embracing interpretation of events, uncluttered by complex theories of causation. It implied that the Revolution had few genuine adherents and exonerated the ancien régime system of suspicions that it had outlived its utility or was essentially unpopular or socially unjust. It also freed the *émigrés* themselves of any guilt at having been complicit in such a system, or wishing to see it reestablished. In the process, the *émigrés* deproblematized the issue of a Bourbon restoration, making it possible to envisage a near integral restoration of the ancien régime: if little had been wrong, little needed to be changed. There was no need to recognize that the Revolution might have been the result of deep-seated disatisfaction with the status quo or serious social or institutional problems. Such observations explain many of the political mysteries of the emigration. These include the intransigence which was so evident in 'pure' *émigré* political circles, and the reluctance of the Bourbon pretender, Louis XVIII, to make significant compromises with the Revolution, even in public manifestos designed to win support inside France, until the Calmar Declaration of December 1804.[20] They also explain, in part, why moderate *émigré* publicists such as Malouet, Montlosier, and from 1795 Calonne were vilified by many fellow *émigrés* whenever they had the temerity to suggest that the Revolution had a wide and entrenched constituency of support and had wrought profound and irreversible changes.[21] Finally, as Darrin McMahon has pointed out, conspiracy theories let the many *émigrés* who had initially supported the Revolution off the hook, allowing them to deflect blame for their actions onto hidden conspirators who had used them as naïve tools.[22]

However, such comforting notions also had profound practical implications. Whether they viewed the Revolution as the work of a few ambitious politicians, a *philosophic* conspiracy or a Masonic plot, all conspiracy theorists believed that the Revolution was the work of a small clique lacking popular support or a secure power base. In consequence, it was quite rational to believe that by eliminating or subverting a few key figures, or building on localized revolts, the Revolution could be reversed. Thus from 1789 onward the *émigré* leadership sponsored attempts to subvert the Revolution from within or overthrow it by stealth tactics, alongside more overt moves to provoke and support insurgency inside France and rally foreign coalitions and *émigré* armies.

The reality of the *émigré* threat seemed ever present, for across the revolutionary and Napoleonic period a long series of plots, both real and imaginary, appeared to bear the hallmarks of *émigré* involvement. It is true that only a small proportion of the estimated 150,000 *émigrés* were ever actively involved in counterrevolutionary activities. The *émigré* armies probably never numbered more than 10,000 men, and the Napoleonic amnesty of 1802 identified and excluded only about 1,000 activists of all varieties. Nevertheless, *émigré* involvement could be detected in many of the most prominent efforts to destabilize revolutionary and Imperial régimes. Nor were their plots always violent in nature. *Émigré* activists were involved in mass production of false *assignats* to undermine the French economy and fund their own clandestine activities, sometimes with the assistance of foreign governments.[23] Others attempted to bribe key members of the revolutionary government to lead a coup d'état, or dreamed of attempting to rescue the king or queen. Yet more were involved in gathering intelligence, or writing and disseminating antirevolutionary propaganda across Europe.

Émigré attempts to penetrate France and foment disturbances began long before the overthrow of the monarchy on 10 August 1792, and hence the early efforts of d'Artois and others might be depicted as treasonous incitements to rebellion against Louis XVI's government. As early as January 1790, François Froment visited d'Artois in his Turin exile to seek authorization to seize control of several towns in the Midi in preparation for an *émigré* invasion. Froment's invasion plan came to nothing, but his activities in the Gard *département* nevertheless had serious repercussions on both the local and the national political scenes. At Nîmes, where Froment established Catholic National Guard units to counteract the influence of the heavily Protestant ones, incipient sectarian unrest gave way to a bloody power struggle, and in June some 300 people were killed as Protestants seized control of the municipality.[24] The modestly-named *bagarre* (brawl) at Nîmes helped to rally Catholic resistance to Protestant advances locally and provided evidence for proponents of the (absurd) proposition that the Revolution was a Protestant plot. In the Gard and the neighboring Ardèche region, Catholic defense began to coagulate under the Allier brothers, who orchestrated the celebrated meetings of local National Guard units at the Camp de Jalès, in the hope of organizing an insurrection. Since most of those who attended were summoned under false pretences, the plans could not be kept secret and collapsed into farce. However, the Alliers did not abandon their plans, and with the backing of the *émigré* princes organized some disastrous and poorly coordinated risings in mid-1792, which culminated in the capture of Saillans, the commander sent by the princes.[25] Nor was the Gard the sole area in which *émigré* agents were active: in France's second city, Lyons, d'Artois appointed a former mayor, Imbert-Colomès, to prepare the way for counterrevolution in 1790.[26]

Emigrés were also heavily involved in planning and coordinating the most decisive political event of the early 1790s: the king's flight to Varennes on 20 June 1791.[27] The key actor was the baron de Breteuil, who had been charged by Louis XVI to orchestrate the royal family's escape some months earlier. This involved liaison with both the royal family and the marquis de Bouillé, who had the dangerous job of organizing troops under his command to rendez-vous with the royal party, and also to negotiate for Austrian financial and military backing. In addition, Breteuil had to head off alternative schemes promoted by d'Artois, who with a self-interested and callous disregard for the lives of his brother, his sister-in-law, and their children called for direct intervention regardless of the risk to the royal family.[28]

The outbreak of war between France and Austria in April 1792 transformed the status of the *émigré* conspirator. On one level it relegated him to the rank of junior partner in foreign intrigues to overturn the Revolution. On another, it elevated him to the spearhead of a vast international plot headed by France's inveterate enemies Austria and, from January 1793, Britain, with whom the *émigrés* now became indelibly linked in the revolutionary imagination. By transmuting *émigré* activists into agents of Pitt and Coburg, war confirmed their status as traitors. No longer protagonists in a purely domestic dispute, the *émigrés* were now perceived as active servants of the foreign enemy.

Often the links between the *émigrés* and France's enemies were quite open. For example, between the disastrous retreat from Valmy in 1792 and 1800, Condé's army – the only one of three *émigré* forces to survive the retreat as an effective unit – passed successively into Austrian, Russian, and finally British pay.[29] Likewise, in 1795, the British conscripted all able-bodied secular *émigré* males of military age who were receiving British government relief payments to serve in the Quiberon expedition. The disastrous failure of this campaign literally decimated London's *émigré* population, for the majority of the *émigré* force was captured under arms and shot. The well-publicized executions of these 640 *émigrés* served as a warning to other *émigrés* who might be considering a return to the territory of the Republic.[30] It also provided a dramatic proof for the Republic's population that the *émigrés* en bloc continued to wage war against it.

More sinister in the revolutionary imagination was the continued threat of clandestine *émigré* conspiracies, although here, too, the threat was subsumed within a bigger international challenge once war was declared. Indeed, *émigré* agents were so important to Britain's clandestine war against France that, as Elizabeth Sparrow has shown, the Alien Office – which was originally created in January 1793 to register foreigners –

rapidly evolved into a front for espionage.[31] The junior role that the *émigré* conspirator now played is perhaps best exemplified by the shadowy Foreign Plot of 1793–94, whose very nomenclature relegates the *émigré* conspirator to a pawn in the great game of international politics.[32]

The Foreign Plot was central to the factional turmoil of the Terror, serving as the pretext and weapon by which Robespierre and his allies purged their rivals, although the true causes of factional rivalry lay elsewhere. It was predicated on the suggestion that the Republic was being undermined by a conspiracy linking corrupt politicians and financiers with the agents of foreign governments. Beginning with a genuine financial scandal involving many of Danton's associates and centering on the liquidation of the *Compagnie des Indes*, it allowed the Robespierristes to eliminate enemies on both the Jacobin left (the Hébertists or enragés) and Jacobin right (the Dantonists or indulgents).[33]

According to Robespierre, whose fevered imagination certainly invented many of the links between the alleged plotters, the orchestrators of the Foreign Plot did not care whether the Dantonist or Hébertist puppets triumphed: 'If it is Hébert, the Convention will be overturned, patriots will be massacred, France will again fall into chaos, and tyranny will be gratified. If it is the moderates, the Convention will lose its energy, the crimes of the aristocracy will go unpunished, and the tyrants will triumph. The foreigner must protect all these factions.'[34] Clearly Robespierre and his associates were now increasingly driven by traditional Anglophobia and Austrophobia, rather than the revolution's more novel obsession with the *émigré* menace. Nevertheless, *émigré* agents were far from absent from the tortured web of financial corruption, factional mistrust, circumstantial suspicions and, quite possibly, genuine intrigues that comprised the Foreign Plot. Indeed, on closer investigation, they may hold the key to the whole affair.

The most obvious *émigré* to investigate is the notorious and shadowy conspirator the Baron de Batz, a descendant of the real-life d'Artagnan.[35] Batz, a noble from the Cantal, made a fortune in financial speculations in the 1780s and sat as a noble deputy in the National Assembly. He emigrated in June 1792 and thereafter undertook numerous missions to France. Robespierre saw Batz as central to the Foreign Plot, and the surviving evidence suggests that, as far as there was a plot, Batz was the main instigator, probably with the backing of Breteuil.[36] Although conclusive evidence that Batz acted in concert with Breteuil is lacking, Munro Price has shown recently that the links between them go back to the 1780s, when the two men were part of an informal consortium speculating profitably on a bear market. Subsequently, in July 1789, Batz played a key role in trying to raise loans to support the royal counter-coup that commenced with the dismissal of Necker and appointment of Breteuil's Ministry of the Hundred Hours and collapsed with the storming of the Bastille. These links continued in the early Revolution, when Batz showed considerable sang-froid by retaining his seat in the National Assembly and, with Breteuil's encouragement, using his position as chair of the Assembly's committee for the liquidation of the national debt to channel over 500,000 *livres* into a secret fighting fund for Louis XVI.[37] Finally, in 1793 he led abortive attempts to rescue Louis XVI and Marie-Antoinette, as we shall see below.

In late 1793, it appears that Batz dreamed up another way of under-mining the Revolution, using bribery and corruption as tools. However, his aim was not to promote a real conspiracy but to create an illusory one, so that the revolutionaries would destroy the régime from within by their mutual suspicions and recriminations. This, at least, is the suggestion of a manuscript he prepared in 1794:

> How can such a formidable power [the revolutionary government] . . . be brought down? I would reply that such a régime is by its very nature a form of delirium, a convulsive state; and . . . according to the immutable laws of nature, of short duration . . . the jealousies, suspicions, hatreds and divisions it produces will set the participants against each other and drag them toward the abyss they themselves have opened . . . preparing these divisions and accelerating them by sowing mistrust and exacerbating rivalries is, in the absence of armed force, the only effective way of conspiring against such a government and hastening its prompt collapse.[38]

Batz's strategy is indicative of his conviction that the Revolution was the unstable result of the actions of a few self-interested and factious men. Moreover, it appears that he began to put it into practice, corrupting members of both the Hébertist and Dantonist camp, and to that extent was indeed the hand behind the Foreign Plot.[39] Unfortunately, however, the mutual allegations that the two factions made against each other as their venality in the *Compagnie des Indes* affair was laid bare did little to hasten a counterrevolution. Instead it helped the Robespierristes to consolidate their grip on power. But in the longer term, the purges of Dantonists and Hébertists left the Robespierristes isolated and hastened their day of reckoning at Thermidor.

An *émigré* connection is less evident in the case of a second figure whom Robespierre linked to the Foreign Plot, but may nevertheless exist. This was Pierre-Jean Berthold, comte de Proly, who served as Hérault de Séchelles's private secretary and was charged with the correspondence of the Jacobin Club. Proly was born in the Austrian Netherlands, and rumored to be the illegitimate son of the Austrian chancellor Kaunitz, who was alleged to have subsidized Proly's revolutionary newspaper *Le Cosmopo-lite*. He was thus a natural target for suspicion, especially as he vigorously defended Imperial foreign policy prior to April 1792, albeit from a revolutionary perspective.[40] It was thus implied that he was an Austrian spy and agent-provocateur, who used radical journalism as a cover to dispel suspicions from the revolutionary left, while perhaps also discrediting extremism. Moreover, Proly was rich. Like Batz, he had made a fortune in speculating in the 1780s. A lover of the finer things in life, it was almost inevitable that Robespierre should see him as a decadent aristocrat and false friend of the Republic.[41] He was tried with the Hébertists and died with them on the scaffold.

When the Hébertists were brought to trial, evidence of their involvement in a vast foreign plot proved to be based on dubious circumstantial evidence and hearsay. No written evidence was presented to support the allegations, which included suggestions that Proly was an Austrian spy and had culpable relations with Batz and the executed Girondin finance minister Etienne Clavière, with whom he had been acquainted before 1789. Nevertheless, several recently discovered documents indicate conclusively that Proly was an Austrian agent. The first evidence to emerge was a document dating from October 1791 found by the present author among the papers of Charles-Alexandre de Calonne, who served as de facto prime minister to the *émigré* princes. It reveals that Proly was sending intelligence to the Austrians and that they were forwarding it to Calonne. It states 'le correspondent de Paris dont vous lisez quelques foibles bulletins est un nommé comte de Proli fils d'une Madame Deproly qui a été maîtresse du prince de Kaunitz, auquel [les?] bulletins sont adressés de suite.'[42] Subsequently, Tom Kaiser has found further evidence that Proly conducted a political correspondence with the Austrian government and attempted to serve as intermediary between Austria and both revolutionary France and the Vonckist rebels in the Austrian Netherlands.[43]

The insinuation that Proly's journalism on the *Cosmopolite* was a 'front' is also supported by strong circumstantial evidence. For Proly's collaborator and the paper's founding financial backer was a certain Jacques Regnier, a contributor to the counterrevolutionary satirical journal *Les Actes des Apôtres*, published between 1789 and 1792.[44] Regnier's background makes him an unlikely candidate for a flirtation with Jacobin extremism, not least because he was a member of two groups who lost out badly during the Revolution, the Saint-Domingue planters and Parlementary magistracy. Moreover, after a spell in prison in 1794–95, Regnier emigrated and between 1802 and 1815 edited a series of outspoken *émigré* propaganda newspapers in London.[45] Evidence concerning Proly given by a schoolmate and erstwhile associate of Regnier, the pamphleteer turned *émigré* journalist Peltier, is even more striking. In April 1794, Peltier asserted that while he was editor of the *Actes des Apôtres*, Proly had supplied him with information on other left-wing revolutionaries. Since this revelation appeared in a notice concerning the death of Proly and the Hébertists, it seems unlikely that Peltier was merely making mischief.[46] Thus Proly certainly had compromising links to the Austrians and, apparently, to counterrevolutionary agitators inside France, and the *émigré* leadership also received his intelligence. Hence there are clear indications that leading actors in Robespierre's 'Foreign Plot' indeed had *émigré* connections, but it remains unlikely that Batz really ensnared any of Hébert's close circle. Nevertheless, Proly's activities suggest that (the surely false) allegations that Hébert too was a crypto-royalist agent-provocateur are less far-fetched than they once seemed. The revolutionaries were not wrong to imagine such things possible.

Long after the Foreign Plot, crude bribery remained a favored tool in the conspiratorial arsenal of another royalist agent, Louis Fauche-Borel.[47] Fauche-Borel remained wedded to the idea that he could overturn the Revolution by corrupting a single key figure. His list of targets is a roll-call of prominent figures: General Pichegru; General Bonaparte; the Director Jean-Paul Barras; Napoleon's archrival General Moreau; and his aide-de-camp Berthier. As this gullible, inept, and indefatigable servant of the Bourbons was involved in most of the major *émigré* conspiracies of the years 1795 to 1804 and beyond, it is worth studying Fauche-Borel's career in some detail.

Originally a bookseller-publisher from the Prussian-ruled Swiss canton of Neuchâtel, Fauche-Borel was recruited to serve the *émigré* cause by the spymaster and multiple turncoat Montgaillard in 1795. Montgaillard, who had just succeeded in persuading the prince de Condé that general Pichegru, the French commander on the Rhine, harbored royalist leanings and might be won over to the *émigré* cause, was looking for someone to act as a go-between to approach Pichegru. This was a dangerous mission, but by appealing to Fauche-Borel's vanity Montgaillard succeeded in finding an agent. Fauche-Borel's approaches were well-received by Pichegru, and financial backing was provided by William Wickham, the British diplomatic agent in Switzerland, who was charged with orchestrating Britain's espionage activities in Eastern France.[48] Unfortunately, the failure of the Vendémiaire rising in Paris in October 1795 persuaded Pichegru that 'converting' to royalism was not yet practicable. However, in 1797, when moderates and royalist candidates, including Pichegru, made significant gains at the polls, he began to plan a restoration of the monarchy by constitutional means, and was even elected President of the legislative Council of 500, a position renewed fortnightly.[49]

Unfortunately, in late 1796 Montgaillard had approached another revolutionary general, Napoleon Bonaparte, who was on campaign in Italy. Bonaparte was not impressed, and when he seized compromising documents relating to the conspiracy on the person of one of Montgaillard's associates, the comte d'Antraigues, he duly forwarded them to Paris. These documents revealed the large sums that Wickham had spent 'corrupting' deputies in the French legislature, and on facilitating the electoral victories of moderate and royalist candidates. As a result, a number of royalist agents were arrested in Paris in January 1797, most notably the abbé Brottier and Duverne du Presle, and the Directory was placed on its guard. It was thus no surprise that following the right-wing victories in the 1797 elections, the Directory organized a preemptive coup d'état on 18 fructidor V (4 September 1797). Royalist-leaning deputies were purged from the legislature and some, including the newly-elected Pichegru, were sentenced to exile in French Guyana, a penal colony so unhealthy that it was known as 'the dry guillotine.' D'Antraigues was apparently allowed to escape, probably in return for doctoring the documents captured with him to remove all reference to Napoleon.[50] The Fructidor coup proved to be a defining moment in Directorial politics, as it stripped the Directory of claims to be a legitimate representative government; permanently deprived royalists of the hope of a peaceful victory at the ballot box; and marked the first decisive intervention of the army in domestic politics. Henceforth force was to be the way to power.

Undetered by these events, Fauche-Borel remained convinced that most revolutionaries were corrupt. He set out to approach further potential targets, and in 1799 he was instrumental in attempts to suborn the director Barras. Together with Pichegru, who had escaped from Guyana, Fauche-Borel met with Barras's agent Guérin in Berlin to discuss the restoration of Louis XVIII. From there, Fauche-Borel travelled to Mittau, where Louis was living in exile, bearing draft powers for Barras to declare a Bourbon restoration. These were approved by Louis XVIII, with minor alterations, on 10 May 1799, and remained valid for six months. Thus they finally expired at the very moment Bonaparte seized power in the coup of 18–19 Brumaire (9–10 November 1799). As Bonaparte was widely perceived to be Barras's man, it is not surprising that the Bourbons long clinged to the delusion that the new First Consul might indeed recall them to the throne. Bonaparte had no such intention. Moreover, Guérin and Barras were playing a double-game. From the outset, Barras kept the Directory closely informed about developments.[51] Even now, Fauche-Borel was none the wiser and was soon duped into conducting a correspondence with a mysterious 'royalist committee' in Paris, which claimed to be devoted to the restoration of the Bourbons. In reality this 'committee' was an invention of the Paris police, who thus kept Fauche-Borel occupied chasing red herrings, while pumping him for information.

In 1804, Fauche-Borel finally fell into Napoleon's clutches. He was arrested in Paris while working with Pichegru to advance a conspiracy orchestrated by the veteran *chouan* leader Georges Cadoudal, to kidnap or murder Bonaparte and whisk a royal prince to Paris to prepare a restoration.[52] Pichegru's role was to persuade general Jean-Victor Moreau to join an attempt to oust Bonaparte and neutralize army opposition. Moreau was an obvious choice. It was he who had delivered the knockout blow to the Austrians at Hohenlinden in December 1800 and hence he enjoyed enormous popularity, particularly in the army. He was also an outspoken critic of Napoleon. Unfortunately for the conspirators, he appears to have refused their blandishments and expressed distaste for a Bourbon restoration. This did not save him from disgrace when the plot was discovered. When Moreau was brought to trial, the prosecution offered no compelling evidence: the judges voted to acquit him by seven votes to five, but were coerced into imprisoning him for two years. The conspirators did not escape so lightly. Cadoudal was executed and Pichegru apparently hanged himself in prison. Bonaparte's enemies insisted he was murdered. Fauche-Borel was imprisoned in the Temple. Then, in the final act of the tragedy, Bonaparte authorized the kidnap from neutral Baden of the (wholly innocent) d'Enghien, who was tried before a kangaroo court and shot in secret, convinced that he was the royal prince the plotters had intended to summon.[53] This step proved decisive for Bonaparte, for it made reconciliation with the Bourbons impossible; alienated other European rulers, especially Tsar Alexander I; and precipitated his decision to proclaim France an empire.

Fauche-Borel was eventually released on 18 February 1805, at the request of the King of Prussia, who claimed him as a Prussian subject.[54] Before being granted his liberty, Fauche-Borel promised to serve Napoleon, though it is unlikely that he kept his word and served consciously as a mole in the Bourbon camp as his enemies later alleged. Instead, he returned to London, where the Napoleonic police drew him into correspondence with an agent named Perlet, who claimed to represent a (fictitious) royalist committee.[55] At this point, the machinations of Perlet and his superiors, including Napoleon's police minister Joseph Fouché, become very murky. From Elizabeth Sparrow's account, it appears that Fouché and his subaltern Veyrat may indeed have contrived to orchestrate a coup d'état, and it certainly seems that they were willing to take money from all camps. Whatever the case, these developments proved disastrous to Fauche-Borel and his family, for in January 1807, with the approval of the British government, he sent his nephew Charles-Samuel Vitel to Paris to meet with Perlet and deliver a letter to Fouché. Instead, Vitel was arrested and shot, in order to prevent the subterfuge from being discovered, and perhaps allay suspicions against Perlet and his associates.[56] Following Vitel's death, Fauche-Borel was marginalized from British plans and apparently concluded that his nephew had been betrayed from London, for he publicly accused two rival *émigré* spymasters, his archenemy d'Antraigues and the comte de Puisaye of complicity in the deed.[57] The result was a long and bitter pamphleteering battle. Meanwhile, Fauche-Borel continued to dream of bribing leading figures in the government – as late as 1811 he suggested a plan to corrupt Berthier.

There was no happy ending for Fauche-Borel after the restoration, for Perlet accused him of betraying the Bourbon cause. A furious pamphlet exchange followed. Eventually Fauche-Borel dragged Perlet before the courts, where he was sentenced to five years in gaol. However, the Bourbons snubbed Fauche-Borel, and he soon fell into financial difficulties. He attempted to extricate himself from this perilous position by publishing his memoirs, which finally appeared in 1828–29 and revealed, among other things, his attempts to suborn Barras. His work did not meet with the success he hoped, although within a year Barras had responded with memoirs of his own, which revealed that he had informed his fellow directors of all Fauche-Borel's machinations.[58] Thus by the time Fauche-Borel commited suicide by jumping from a clock tower in Neuchâtel on 4 September 1829, apparently because of his financial troubles, he was well aware that he had been a serial dupe, that his gullibility had led to his nephew's execution, and that his career as a spy and conspirator had been a spectacular failure.

If Fauche-Borel's conspiracies seem naive in their simplicity and ambition, they also reached the heart of successive revolutionary governments. In Pichegru, Bonaparte, and Moreau he attempted to suborn the most successful generals of the republic; in Barras he hoped to buy the most influential and longest-serving member of the Directory; and in Berthier he targeted Napoleon's most trusted military aide. He was also not altogether without success. Pichegru, whose military prestige gave him tremendous influence in 1795–96, appears to have been genuinely converted and committed to the royalist cause, and it is possible that the archsurvivor Barras, too, wished to keep his options open. Moreover, at different times, Fauche-Borel enjoyed the backing of both the British and the Russian governments. The former was closely involved in the conspiracy to use Pichegru to achieve a Bourbon restoration;[59] the latter gave its blessing to the attempt to suborn Barras and continued to listen to him well into the Napoleonic period.[60] That his attempts came to nothing does not mean that they lacked substance. On the contrary, such serious and well-financed attempts to subvert and transform the government of France kept alive and added substance to fears of conspiracy and mutual suspicions among the revolutionary political elite even after the fall of Robespierre. Retrospectively, they must also have seemed to add weight to the allegations circulating since 1789 that the British ambassador, the Duke of Dorset, had spent considerable sums to 'arrange' the disturbances of July 1789 in Paris. No longer could informed French citizens doubt the perfidy of Albion.

The careers of Fauche-Borel and Pichegru also illustrate the existence of competing networks of spies and conspirators. D'Antraigues, Puisaye, Montgaillard, and Mallet Du Pan, for example, all had their own networks of agents and informers inside France, often pursuing different aims.[61] The rivalry between these organizations was exacerbated by struggles for the patronage of the allied powers and the fragmentary nature of political authority within the emigration. This latter problem persisted almost to the end of the emigration. During the period 1789–92, d'Artois and the *émigré* political leadership claimed to speak on Louis XVI's behalf, asserting that the king was effectively a prisoner. Such claims were largely undermined by the existence of a parallel network of diplomats and agents orchestrated by Breteuil, himself living in exile, who in November 1790 had been invested with full authority to approach the powers of Europe on Louis XVI's behalf.[62] This situation was not greatly improved by the execution of Louis XVI and the assumption of power by his brother, the comte de Provence. Provence, who had escaped France during the flight to Varennes, claimed to rule first as regent on behalf of his nephew Louis XVII, and then, from 1795, in his own right as Louis XVIII. Provence spent the later 1790s living in various refuges around Europe, while his brother d'Artois was in Britain, sometimes pursuing variant policies.[63]

Only in 1807, when the British government allowed Louis XVIII to come to England, did the two brothers find themselves in the same country once again. In the interim, Louis often found the actions of d'Artois and his agents an embarrassment. This was particularly obvious in the aftermath of the Opéra bomb plot, in which royalist conspirators operating on the ultimate authority of d'Artois's agent, Nicolas Dutheil, blew up a cart full of explosives in a Paris street just as the emperor's cortege was passing.[64] This *machine infernale* missed its target, but large numbers of bystanders were killed or wounded. It also shocked a Europe unused to terrorist outrages, and angered Louis XVIII who disapproved of such methods.[65] Moreover, the conspiracy proved counterproductive.

Although the culprits were quickly identified, Napoleon used the bomb plot as a pretext to strike against Jacobins as well as royalists, thereby cementing his throne yet further.

Equally, Louis XVIII apparently disapproved of Cadoudal's plot to kill or kidnap Napoleon in 1804, which d'Artois had concealed from him: indeed, Louis's private secretary Bonnay denounced it as 'une lâche atrocité' ['a cowardly atrocity'].[66] The power struggle and rivalry between the two royal brothers was so intense that Louis kept the names of his agents secret from d'Artois. In response, d'Artois attempted to win over Louis's representatives, and in 1800, with British government backing, tried to lure Louis's agent d'André to London to discover Louis's plans and the identities of his operatives.[67] Yet had the rivalry not existed, Louis XVIII's policy would nevertheless have been prudent. The more people were aware of his networks, the more the risk that it would be compromised. On the other hand, the existence of comparable and competing networks ensured that some would be discovered from time to time, whether through loose talk, betrayal, bungling, counterespionage, or the disputes of rival operatives. Hence across the revolutionary and Napoleonic period there were a series of explosive exposés of the espionage activities of *émigré* agents and their allies, which in turn reinforced the image of the *émigré* conspirator. Some of these reports, though by no means all, appeared in official reports of French legislatures into the various conspiracies that punctuated this period, or memoirs of French agents, often published with official blessing.[68] But others were produced in London and elsewhere by aggrieved operatives.[69] Thus even after the *émigré* amnesty of 1802, which resulted in the reconciliation of perhaps 90 percent of the surviving *émigrés* with the Consular régime, the image of the *émigré* conspirator continued to thrive and develop.

An additional problem for the *émigré* leadership was that many conspiracies, particularly in the early period, appear to have been freelance efforts. For example, several different *émigrés* hoped to rescue the king or queen from prison, although their plans came to nothing. Just how seriously these efforts should be taken is open to question, as some conspiracies seem to have been little more than attempts to fleece supporters of funds. For example, according to his biographer, Peltier's involvement in a plot to spring Marie-Antoinette from the Temple using funds supplied by the British actress Charlotte Atkins was probably nothing but an attempt to embezzle the latter's money.[70] However, Atkins found a more reliable agent in Batz, whose attempts to infiltrate his agents into the guards at the Temple prison in order to secure the queen's evasion failed apparently only due to a last-minute betrayal.[71] Batz was also the orchestrator of an ambitious last-ditch attempt to rescue Louis XVI. At the head of a small band of royalist co-conspirators, he led an ambush on the wagons carrying the king to the scaffold on 21 January 1793. Batz had hoped that his companions would be joined by some 500 royalist enthusiasts, summoned, he claimed, by letter from around France. However, none of his epistolary contacts turned up, and none of the crowd answered his rallying call, 'Here friends here! – all who wish to save their King!'[72] Hopelessly outnumbered by the National Guards lining the king's route, Batz's party failed even to reach the escort, and the king probably remained ignorant of the attempt to save him. Batz, true to his vampiric name, vanished like smoke in the ensuing chaos, and lived to fight another day.[73]

Given the ceaseless efforts of figures such as Batz, d'Antraigues, Dutheil, and Fauche-Borel to subvert, corrupt, or assasinate revolutionary leaders, fears of *émigré* conspirators were both rational and well-grounded. The belief that their tentacles reached into the heart of government were perhaps exaggerated, but the potential was always there. Nor were fears unfounded that they would use other insidious means such as economic warfare (including false *assignats*, and attempts to undermine confidence), propaganda, and quite possibly agents provocateurs such as Proly. While it is difficult to trace such activities due to the problematic nature and survival of the sources and the 'freelance' nature of many counterrevolutionary operatives, an overall picture emerges suggestive of sustained efforts at internal subversion across a broad front. If both the revolutionaries and the counterrevolutionaries overestimated their chances of success and the danger that they represented, due to a shared intellectual commitment to conspiratorial modes of explanation, the plots themselves were real enough to suggest that revolutionary fears – and hence the Revolution itself – were driven not by their own paranoia or opportunism, but the repeated attempts of royalists to realize their own fantasies.

Notes

1 On the career of d'Artois during the emigration see: O. du Beaudieu de Messières, *Le Comte d'Artois: un émigré de choix* (Paris, 1996).

2 A. Mathiez, *La Conspiration de l'étranger* (Paris, 1918); M. Slavin, *The Hébertistes to the Guillotine: Anatomy of a 'Conspiracy' in Revolutionary France* (Baton Rouge and London, 1994).

3 For Burke's view of *émigré* propaganda efforts see *The Correspondence of Edmund Burke* (Chicago and Cambridge, 1958–1970), VI, 241–243, Burke to the Chevalier de Bintinaye, March 1791. In fact, Burke's comments galvanized Calonne into action: see S. Burrows, *French Exile Journalism and European Politics* (Woodbridge, 2000), pp. 95–96.

4   See for example J. Godechot, *The Counter-Revolution: Doctrine and Action*, trans. Salvator Attanasio (Princeton, 1971).

5   There is no systematic comparative study of the anatomy of conspiracy theories current among the *émigrés* and the revolutionaries. Such a study is beyond the scope of this chapter. Suffice it to note here that conspiratorial *modes* of thinking were common to both sides.

6   H. Maspero-Clerc, *Un Journaliste contre-révolutionnaire: Jean-Gabriel Peltier, 1760–1825* (Paris, 1973), pp. 19–26, 57, 78; Burrows, *French Exile Journalism*, p. 146.

7   G. Gengembre, *La Contre-révolution ou l'histoire désespérante* (Paris, 1989), p. 51.

8   D. M. MacMahon, *Enemies of Enlightenment* (Oxford, 2002), pp. 19–55, 58–59, pp. 56–88 of the same work discusses the evolution of these ideas during the revolution.

9   Charles-Louis Cadet de Gassicourt (atrib.), *Le Tombeau de Jacques Molai, ou le secret des conspirateurs. A ceux qui veulent tout savoir. Oeuvre posthume de C. L. C. G. D. L. S. D. M. B. C. D. V.* (Paris, l'an IV de l'ère française [1796?]). According to the British Library Catalogue, the initials in the title stand for Charles-Louis Cadet Gassicourt, de la section de Montblanc, condamné de Vendémiaire.' Jacques Molai was the last Grand Master of the Templars.

10   J. Osen, *Royalist Political Thought during the French Revolution* (Westport CT, 1995), pp. 7–8; W. J. Murray, *The Right-Wing Press in the French Revolution, 1789–1792* (Woodbridge, 1986), pp. 255–256; J.-P. Bertaud, *Les Amis du roi: journaux et journalistes royalistes en France de 1789 à 1792* (Paris, 1986), p. 69.

11   Charles Jenkinson (1727–1808), President of the Board of Trade (1786–1804) and father of the future Prime Minister.

12   Balliol College Library, Mallet Papers, file #3, Liverpool to Reeves, 5 January 1798.

13   On this incident see ibid. and J. L. Mallet, *An Autobiographical Retrospective of the First Twenty-Five Years of his Life* (Windsor, 1890), pp. 200–201.

14   *British Mercury*, 14 (15 March 1800), pp. 335–363. The *British Mercury* was the English translation of Mallet Du Pan's *Mercure britannique*. The latter was generally published five days before the former.

15   Ibid., p. 356.

16   Ibid., p. 357.

17   Ibid., p. 358.

18   Ibid.

19   See, for example, Godechot, *Counter-Revolution*, pp. 67, 83.

20   On Louis XVIII's political evolution see: P. Mansel, *Louis XVIII* (London, 1981), pp. 56–136.

21   On the arguments of these individuals, and the vilification they suffered, see: R. Griffiths, *Le Centre perdu: Malouet et les 'monarchiens' dans la révolution*

française (Grenoble, 1988), especially pp. 161–227; Burrows, *French Exile Journalism*, especially pp. 47–48, 157–163.

22 MacMahon, *Enemies of Enlightenment*, p. 81.

23 The classic study of falsification of the currency in the revolution is J. Bouchary, *Les Faux-monnayeurs sous la révolution française* (Paris, 1946).

24 On Froment and the Gard see especially G. Lewis, *The Second Vendée: the Continuity of Counter-Revolution in the Department of the Gard, 1789–1815* (Oxford, 1978).

25 Roberts, *The Counter-Revolution in France, 1787–1830* (Basingstoke, 1990), p. 26.

26 Godechot, *Counter-Revolution*, p. 153.

27 The most recent study of the flight to Varennes is T. Tackett, *When the King Took Flight* (Cambridge, MA, 2003).

28 On Breteuil's role in the planning and execution of the King's flight see M. Price, *The Fall of the French Monarchy: Louis XVI, Marie-Antoinette and the Baron de Breteuil* (London, 2002), pp. 136–205.

29 On Condé's army see F. d'Agay, 'A European Destiny: the Armée de Condé, 1792–1801,' in K. Carpenter and P. Mansel, eds, *The French Émigrés in Europe and the Struggle against Revolution, 1789–1814* (Basingstoke, 1999), pp. 28–42.

30 Recent studies of Quiberon include P. Huchet, *1795, Quiberon ou le destin de France* (Rennes, 1995). For the disaster's effect on the London *émigré* community see K. Carpenter, *Refugees of the French Revolution, Émigrés in London, 1789–1802* (Basingstoke, 1999), pp. 90–95.

31 E. Sparrow, *Secret Service: British Agents in France, 1792–1815* (Woodbridge, 1999), pp. 19–26.

32 The main studies of the Foreign Plot are A. Mathiez, *La Conspiration de l'étranger* (Paris, 1918) and *L'Affaire de la Compagnie des Indes: un procès de corruption sous la Terreur* (Paris, 1920); N. Hampson, 'François Chabot and his Plot,' in *Transactions of the Royal Historical Society*, 5th series, 26 (1976), pp. 1–14; M. Price, 'The "Foreign Plot" and the French Revolution: A Reappraisal,' in B. Coward and J. Swann, eds, *Conspiracy and Conspiracy Theories in Early Modern Europe: From the Waldensians to the French Revolution* (Aldershot, 2004), pp. 255–268; and the works on the Baron de Batz cited below note 35. See also T. Kaiser, 'From the Austrian Committee to the Foreign Plot: Marie-Antoinette, Austrophobia, and the Terror,' *French Historical Studies*, 26:4 (2003), pp. 579–617, pp. 605–615.

33 The classic study of the Compagnie des Indes scandal is Mathiez, *L'Affaire de la Compagnie des Indes*.

34 *Le Moniteur*, 25 March 1794, cited and translated in Kaiser, 'From Austrian Committee to Foreign Plot,' p. 608.

35 On Batz see: Baron de Batz, *La Vie et conspirations de Jean, Baron de Batz* (Paris, 1908) and *Les Conspirations et la fin de Jean, Baron de Batz* (Paris, 1911); M. Minnigerode, *Marie-Antoinette's Henchman: The Career of Jean, Baron de Batz, in the French Revolution* (New York, 1936); A. de Lestapis,

La 'Conspiration de Batz' (1793–1794) (Paris, 1969); M. Grey, *Le Baron de Batz: le d'Artagnan de la révolution* (Paris, 1991); G. Lenôtre, *Le Baron de Batz* (Paris, 1896). In preparing this chapter I have had to consult the edition of Lenôtre's study translated into English by Mrs Rodolph Stawell under the title *A Gascon Royalist in Revolutionary Paris: The Baron de Batz, 1792–1795* (London and New York, 1910).

36 See Price, '"Foreign Plot",' pp. 261–266; Price, *Fall of the Monarchy*, pp. 346–351.

37 Price, '"Foreign Plot",' pp. 255–268.

38 Batz, *Conspirations et fin de Batz*, pp. 30–31: quote translated in Price, '"Foreign Plot",' pp. 259–60.

39 Price, '"Foreign Plot",' pp. 257–266.

40 Kaiser, 'From Austrian Committee to Foreign Plot,' p. 611.

41 Ibid.

42 National Archives, PC 1/124 piece 263, undated fragment. I first noted the importance of this document in print in S. Burrows, 'British Propaganda for Russia in the Napoleonic Wars: the *Courier d'Angleterre*,' *New Zealand Slavonic Journal* (1993), pp. 85–100.

43 Kaiser, 'From Austrian Committee to Foreign Plot,' p. 611.

44 Archives nationales, Paris, F⁷ 6330 dossier 6959, 'Note sur M. Peltier'; *Courier de Londres et de Paris*, 21 (5/10 August 1802); Slavin, *Hébertistes*, p. 176.

45 On Regnier see Burrows, 'British Propaganda for Russia,' esp. pp. 85–86; Burrows, *French Exile Journalism*.

46 Correspondance politique 71 (15 April 1794).

47 On Fauche-Borel see G. Lenôtre, *Two Royalist Spies of the French Revolution*, transl. Bernard Miall (London, 1924); Peter de Polnay, *Napoleon's Police* (London, 1970), ch. 14, 'The Tragedy of Fauche-Borel.' For autobiographical accounts see L. Fauche-Borel, *Précis historique des différentes missions dans lesquelles M. Louis Fauche-Borel a été employé pour la cause de la monarchie* (Paris, 1815) and *Mémoires*, 4 vols. (Paris, 1829).

48 On Wickham's missions see W. R. Fryer, *Republic or Restoration in France? 1794–1797* (Manchester, 1965); H. Mitchell, *The Underground War against Revolutionary France* (Oxford, 1965); Sparrow, *Secret Service*, passim.

49 On Pichegru, see E. Daudet, *La Conjuration de Pichegru et les complots royalistes de midi et de l'est, 1795–1797* (Paris, 1901); G. Caudrillier, *La Traison de Pichegru et les intrigues des royalistes dans l'Est avant Fructidor* (Paris, 1908); Sir J. Hall, *General Pichegru's Treason* (London, 1915).

50 On d'Antraigues's role see C. Duckworth, *The d'Antraigues Phenomenon. The Making and Breaking of a Royalist Espionage Agent* (Newcastle, 1986), pp. 215–252; J. Godechot, *Le Comte d'Antraigues: Un espion dans l'Europe des émigrés* (Paris, 1986), pp. 151–175.

51 On this incident see Burrows, *French Exile Journalism*, p. 104; Sparrow, *Secret Service*, pp. 181–185. The *pleins pouvoirs* and related correspondence

are in the Archives du Ministère des affaires étrangères, mémoires et documents, France, 607 fos 153–170.

52 On this conspiracy see C. Huon de Penarster, *Une Conspiration en l'An XI et en l'An XII* (Paris, 1896); E. M. de Saint-Hilaire, *Cadoudal, Moreau, Pichegru* (Paris, 1977); H. Gaubert, *Les Conspirateurs au temps de Napoléon Ier* (Paris, 1962), pp. 161–261; de Polnay, *Napoleon's Police*, pp. 59–93; G. de Cadoudal, *Cadoudal et la chouannerie par son neveu, Georges de Cadoudal* (Paris, 1887); J.-F. Chiappe, *Cadoudal et la liberté* (Paris, 1971); and works on Pichegru cited above in note 49.

53 On d'Enghien's kidnap and execution see M. Dupont, *Le Tragique Destin du duc d'Enghien* (Paris, 1938); J.-P. Bertaud, *Bonaparte et le duc d'Enghien: le duel des deux France* (Paris, 1972).

54 His release is recorded in Fouché's daily police bulletin of 19 February 1805, published in E. d'Hauterive, *La Police secrète du premier empire*, 5 vols (Paris, 1908–1968), 1, paragraph 931.

55 On Perlet see G. Lenôtre, *L'Affaire Perlet* (Paris, 1923).

56 Sparrow, *Secret Service*, pp. 316–323.

57 L. Fauche-Borel, *Exposition of the Persecutions which Louis Fauche-Borel has experienced from MM. d'Antraigues and de Puisaye in Consequence of the Zeal he has Manifested in the Service of England and in the Cause of Legitimacy* (London, 1812).

58 J.-P. Barras, *Mémoires*, 4 vols (Paris, 1829), 2, pp. 634–637.

59 National Archives, London, FO 27/54, pt. I, fo. 210, translation of 'Rescript of [Tsar] Paul,' 14/25 May 1799.

60 Sparrow, *Secret Service*, pp. 316–323.

61 On these networks see Godechot, *Counter-Revolution*, pp. 173–200; J. Chaumié, *Le Réseau d'Antraigues et la contre-révolution, 1791–1793* (Paris, 1965); F. Acomb, *Mallet du Pan (1749–1800): A Career in Political Journalism* (Durham, NC, 1973), pp. 255–266; M. Hutt, *Chouannerie and Counter-Revolution: Puisaye, the Princes and the British Government in the 1790s*, 2 vols (Cambridge, 1983).

62 Price, *Fall of the Monarchy*, p. 115.

63 On Provence's activities, see Mansel, *Louis XVIII*, ch. 5.

64 On this atrocity see J. Lorédan, *La Machine infernale* (Paris, 1924); J. Thiry, *La Machine infernale* (Paris, 1952).

65 Roberts, *Counter-Revolution*, p. 57.

66 Mansel, *Louis XVIII* (London, 1981), p. 102.

67 Ibid.

68 Reports, memoirs and documents depicting *émigré* conspiracies include: *Correspondance originale des émigrés, ou les émigrés peints par eux-mêmes* (Paris, 1793); *Rapport fait au nom des Comités réunis de Salut public et de Sureté générale sur la conspiration de Batz, ou de l'étranger* (Paris, 1794); *Rapport fait par Jean Debry, au nom d'une commission spéciale, sur la conspiration découverte la 12 pluviôse an V, tendante au renversement du gouvernement républicain et au rétablissement de la royauté* (Paris, 1797); *Recueil des pièces sur la conspiration anglaise en l'an XI*, 2 vols (Paris, 1809);

J.-C.-H. Méhée de la Touche, *Alliance des Jacobins français avec le ministère anglais* (Paris, germinal an XII [1804]).

69 Fauche-Borel, *Exposition*, is a classic example.
70 Maspero-Clerc, *Peltier*, pp. 100–117.
71 Lenôtre, *Gascon Royalist*, pp. 17–23. Price, ' "Foreign Plot" ', p. 259, indicates that it is not certain whether Batz orchestrated the plot to save the queen.
72 Lenôtre, *Gascon Royalist*, p. 8.
73 Ibid., p. 11.

8

Never was a plot so holy: Gracchus Babeuf and the end of the French Revolution

Laura Mason

We are, it seems, absorbed by conspiracy obsessions. This volume represents neither the first nor, undoubtedly, the last word on French revolutionaries' conviction that they struggled against a world populated by duplicitous and seditious enemies. There are, indeed, two generations of scholarship on this issue. Whereas historians writing twenty or thirty years ago offered psychological, cultural, and linguistic explanations for what they treated principally as the invention of revolutionary minds, a newer cohort – which includes the authors gathered here – consider the events, personalities, and political structures that shaped revolutionaries' perception of the world around them. But the stress, in all cases, remains on the charge of conspiracy, not the act itself.[1]

I propose to invert that optic by focusing on the single most famous conspirator of the French Revolution: the radical egalitarian and journalist Gracchus Babeuf. In 1796, Babeuf joined a small circle of displaced Jacobins and Hébertists to foment popular insurrection and overthrow the sitting government of the Directory. Calling themselves Equals, these men and women proposed to restore the democratic constitution of 1793 and resurrect the National Convention in the wake of their new revolution. Some, most notably Babeuf, also considered abolishing private property. But they were denounced to the police and arrested, to become the principal defendants in one of the Revolution's most widely publicized trials.

What is striking about the case is that Babeuf and the Equals rejected the prevailing revolutionary notion of conspiracy as a reprehensible violation of republicanism to appropriate plotting as a selfless gesture of revolutionary devotion. In so doing, they imparted to their nineteenth-century heirs a new definition of political activism that would sustain republicans through years of repression. Most remarkably, they came to believe that political secrecy was not at odds with their identities as latter-day Jacobins. Rather, they hoped to restore the transparency of the year II by means of the plot.

The paradox of the democratic Equals' turn to conspiracy has been largely ignored or dismissed. Historians who follow Marx in labeling Babeuf the first modern communist treat conspiring as the simple means to realize a more important project: that of transforming community of goods from utopian fantasy to social fact.[2] On the other hand, when the revisionist Richard Andrews challenged this interpretation in the early 1970s, he focused on the plot only to slight it. Neither Jacobins nor *sans-culottes*, he concluded, could successfully conspire. 'Secrecy? . . . Democratic challengers, imprisoned by their training and sites of action, proved unable to transform their identities and behavior.'[3] Hence, the Equals' failure.

In recent years, Pierre Serna has refuted Andrews' assertions about democrats' inability to change. Faced with limits that the Directory imposed on political activism, Serna argues, many of the régime's left-wing opponents bowed to the force of circumstance and adopted secrecy for strategic rather than principled reasons.[4] The exception was Babeuf. Insisting that the journalist remained irrevocably committed to the values of the year II, Serna concludes: 'Babeuf associates democracy with publicity. Antithetical to the secret society, it can only function through the expression of universal laws.'[5]

Undeniably, force of circumstance played a part in democrats' decision to accept secrecy during the directorial years. But the Equals' choice to conspire was principled as well as pragmatic. And it was Gracchus Babeuf who systematically elaborated those principles. Developing what would become a philosophy of opposition for generations of activists, Babeuf gave voice to a classical republicanism that is the most consistently undervalued dimension of his thought. However, because Babeuf's republicanism has been so much overshadowed by his economic thinking, and because of the difficult circumstances under which he made his case, he remains a hold-out for transparency in Andrews' and Serna's accounts. Indeed, both historians consider him a man so incapable of conspiring as to be responsible for the Equals' defeat. I mean to turn this formulation on its head by illuminating Babeuf's embrace of the plot in the name of the republic.

The son of a low-level employee of the tax farm, Gracchus Babeuf spent much of his short life in his native Picardy.[6] Although employed as a feudal notary, Babeuf welcomed the Revolution in 1789 and quickly became a visible figure in local politics. Moving to Paris in 1793, he involved himself with the Enragés until arrested on a civil charge, after which he spent the height of the Terror in prison. When released after Thermidor, Babeuf turned to journalism, devoting his newspaper, *Le Tribun du peuple*, to championing the renewal of *sans-culottes'* activism and economic power that was then being eroded by reaction. But he pushed too hard. His editorial urging a popular insurrection for bread and the constitution of 1793 drew the government's ire and won a new arrest. Babeuf remained in prison for another seven months, freed only by the amnesty issued on the eve of the Directory's installation.

More important than the details of Babeuf's political life are those of his intellectual evolution. An autodidact who owed his early philosophical education to books received as a corresponding member of the academy of Arras, Babeuf addressed the problem of social inequality while still a young man. As he combined a growing knowledge of classical and Enlightenment texts with a widening experience of the world – which came to encompass stricken peasants of the ancien régime Somme and starving workers in post-Thermidoran Paris – he penned increasingly radical proposals for the redistribution of resources. In his search for the means to guarantee a natural right to subsistence, Babeuf would journey from proposing the imposition of progressive taxes under the ancien régime to demanding a wholesale redistribution of land and goods by the late summer of 1795.

As the Revolution progressed, Babeuf's commitment to social equality was matched by his growing interest in democratic politics. In private notes, written in 1791, he described a political philosophy that navigated between pessimism about human nature and faith in the plebs' ability to check their rulers' worst impulses. Because men are driven by the will to dominate, he asserted, those who govern inevitably attempt to subordinate their fellows. Worse yet, the people may be misled by such leaders. None-theless, the people retain the necessary force to preserve their fundamental rights, a force they may express through the institutions of direct democracy or by insurrection. Babeuf would revisit these principles when he confronted the Directory.[7]

The political world of the Directory that Babeuf found in place after his final release from prison was very different from the one he had left behind. Although still a republic, the Directory marked a significant retreat from the polity to which legislators aspired in the year II, and which activists still hoped to resurrect during the Thermidoran Reaction. During Babeuf's months in prison, the constitution of 1793 – which promised universal male suffrage, and rights to instruction, work, public assistance, and insurrection – was abandoned in favor of the constitution of 1795 – which restricted suffrage and defined equality as a legal category without

implications for differences of capacity or property.[8] The disenfranchise-
ment of the working poor was matched by their pitiable material
conditions.[9] Devastated by the repeal of the maximum, the murderous
winter of 1794–95, and spiraling inflation, many turned to begging or
banditry; others – Babeuf among them – saw their children wither and die
of starvation. By the fall of 1795, immiseration had joined memories of
the violent repression of the Prairial insurrection the preceding spring
to drive the mass of people into cynicism and political apathy.

Resurrecting *Le Tribun du peuple*, Babeuf condemned the Directory
and the dire condition of the people. This is the newspaper that Richard
Andrews and Pierre Serna cite as key evidence of Babeuf's rejection of
political secrecy, and it does stand as the Directory's most singular
example of unreconstructed Jacobinism. When Babeuf founded the
newspaper in the fall of 1794, during the early months of the Thermidoran
Reaction, he leveled a few charges of conspiracy against the people's
enemies. But his tone was still relatively moderate, undoubtedly because
he hoped that the suspended constitution of 1793 might yet be restored
and popular activism reinvigorated. By the fall of 1795, however, the
democratic constitution had been definitively abandoned and popular
activism vanquished. Now, Babeuf gave voice to unbridled rage, resurrecting the anticonspiracy rhetoric of the year II with all its fear and
defensiveness. Like Robespierre and Saint-Just, he denounced conspiracies
particular and general as systems of deceit, intrigue, and corruption aimed
at restoring the despotism of the ancien régime. And like Marat, he offered
himself as a bulwark against the popular credulity that hypocrites
exploited. Babeuf promised to expose the counterrevolutionary artifice
that enchained the people and threatened the Revolution.[10]

Le Tribun du peuple described the people's representatives as instruments of a wealthy elite poised to defeat the Revolution.[11] It portrayed
legislators and patricians joining their voices to slander the Revolution and
vilify the people, as the people themselves sank into despair.[12] 'What does
it matter to us which of these crooks wins?' Babeuf imagined the latter
asking. 'In either case, we will always be ruled by lawlessness.'[13] Trying
to shake them from their torpor, Babeuf replied that the people must
conspire in turn: 'To make revolution . . . is to conspire against an
unsuitable state of affairs.'[14]

In asserting that the people must 'conspire,' Babeuf adopted the double-
edged use of the word that Camille Desmoulins had put to good effect
during the Terror. Defining the 'conspiracy' of elites as secret association
against the Revolution, he treated that of the people as open and virtuous
struggle. To underscore this differential sense of conspiracy (*conspirer*),
Babeuf applied the word 'plot' (*conjurer*) to the activities of elites alone:

'[T]he outgoing senate, and the one that replaced it, shared a single and indivisible system; . . . their acts before and after Vendémiaire were no more than a series of crimes and plots against the People.'[15] Used in this sense, plotting was secretive and criminal. However, having so applied the word to the activity of the people's enemies in the pages of *Le Tribun du peuple*, Babeuf began to use it privately to describe the secret but loyal activism of the republic's friends.

Babeuf's devotion to the plot is illuminated by papers he composed while himself organizing secretly. He turned to plotting in the spring of 1796, at the invitation of political allies angered by the Directory's closure of the democratic Pantheon Society. The Equals, as Babeuf and the others called themselves, hoped to generate popular insurrection and thereby install a new government. To that end, they appointed former *sans-culottes* militants as their agents in Paris neighborhoods to report on opinion, encourage popular dissatisfaction, and gather information about the availability of arms and men. But all were denounced. When the police arrived at Babeuf's lodgings, they found his 'archives': hundreds of pages of notes and private correspondence that detailed the Equals' practices and objectives. These 'archives' give voice to Babeuf's growing conviction that secrecy had become essential to sustain republicanism.

Babeuf's instructions to the Equals' agents revel in intrigue. They leave no doubt about the kind of activity to which he aspires, for he describes it not as conspiring (*conspirer*), which might yet be public, but as the far more clandestine plotting (*conjurer*): 'Never has a plot been as sacred as ours in either motive or object; nor has there ever been a plot whose agents so deserved the trust placed in them. No one ever struggled secretly against a treacherous government as long and as successfully as we.'[16] He used the same word when reminding the neighborhood agents of the trust, skills, and unique commitment their secrecy required.

> Plotters use no one without first taking his measure; and understand that once having bestowed their confidence, they will not permit their chosen ones to fail. The reasons you give [for failing to execute your mission] . . . are too petty to dissuade revolutionaries; we are surrounded by inquisitors as well; plotters know how to outwit their watchfulness and defy them.[17]

Even when not stirring devotion to the plot, Babeuf was explicit about the need and means to preserve secrecy. Local agents should foster clandestine gatherings by encouraging citizens to meet in private homes, where participants could speak more freely than in cafés because safe from the prying eyes of the police. Such agents ought to restrict the size of these gatherings to make them still less obvious. With these methods, Babeuf promised, patriotic circles would soon flourish in every garret of the capital: 'in seeking the lodgings of every truly patriotic family, you will find small cliques formed independently. In each family, there is a club.'[18]

Turning to secrecy did not, however, obviate the need for public activism like that of *Le Tribun du peuple*. Like other directorial demo-crats, Babeuf regarded public activism as complementary to clandestine organizing. Thus, he asked militants to distribute popular newspapers at secret gatherings and explained that a particular issue of his newspaper would supplement his private instructions.[19] As well, he may have believed that public activism would smooth the transition to a secrecy many still regarded with suspicion. For, Babeuf also reminded his agents, they had not only to avoid the prying eyes of police, but to play a double-game with the very citizens to whom they appealed: 'One must be somewhat bold to inspire others; furtiveness makes the uneducated masses wary.'[20]

Babeuf acknowledged force of circumstance when explaining the need to preserve secrecy – directorial tyranny chased patriotic expression from the public squares where it flourished best – but he did not abandon transparency out of pragmatism alone.[21] As the republic changed in the wake of Thermidor, he reoriented his definition of the relationship between republicanism and secrecy. In so doing, he sustained a long-standing practice of incorporating new texts into his evolving under-standing of politics, turning now to Machiavelli's *Discourses on Livy*. A note in Babeuf's hand from this period identifies chapters in the *Discourses* that detail the means to preserve and restore republican liberty: 'The creation of tribunes perfected the Roman constitution;' 'A corrupt people that becomes free can remain so only with the greatest difficulty.' And, most importantly: 'How to preserve liberty in a corrupt state, if its constitution guarantees freedom . . .'[22]

Drafted by Machiavelli in the wake of his exile from Florence, the *Discourses on Livy* gives fullest expression to his republicanism. In this, his commentary on Livy's history of Rome, Machiavelli considered how to guarantee republican government against human weakness; in particular, against nobles' permanent lust for power and wealth. Although he claimed that 'the desires of a free people are rarely harmful to liberty,' Machiavelli's fundamental pessimism about human nature prevented him from making the people final guarantors of liberty: that task he accorded to good laws and institutions.[23] But even laws and institutions cannot guarantee liberty permanently, for they cease to function properly when a people becomes corrupt. At such time, only an extraordinary man can save the republic by using exceptional means to change them.[24]

As his notes from 1791 suggest, Babeuf had long shared some of Machiavelli's founding beliefs. In particular, both men mingled a wary faith in the people with fundamental pessimism about human nature. What Babeuf now took from Machiavelli was the Italian's emphasis on the exceptional man who might save the republic by wrenching citizens from their comfortable path of decline. So appealing was this argument that Babeuf echoed it in his first directive to the neighborhood agents. 'Times of crisis are not like ordinary times,' he argued. When a people is in full enjoyment of its rights, no one may legitimately appoint himself magistrate or attempt to initiate change without popular referenda.

> This is not so when a people is enslaved and prevented by tyranny from expressing its wishes about all that concerns it . . . Then, it is just and necessary that the boldest, the most devoted . . . assume the dictatorship of insurrection, take the initiative, adopt the glorious title of plotters for liberty, and establish themselves as the redemptive magistrates of their fellow citizens.

This not only justified the Equals' resolution to organize insurrection secretly, he concluded, but invested their efforts with 'grandeur and magnanimity.'[25]

The Equals did not become redemptive magistrates. Denounced and arrested, they were remanded to a high court. During their months in prison before the trial, Babeuf coordinated his defense with co-conspirator Filippo Buonarroti, the future *carbonari*. Pleading not guilty, the men nonetheless explained why conspiracy was legitimate. This defense has baffled Babeuf's biographers, for with it he seems to reveal all even as he claimed to be innocent. Not surprisingly, it is taken as further evidence of Babeuf's fundamental discomfort with secrecy.[26] But that interpretation fails to take into account either the nature of revolutionary jury trials or, more importantly, the extent to which Babeuf was announcing a republican philosophy of conspiracy to fellow democrats.

Juries, introduced in France by revolutionaries, did not issue judgments on the totality of an incident but responded to a series of questions that broke down the alleged infraction. Did a specific act take place? Had the accused committed it? Had he done so with malicious intent?[27] These questions were meant to preserve the autonomy of the laymen who sat on juries, by protecting them from coercion by professional judges and defenders. However, they allowed jurors to shape verdicts according to their opinions of defendants' political motivation. At the time of the Equals' trial, the most notorious such verdicts were being delivered in the south of France, where jurors used the question of intent to acquit locals accused of battering and even murdering former Jacobin officials.[28] But juries sometimes bent in the opposite direction. So even as one Parisian jury acquitted right-wing journalist Richer-Serisy of inciting the Vendémiaire insurrection, another exonerated *sans-culottes* charged with participating in the September massacres of 1792.[29] Both trials concluded in the same week that the Equals were arrested.

This was the context within which Babeuf and Buonarroti set out to defend themselves in apparently contradictory ways. Denying that they committed particular acts, they nonetheless explained why such acts were justifiable. Thus, if they failed to persuade the jury that they were innocent of the deeds of which they stood accused, they might still hope for acquittal on grounds of intent.

Babeuf and Buonarroti began by describing the decay of the Revolution. Echoing *Le Tribun du peuple*, Buonarroti detailed the nation's decline after 9 Thermidor, when the people's erstwhile defenders turned on them.[30] The Convention attacked popular sovereignty by adopting the constitution of 1795, thereby 'depriv[ing] the nation of the right to deliberate on laws, seiz[ing] citizenship from a mass of Frenchmen, [and] divid[ing] the people between rich dominators and poor slaves.' Then the Directory 'add[ed] tyranny to usurpation' by violating even this code, closing popular associations, abridging freedom of the press, and threatening to execute its critics.[31]

Such injustice might legitimately provoke the loyal citizen who understood that revolutionary liberty is founded on popular sovereignty, 'the right to regulate what is useful to society, or prohibit what is harmful.' Even the constitution of 1795, Buonarroti insisted, emphasized that 'the collectivity of French citizens is sovereign.'[32] Like its predecessors, this constitution acknowledged that unconstrained expression is indissolubly linked to the proper exercise of sovereignty, for citizens must be free to deliberate on laws and propose change if necessary. Each and every citizen may contribute to this dialogue, offering knowledge, advice, and opinions on the best means to realize the popular good. Therefore, Babeuf concluded, 'if deliberation is legitimate, encouraging it cannot be wrong.'[33]

Whereas Babeuf drew on Machiavelli in his private writings to highlight the responsibility of the activist in times of crisis, in court he emphasized the work of Gabriel Bonnot de Mably to stress the rights of the collectivity. Written in mid-century, Mably's republican treatise, *Des droits et des devoirs du citoyen* was not published until 1789, when its prescient prescriptions for the reformation of French politics won a broad readership.[34] Asserting the citizen's natural right to exercise reason and enjoy liberty, Mably argued that governments remain legitimate only as long as they are endorsed by an active, popular will.[35] Citizens retain a perpetual right to modify or replace the social contract, defending liberty by 'repairing the insensible damage inflicted upon [the] constitution and contesting the minor abuses that accumulate and combine to produce arbitrary power.'[36]

Babeuf's indebtedness to Mably's utopian reflection on community of goods is well-known, but he was equally indebted to Mably's republicanism. During the trial, Babeuf and Buonarroti cited Mably as an authority when defending free expression and the citizen's right to revise the law. Babeuf quoted him directly when explaining that society must improve the condition of all its members. Mably, he reminded the court, wrote:

> Each citizen has the right to aspire to the government best-suited to guarantee public good, and it is his duty to use every reasonable means at his disposal to establish it . . . Thus, . . . a citizen is neither a plotter nor a disturber of the peace, if he proposes to his fellows a wiser form of government than that which they freely adopted, or which events, passions, and circumstances imperceptibly established.

Therefore, Babeuf continued, whether an association of citizens secretly organized their fellows – in other words, conspired – to discuss rights or to rise up and restore them, they ought not to be treated as the republic's enemies; they should be hailed as friends. Those who feared that such reasoning would expose the nation to illegitimate insurrection need only recall that 'the collective people is no fool.'[37]

Buonarroti developed this line of thinking in his summary defense, as he warned the jury to take intent seriously.

> Conspiracy does not necessarily mean crime, because one may imagine several men acting collectively to achieve a common end without their goal being criminal . . . [S]omething more is necessary to render a conspiracy truly criminal; we say the only circumstance legitimating punishment should be that in which the project characterized as conspiracy visibly endangers society.[38]

Buonarroti continued: if a man were to rob a house to feed a crowd starving outside, he would be judged by his motives. How much more important, then, for jurors in cases like this to consider a citizen's patriotism, commitment to the public good, and conviction that his act reinforced rather than contravened revolutionary law? 'This sacred love of the fatherland . . . is sometimes violent, ill-considered, but never criminal; take care not to smother it by attempting to suppress its idiosyncrasies.'[39]

Babeuf went further still. He concluded that whether citizens conspired against 'established government,' 'a freely-accepted constitution,' or 'legitimate authority,' as the prosecution charged the Equals had, they might yet be well-intentioned. It would be absurd, for example, to claim that any conspiracy against established government is criminal, for this would compel a people to live with whatever government it found in place. By such logic, 14 July 1789 was a criminal conspiracy. Even a freely accepted constitution might fail to serve the people's best interests, in which case the crime lay not in agitating against the constitution but in failing to enlighten one's fellows about how to improve it. 'The first and most critical condition of all human association is a natural tendency to perfect its civil organization to realize the greatest benefits for each and all.'[40] That left legitimate authority. 'But what is legitimate authority? I understand it to be that which corresponds to the true principles of popular sovereignty, which governs according to those same principles, which functions only for its good, its glory, and to preserve liberty.' Those who resist authority to promote despotism are guilty of the worst sort of conspiracy. But no matter how perfect a system might appear, it can never be criminal to propose improvement.[41]

In his final speech, Babeuf claimed repeatedly that he simply exercised his right of free expression by enlightening the people about their own rights. But he had made clear in the course of the trial that generating popular insurrection was equally legitimate. Marrying the right to insurrection guaranteed by the constitution of 1793 with the authority of Mably, Babeuf seemed to allude to Machiavelli one last time. He concluded that, if the people are unable to resist the oppression of their governors, it becomes the duty of 'the bravest, the boldest, the most zealous . . . to apply themselves cautiously to the means of liberation.' To do so was not to usurp popular sovereignty, but to seize it 'from the hands of its usurpers to return it to the people.'[42]

Gracchus Babeuf and Filippo Buonarroti lost their case: Babeuf went to the guillotine and Buonarroti into exile. More important for our purposes is the fate of the arguments they developed before the court that tried them in 1797. The implications of Babeuf's and Buonarroti's arguments could be difficult to discern, developed as they were within the give-and-take of the courtroom and interweaving justifications of 'hypothetical' conspiring with outright denials of personal involvement. So, for those who may have missed their broad intent, Jean-Nicolas Pache provided a map in the final weeks of the trial.

A former Montagnard and mayor of Paris during the Terror, Pache published *Sur les factions et les partis, les conspirations et les conjurations; et sur celles à l'ordre du jour* with an imprint date that all concerned with the affair would immediately recognize: one year to the day from the Equals' arrest.[43] The pamphlet echoes Babeuf's and Buonarroti's court-room arguments. Without naming either man or mentioning the trial throughout the first half of the pamphlet, Pache too mingled outright denials of activism with justification of principled opposition to despotism. 'Conspiracy,' he argued, adopting the distinction Babeuf had already made, merely signified a common state of mind: 'People conspire without knowing one another, without communicating . . . Conspiracy is a simple inclination.' 'To plot' on the other hand, 'is to make a common promise, to swear to join together to achieve . . . a common political end.'[44]

Lest readers suppose that such a pact was necessarily evil, Pache extended his definition. In so doing, he dismissed with a single clause the republican commitment to transparency that placed plotting beyond the pale: 'In and of itself, the plot is as neutral as the conspiracy.' Nor did the plot's success or failure determine how it would be judged. Echoing a chapter from Machiavelli's *Discourses* that Babeuf had highlighted, Pache continued: 'It is the objective of the plot that determines its character. A plot is in favor of or opposed to the principles of government, the former is as virtuous as the latter is criminal.'[45]

Finally, Pache evoked Mably by defending the right to revolutionary activism. If men in power plotted, they did so only to defend despotism. However, if patriots, 'as patriots, attack bad governors who are enemies of the principles of government . . . the plot, far from being dangerous, is salutary, is desirable . . . It saves the public good [*la chose publique*].'[46]

This would prove a durable definition of republican conspiracy. Revolutionary democrats were still distinguishing between 'conspiring' and 'plotting' a few years later, on the eve of Napoleon Bonaparte's seizure of power. Although that distinction died with the next generation, the notion of plotting for transparency was carried into the nineteenth century by Filippo Buonarroti himself.[47]

Described as the first professional revolutionary, Buonarroti devoted the rest of his life to restoring the republic of virtue. Even while imprisoned in a Breton island fortress after the trial, he corresponded with former activists.[48] Exiled to Geneva, he would spend the 1810s and 1820s schooling young men in the plot and founding the Sublimes Maîtres Parfaits, a secret society committed to preparing Europe for republican egalitarianism.[49] In Geneva, too, he would collaborate with Giuseppe Mazzini, and then break with him when their differences over strategy become irremediable.[50]

In 1828, Buonarroti published the book that would carry his and Babeuf's names into the twentieth century. *La conspiration pour l'égalité, dite de Babeuf* abandoned the courtroom intermingling of denial and assertion, to announce that the Equals truly conspired. Now, Buonarroti celebrated the Equals' methods of secrecy as he reclaimed Jacobinism for a new generation of republicans.[51] Returning to France after the

Revolution of 1830, he found the book prized by republicans and socialists. So he remained, to spend the final years of his life participating in French secret societies and encouraging potential revolutionaries with whom he debated timing, tactics, and ends. When Buonarroti died in Paris in 1837, more than a thousand mourners marched in his funeral procession.[52]

Buonarroti's book lived well beyond its author. Although out of step with nineteenth-century social and political concerns, because it celebrated radical republicanism forged within a pre-industrial economy, *La Conspiration pour l'égalité* was read approvingly by the republican Louis Blanc, the utopian Etienne Cabet, and the socialist August Blanqui, who appropriated the Equals' organizational strategies to attempt a revolutionary insurrection in 1839.[53] Russian anarchists Peter Kropotkin and Mikhail Bakunin were also familiar with the book; Bakunin claimed that Buonarroti was his century's greatest conspirator.[54] Finally, and most importantly, it introduced Karl Marx and Friedrich Engels to Babeuf. Arguing that Babeuf's wedding of egalitarian aspirations with practical activism made him the first modern communist, Marx and Engels cemented his and the Equals' reputations.

But the impact of the Babouvist idea of conspiracy was not restricted to the left. As Richard Cobb and Isser Woloch have demonstrated, each sign of political unrest in France throughout the next decade reflexively prompted authorities to arrest old Jacobins and Hébertistes, who they perpetually suspected of attempting a new conspiracy of Equals.[55] And as conservative fears of subversive, secret societies expanded in the nineteenth century, the Babouvists were drawn into this widening circle by Buonarroti's reinvigoration of Babeuf's reputation. As Babeuf's antagonistic biographer, Edouard Fleury, complained in 1851:

> Socialists under whatever name – Egalitarians, Fraternitarians, Icarians, Fourierists, Proudhonists – . . . have been . . . exalted by Buonarroti. For us, it is still Babeuf alive again in our own times. It is Babeuf with a hundred heads. It is Babeuf who torments our age more successfully than he tormented his own. It is Babeuf from the grave revolutionizing society, as he had failed to do while alive.[56]

Fleury was indulging in hyperbole, but Babeuf and Buonarroti did foster an appreciation of secrecy that was wholly absent from republican thinking a mere two years before the Equals initiated their conspiracy, and which lived on into the nineteenth century. They were able to make such a novel contribution because, faced with the narrowing parameters of political life in the wake of Thermidor, Babeuf shifted the emphasis of his thinking from Rousseau's abstract assertions about how the ideal republic ought to function, to Machiavelli's and Mably's more historical accounts of how republics emerge, decline, and defend themselves from hostile elements that remain within. Joining Mably's conviction that citizens retain a perpetual right to propose reform with Machiavelli's assertion that extraordinary measures are sometimes necessary to save the republic, Babeuf abandoned – temporarily, he believed – the dream of a transparent polity.

In looking to Machiavelli and Mably, as well, Babeuf abandoned the revolutionary definition of conspiracy in favor of its more classical understanding. For whereas Jacobins, among others, believed conspiracy signified the hidden orchestration of political life in a Manichaean world, classical and Renaissance political theorists tended to represent the plot in more neutral and mechanistic terms, as a means by which to defeat specific rulers.[57] In making this shift, however, Babeuf did not mark the defeat of the revolutionary conception of conspiracy: he positioned himself on the cusp of fluctuating modes of thinking. For the Directory's handling of the Equals' case suggested that revolutionary authorities still believed there was political capital to be wrung from the conspiracy obsession.

Like the leaders of the Terror who preceded them, the Directors and their agents painted the Equals as the mere tip of the iceberg, leaders of a mass of plotters stretching from one end of France to the other and preparing to destroy the nation. As well like the leaders of the Terror, the Directors believed in the conspiracy they pursued but also recognized that its existence might strengthen them politically, allowing them to pose as guardians of domestic peace and order. But the Directors faced a citizenry hardened in the wake of Thermidor, as well as a revived and fearless press. So their pronouncements about the extent of the Equals' conspiracy fractured the polity, rather than uniting it. Democrats, whom the Directory needed as political allies, received the news with disbelief that became outrage. Royalists, for their part, readily accepted the most terrifying assertions but denied that frustration of the plot evinced the government's strength – they considered the mere existence of the Equals a sign of official weakness. These positions were hardened by a controversial trial and a series of contradictory verdicts, which persuaded democrats that the Directory used the bogey of conspiracy to attack the republic's truest friends, and convinced royalists that the government was unable to counter the ever-widening threat of resurgent Jacobinism.

In sum, the two conceptions of conspiracy that would dominate the nineteenth century were fought around the arrest and trial of the Equals. Looking to the example of men they considered heroes martyred by a corrupt government, democrats and socialists might henceforth accept the plot as legitimate means of opposition against invasive and anti-popular authority. Meanwhile, conservative republicans, monarchists, and royalists took the conspiracy obsession for their own, treating plots discovered or suspected as evidence of the boundless conspiracy that threatened to engulf them all.

Notes

1 The first generation of texts include G. Wood, 'Conspiracy and the Paranoid Style: Causality and Deceit in the Eighteenth Century,' *William and Mary Quarterly*, 39(3) (July 1982), pp. 401–441; F. Furet, *Interpreting the French Revolution*, trans. E. Forster (Cambridge, UK and New York, 1981); L. Hunt, *Politics, Culture and Class in the French Revolution* (Berkeley, 1984); G. Cubitt, 'Denouncing Conspiracy in the French Revolution,' *Renaissance and Modern Studies*, 33 (1989), pp. 144–158. T. Tackett inaugurated the new generation of scholarship with 'Conspiracy Obsession in a Time of Revolution: French Elites and the Origins of the Terror, 1789–1792,' *American Historical Review*, 105(3) (June 2000), pp. 691–713.

2 C. Mazauric, *Babeuf et la conspiration pour l'Egalité* (Paris, 1962); M. Dommanget, *Babeuf et la conjuration des Egaux*, 2nd edn (Paris, 1989); I. Birchall, *The Spectre of Babeuf* (New York, 1997).

3 R. M. Andrews, 'Réflexions sur la Conjuration des Egaux,' *Annales: économie, société, civilisation*, 29(1) (Janvier/Février 1974), pp. 73–106.

4 P. Serna, 'Pistes de recherches: Du secret de la monarchie à la république des secrets,' in P. Serna and B. Gainot, eds, *Secret et République, 1795–1840* (np, 2004), p. 32; P. Serna, *Antonelle: Aristocrate révolutionnaire, 1747–1817* (Paris, 1997), pp. 297–319. S. Luzzatto more uncritically recycles Andrews's account of the Equals in *L'automne de la Révolution: Luttes et cultures politiques dans la France thermidorienne*, trans. from Italian by S. C. Messina (Paris, 2001), pp. 229–235.

5 Serna, 'Du secret de la monarchie,' p. 32. For his assessment of Andrews, see *Antonelle*, pp. 298–300.

6 This summary of Babeuf's life and the evolution of his thought is drawn from R. B. Rose, *Gracchus Babeuf: The First Revolutionary Communist* (Stanford, CA, 1978).

7 Ibid. pp. 99–101; 158–161; 173.

8 J. Godechot, *Les institutions de la France sous la Révolution et l'Empire* (Paris, 1951), pp. 457–467; A. Jainchill, 'The Constitution of the year III and the Persistence of Classical Republicanism,' *French Historical Studies*, 26(3) (Summer 2003), pp. 399–436.

9 M. Lyons, 'Les Gros' and 'Les Maigres,' *France under the Directory* (Cambridge, UK and London, 1975).

10 G. Cubitt 'Denouncing Conspiracy.' See also his 'Robespierre and Conspiracy Theories,' in C. Haydon and W. Doyle, eds, *Robespierre* (Cambridge, UK and New York, 1999).

11 *Le Tribun du peuple*, 34, pp. 13–18; 40, pp. 221–222.
12 *Le Tribun du peuple*, 34, p. 7. See also 34, pp. 15–16; 36, pp. 113–117; 39, p. 185.
13 *Le Tribun du peuple*, 34, p. 7.
14 *Le Tribun du peuple*, 36, p. 115.
15 *Le Tribun du peuple*, 39, p. 187.
16 'Le directoire de salut public aux agents de douze arrondissements' (18 floréal IV), in Haute Cour de Justice, *Copie des pièces saisies dans le local que Baboeuf occupoit lors de son arrestation* (Paris, 1796), 1, pp 80–86. Most texts discussed here were written in Babeuf's hand, or his authorship was confirmed during the Equals' trial. I attribute to him additional unsigned texts from the *Pièces saisies* on the basis of Buonarroti's assertion that Babeuf was sole author of most of the committee's letters and instructions. Buonarroti, *La Conspiration pour l'égalité, dite de Babeuf*, preface G. Lefebvre (Paris, 1957), 1, p. 109.
17 'a C. . . . .' (14 germinal), *Pièces saisies*, 1, pp. 331–332.
18 'Le directoire de salut public aux agents de douze arrondissements' (6 floréal IV), *Pièces saisies*, 2, pp. 158–161.
19 On democrats' ideas about the complementarity of public and private activism, see Serna, *Antonelle*, pp. 297–300; 'Pistes de recherches.' For instructions to agents: 'Le directoire secret de salut public aux principaux agents . . .' (26 germinal IV), *Pièces saisies*, 1, pp. 201–204.
20 'Le D. de S.P. à l'agent du douzième arrondissement' (22 germinal IV), *Pièces saisies*, 1, p. 328.
21 On force of circumstance: 'Le directoire de salut public aux agents de douze arrondissements' (6 floréal IV), *Pièces saisies*, 2, pp. 158–161.
22 'Titres de quelques chapitres du premier livre de Machiavel,' *Pièces saisies*, 2, pp. 70–71.
23 Machiavelli, *Discourses on Livy*, trans., intro., and notes J. C. Bondanella and P. Bondanella (Oxford and New York, 1997), p. 30.
24 Ibid., Chapter 17, 'A Corrupt People Which Becomes Free Can Remain So Only With the Greatest Difficulty,' pp. 65–67.
25 'Première instruction du directoire secret,' *Pièces saisies*, 1, pp. 172–173.
26 Serna, *Antonelle*, pp. 331–336.
27 I. Woloch, *The New Regime: Transformations of the French Civic Order, 1789–1820* (New York and London, 1994), p. 361.
28 Ibid., pp. 364–367; C. Lucas, 'The First Directory and the Rule of Law,' *French Historical Studies*, 10(2) (Fall 1977), pp. 231–260.
29 *L'Ami du peuple* (26 floréal IV); *Courier républicain* (28 floréal IV).
30 *Débats du procès instruit par la haute-cour de justice séante à Vendôme, contre Drouet, Baboeuf, et autres* (Paris, 1797), 3, pp. 217–220.
31 Ibid., pp. 221–22, 224. Babeuf echoed these concerns in his defense. 'Défense générale de Gracchus Babeuf devant la haute-cour de Vendôme,' in V. Advielle, *Histoire de Gracchus Babeuf et du Babouvisme* (Geneva, 1978), 2, pp. 26–27.

32 *Débats du procès*, 2, pp. 239–240.
33 'Défense générale de Gracchus Babeuf,' 2, pp. 134–135.
34 K. M. Baker, 'A Script for the French Revolution: the Political Consciousness of the abbé Mably,' *Inventing the French Revolution* (Cambridge, UK and New York, 1990). See also J. K. Wright, *A Classical Republican in Eighteenth-Century France: the Political Thought of Mably* (Stanford, CA, 1997), pp. 70–80.
35 Baker, 'A Script for the French Revolution,' pp. 92–94.
36 Ibid., p. 95.
37 *Débats du procès*, 2, pp. 303–306. Citing Mably, Babeuf's conclusion also echoes Machiavelli's argument that the desires of a free people are never harmful to liberty.
38 *Débats du procès*, 4, pp. 253–254.
39 *Débats du procès*, 4, pp. 259–261.
40 G. Babeuf, 'Défense générale,' 2, pp. 23–24.
41 Ibid., 2, p. 24.
42 *Débats du procès*, 2, p. 305.
43 The pamphlet is dated 21 floreal V; arrested on 21 floréal IV, the Equals were, for months, referred to as the 'floréal conspirators.' J.-N. Pache, *Sur les factions et les partis* . . . (Thym-le-Moutier, an V). See also B. Gainot, 'Espace public et conjuration sous le Directoire. À propos d'un texte de Jean-Nicolas Pache,' P. Serna and B. Gainot, eds, *Secret et République, 1795–1840*. Gainot acknowledges the importance of Pache's distinction between 'good' and 'bad' conspiracies but overlooks its fundamental link to Babeuf's and Buonarroti's courtroom arguments.
44 Pache, *Sur les factions et les partis*, pp. 6–7.
45 In Book I, chapter 9, Machiavelli justifies Romulus' murder of his brother and consent to the execution of Titus Tatius: 'a wise mind [will never] reproach anyone for some illegal action that he might have undertaken to organize a kingdom or to constitute a republic . . . [O]ne should reproach a man who is violent in order to ruin things, not one who is so in order to set them aright.' Machiavelli, *Discourses*, p. 45.
46 Pache, *Sur les factions et les partis*, p. 14.
47 Serna, 'Pistes de recherche,' pp. 25–26.
48 G. Weill, 'Philippe Buonarroti,' *Revue historique*, 76 (1901), pp. 241–275, 257.
49 E. Eisenstein, *The First Professional Revolutionary: Filippo Michele Buonarroti* (Cambridge, MA, 1959), pp. 34–54; A. Lehning, 'Buonarotti and his International Secret Societies,' *International Review of Social History*, 1 (1956), pp. 112–140.
50 Weill, 'Philippe Buonarroti,' pp. 272–273.
51 Eisenstein, 'The Revolutionist at Home,' *First Professional Revolutionary*; Pamela Pilbeam, *Republicanism in Nineteenth-Century France, 1814–1871* (Houndmills and London, 1995), pp. 107–109.
52 Eisenstein, *First Professional Revolutionary*, p. 149.

53 Although Blanqui never directly cited Buonarroti, the similarities between his thinking and that of Babeuf are sufficiently striking to encourage commentators to assume that he read *La conspiration pour l'égalité*. Pilbeam, *Republicanism in Nineteenth-Century France*, pp. 129–140; A. B. Spitzer, *The Revolutionary Theories of Louis Auguste Blanqui* (New York, 1957), pp. 126–134.

54 Eisenstein, *First Professional Revolutionary*, p. 1.

55 R. Cobb, *The Police and the People: French Popular Protest, 1789–1820* (London and Oxford, 1970), p. 166; I. Woloch, *Napoleon and his Collaborators: The Making of a Dictatorship* (New York and London, 2001), pp. 67–80.

56 E. Fleury, *Babeuf et le Socialisme in 1796* (1851) quoted in D. Thomson, *The Babeuf Plot: the Making of a Republican Legend* (London, 1947), p. 78. On nineteenth-century fears of secret societies see J. M. Roberts, *The Mythology of the Secret Societies* (London, 1972), especially chapter 9: 'The Restoration and After.'

57 Wood, 'Conspiracy and Paranoid Style,' pp. 409–411.

9

Conclusion: Catilina's revenge – conspiracy, revolution, and historical consciousness from the ancien régime to the Consulate

Thomas E. Kaiser

In several of his stimulating publications, Keith Baker has argued that late eighteenth-century French republicanism subscribed to two conflicting notions of history.[1] On the one hand, it embraced the concept of history as 'progress,' a notion rooted in the Enlightenment's conviction that modern advances in the arts, letters, and sciences had engendered a fitful but inexorable improvement in the human condition. On the other, it represented history as an escalating 'crisis' generated by the advance of despotism and the corruption of the body politic; according to this view, only immediate and decisive political action could prevent humanity's fall into an abyss from which it might never re-emerge. The conviction that a new enlightened age was dawning, Baker contends, competed with the anticipation of an imminent victory of despotism from the very onset of the Revolution, and it eventually engendered the Terror as a means to secure the liberty promised by nature but hitherto denied by history.

Whatever its value as an explanation of the Terror, Baker's construct does provide a useful framework for concluding this volume on conspiracy during the French Revolution. In particular, it provides a structure for further exploration of a question underlying all the chapters in this work – namely, how Revolutionaries conceived of their own project in relation to the conspiracies, real and imagined, leveled against the new regime. At first look, one might suppose that the answer to this question is obvious. The dominant republican political language of 1789 most commonly represented 'conspiracy' as the preferred weapon of 'despotism.' Both were antithetical to the Revolution: secretive, whereas the Revolution was transparent; corrupt, whereas the Revolution was virtuous; aristocratic, whereas the Revolution was popular; and retrograde, whereas the

Revolution was progressive. As one pamphleteer put it with regard to counterrevolutionary subversion generally, 'truly the enemies of the Revolution, whose means are exhausted, have only this infernal expedient to finish their enterprises victoriously, to enslave their country, and to resurrect everything that reason and justice have destroyed.'[2]

In fact, the discursive antinomy 'conspiracy'/'Revolution' – however simple and elegant – was never easy to sustain during the Revolutionary decade. Indeed, I shall contend, it continually threatened to collapse for two principal reasons. First, the proliferation of defections, betrayals, and insurgencies that often did place the Revolution's triumph in jeopardy provided more than enough grounds for a widening hunt for counter-revolutionary 'conspirators' among leaders who had once been, or at least appeared to have been, the Revolution's most conspicuous champions. The cumulative impact of unmasking so many *ci-devant* 'patriots' as counterrevolutionary agents was to place in doubt the integrity of the Revolution they had once led, for it made the Revolution appear as little more than a vast chain of interlocking conspiracies. Second, as the number of real and imagined conspiracies increased despite the deployment of violent countermeasures, Revolutionaries became increasingly inclined to construe the seemingly endless profusion of plots against the new order as *necessary* byproducts of the Revolution and no less 'natural' than the Revolution itself. This characterization not only further blurred the distinction between 'Revolution' and 'conspiracy,' but also clouded the Revolutionaries' vision of the future. For if the Revolutionaries never abandoned their belief in an ultimate victory of 'liberty' as part of the historical scenario of 'progress,' the apparently endless proliferation of conspiracies indicated that the Revolution had entered an enduring state of 'crisis,' which could be contained only through the indefinite prolongation of repression. To be sure, in trying to avoid the taint of the Terror they so emphatically denounced, the Directory and First Consulate made some limited efforts to rise above the politics of counterconspiracy. But ultimately these régimes found conspiracies too threatening and too useful as political myths to abandon the repressive political logic of previous Revolutionary régimes. For these reasons, I conclude, the tension between history as 'progress' and 'crisis' was never resolved during the Revolutionary decade, nor would it be until the republic it had sought to establish was far better secured in the later nineteenth century.

The ancien régime

Peter Campbell has demonstrated in Chapter 1 that conspiracies were built into the very fabric of ancien régime politics, but it is no less true that familiarity with them bred, for the most part, contempt.[3] To be sure, there were lingering vestiges of the venerable tradition of aristocratic conspiracy undertaken in the name of the 'public.'[4] Nevertheless, by 1750 nearly two centuries of absolutist rule had so stigmatized aristocratic conspiracy as disruptive to public law and order that all the terms referring to it were strongly pejorative. Defined in the *Encyclopédie* as a 'union of several people seeking to do harm to someone or something,' *conspiration* closely resembled *complot*, which Richelet defined as a 'dark and cunning plan to do harm to a person, to ruin him, to destroy him, or to ruin him'; it also resembled *conjuration*, which the *Encyclopédie* defined somewhat more narrowly as 'a plot of badly intentioned people against the prince or the state.'[5] In view of such definitions, it is not surprising that the abbé de Vertot, who wrote several notable works about conspiracies, concluded that history would find virtually none of them to have been 'just.'[6]

Although French history – especially the Wars of Religion and the Fronde – provided memorable instances of conspiracy closer to home, the conspiracy with the greatest impact upon the eighteenth-century political consciousness was doubtlessly that of Lucius Sergius Catilina.[7] The Catiline conspiracy erupted in Rome during the first century BCE, when a band of aristocratic malcontents and their minions plotted to seize power under Catilina's leadership but were eventually hunted down and executed on the instigation of Cicero. This bloody tale was widely known to eighteenth-century readers primarily from the dark accounts written by Cicero himself and by Sallust.[8] Widely used text in the *collèges* of the ancien régime, the Ciceronian version was especially familiar to future French Revolutionaries and left a profound impression. 'How many times,' Camille Desmoulins reminisced, '. . . did I embrace Cicero, my eyes wet with tears.'[9]

In their recounting of the Catiline conspiracy, Cicero and Sallust emphasized the moral dimension of this paradigmatic study of political subversion, focusing particular attention on the character of the archvillain and his accomplices. Catilina was represented as a creature driven, above all, by insatiable ambition, which he hid under a false commitment to republican liberty. Among the many tools Catilina used to promote his concealed self-aggrandizing plots, Cicero and Sallust stressed his eloquence. 'His skill and audacity at accosting and sounding and swaying his fellow-men were extraordinary,' Cicero observed. 'In everything he planned, his tongue and his hand never failed him.'[10] In addition to seductive language, Catilina used promises of sex and lucre to entrap his confederates, making him appear in eighteenth-century eyes as the very antithesis of the virtuous republican.[11] Ultimately, however, the corrupt nature of their enterprise, indeed, the very countenance of the conspirators betrayed them, for although there was also material evidence of their guilt, it was 'their pallor, the look in their eyes, the set of their features, their silence which spoke most eloquently against them when they were finally caught.'[12] Revolutionaries would pay close attention to all these aspects of the Catiline story, down to the physiognomic criteria for distinguishing true republicans from their conspiring counterfeits.

If the Catiline plot lent to 'conspiracy' a fairly well-defined profile in the eighteenth century, it was still possible to confuse the term with another, still broader category of political analysis, namely 'revolution.' As the many studies of this political term have amply demonstrated,[13] 'revolution' had multiple, even contradictory meanings in the eighteenth century. Most senses of the term, like those of 'conspiracy,' were pejorative. Before 1750, 'revolution' generally denoted a sudden socio-political crisis profoundly disruptive to public order that was likely to end at best with retrogression to an acceptable *status quo ante*. After 1750, the meanings assigned to 'revolution' gradually expanded to include a benign transformation of the social order, strongly associated in Enlightenment circles with the progress of the sciences and the arts. Yet the attribution of a new, more positive meaning to the term hardly effaced older connotations. Indeed, a 'revolution' could as easily refer to an instrument of 'despotism' as to a prescription for 'liberty,' and thus the publicist Pidansat de Mairobert condemned the Maupeou coup against the parlements in 1771 as a 'revolution perpetrated on the constitution of the French monarchy.'[14] Some publicists may have seen a slightly greater merit in 'revolutions' than in 'conspiracies,' yet the distinction between the two remained fragile. Citing them as examples of 'great enterprises,' Montesquieu confounded 'revolutions' and 'conspiracies' (*conspirations*),[15] as did the historian Duport de Tertre in his ten-volume *Histoire des conjurations, conspirations et révolutions célèbres* (1754–60).[16]

The partial elision of 'conspiracy' with 'revolution' allowed the more positive meaning ascribed by some authors to the latter term to rehabilitate the former, especially after 1750. Thus, although Duport de Tertre embraced the standard view that most conspiracies had been 'dangerous' and that their 'success had occasioned the most terrible calamities,' he allowed that their leaders had often exhibited 'great qualities.'[17] Although he did not endorse any particular French conspiracy, he did applaud insurgencies conducted against 'oppression' elsewhere, such as the heroic Dutch revolt against Spain, which he attributed to 'the love of liberty, especially when one suffers the horrors of tyranny.'[18] By the end of the ancien régime, 'conspiracy' had acquired enough positive spin for Mirabeau to baptize the Society of Thirty – the celebrated prerevolutionary agency of oppositional political consciousness-raising – a 'conspiracy of well-intentioned men (*honnêtes gens*).'[19] Such usage indicates that by the 1750s the language of liberty had begun to inflect contemporary political usage generally and that a 'conspiracy,' like a 'revolution,' might in some instances be regarded as an engine of 'progress.'

From 1789 to the Terror

In the crisis of 1788–89, the relationship of 'revolution' to 'conspiracy' was once again reconfigured. Use of 'revolution' and 'revolutionary,' which had referred – sometimes favorably, more often unfavorably – to a wide variety of historical insurgencies, became restricted in patriot discourse to upheavals that promoted the ideals of 1789. 'The word *revolutionary*,' Condorcet flatly declared, 'applies only to revolutions that have liberty as their object.'[20] Indeed, the word 'revolution,' so often used previously in the plural form, was almost immediately confined in patriot discourse to denote and celebrate the events of 1789 alone.[21] One immediate consequence of this singularization was to represent '*the* Revolution' as an epochal act of self-liberation that even the most radical previous political revolutions had at most dimly foreshadowed. 'The history of revolutions [note plural form],' explained the journal *Révolutions de Paris*, 'is the recitation of the usurpations of power, the demands of reason and the vengeance of force. It is the history of despotism.'[22] *The* Revolution was surely different. 'What stuns the universe today is the new spectacle of a people who in one instant liberates itself from the chains it has worn for centuries.'[23]

But how definitive was this fresh victory? As Pierre Rétat and Keith Baker have emphasized, the fate of the Revolution appeared highly uncertain to the patriots even after 14 July 1789; indeed, far from concluding that the storming of the Bastille had ended their struggle, the patriots were convinced they faced a continuing combat with the enemies of liberty.[24] Baker has attributed this protracted sense of uncertainty about the future to the temporal extension of a prerevolutionary, republican belief in 'revolution' as 'crisis,' that is, as a decisive moment in the body politic when the entire fate of liberty hung in the balance. In Baker's interpretation, prerevolutionary republicanism had preconditioned the patriots to conceptualize their Revolution as such a 'crisis,' which the patriots now projected indefinitely into the future. Not a single critical moment but a prolonged period of 'infinite dangers and unending risks,' the Revolution might well be derailed if the appropriate countermeasures were not taken.[25]

Now it is no doubt true that the patriots' prerevolutionary expectations of 'crisis' shaped their views of the Revolution and that the aggressive actions they took as a consequence made their prophecies of imminent danger to some extent self-fulfilling. But a plausible explanation of the prolongation of 'crisis' ought to take at least some account of the very real opposition encountered by the patriot movement in 1788–89, notably the resistance of most nobles to the demands of the Third Estate and the monarchy's devious politics. Breaking with the 'revisionist' orthodoxy of François Furet, et al., historians such as Michael Fitzsimmons and Timothy Tackett have shown that there were, after all, significant differences between the outlooks and agendas of the Third and Second Estates before, during, and after 14 July; [26] and Munro Price's superb account of decision-making at the top during the July crisis indicates that Third Estate had good reason to suspect the Queen's circle was plotting with noble leaders to crush the patriot insurgency. [27] In sum, what allowed the patriots' expectation of 'crisis' to harden into the firm conviction that they had entered a protracted one was not simply the self-confirming nature of their ideology, but also their harrowing experience during the early phase of the Revolution.

It is here that we can return to conspiracy. Tackett may be correct to argue that belief in conspiracy before Varennes was less intense among political elites than afterward. Yet there is ample evidence that the conflicts he and others have so ably documented during the period 1788–89 were fanning widespread belief in an 'aristo-ministerial' plot directed against the liberty of the nation.[28] Belief in this plot devolved, on the one hand, from long-standing warnings of the Jansenist movement in association with the *parlements* that the monarchy was falling headlong into a 'ministerial despotism.' On the other hand, they devolved from the polemics of opponents of 'aristocracy,' such as Volney, who in November 1788 radicalized the ancient anti-aristocratic discourse sponsored by the monarchy to denounce a so-called 'Conspiracy of Noble Leaguers.'[29] As Dale Van Kley has argued, these two sets of fears fused in late 1788, giving rise to what he has picturesquely termed the 'twin *bêtes noires* of the apocalypse.'[30] Henceforth, it was not the nobility acting by itself, but rather the nobility working in combination with the court – the 'aulic aristocracy' – whom the Third Estate most feared, as evidenced by Sieyès's celebrated *Qu'est-ce que c'est le tiers état?*[31] Such conspiracy charges were diffused among the reading public in many of the thousands of pamphlets and nearly 200 newspapers published in 1789 alone.[32]

If the 'twin *bêtes noires*' of aristocracy and despotism stalked the pages of political journals before the meeting of the Estates-General, they also featured prominently in contemporary accounts of the storming of the Bastille. Thus, in his journal entry of 12 July, Nicolas Ruault noted with alarm the imminent igniting of a 'kind of conspiracy against public order.'[33] Tackett argues that fears of an imminent conspiracy ebbed somewhat in the weeks after 14 July. But belief in an aristo-ministerial plot, which had allegedly failed only because of the people's defense of Paris and might well rise again, hardly faded. Indeed, reminders of such dangers appeared frequently in the many commemorations of 14 July over the course of the Revolution[34] and by the legion of contemporary reports that denounced the 'plot' concocted by 'drunk Catilinas' and 'conspirators' who intended to reestablish 'tyranny' by means of 'their execrable orgies.'[35] Several months after 14 July, the deadly 'conspiratorial' nature of the barely foiled July plot was reconfirmed in the wide-ranging report published by the *comité de recherches* of the Paris Commune. Condemning the July criminals by name, this report showed that they had violated not only the French legal injunction against 'those who will conspire . . . against the republic,' but also the law of ancient Rome, that is, the intended target of Catilina and his henchmen.[36]

Once the reality of this plot was established, it became all the easier to perceive others through the same Catilinian lens. Indeed, the events that had prompted the march to Versailles on 5/6 October – most notoriously, the banquet hosted by Marie-Antoinette – were retrospectively represented as a 'plot' of palace 'Catilinas' that immediately recalled the same cast of characters and events surrounding the crisis in July. 'When,' demanded *Le Moniteur* in a question to be posed again and again, 'will their plots come to an end?'[37] To be sure, certain allegations of conspiracy were rejected by skeptics, who earnestly sorted through the available evidence to distinguish fact from fiction. But even so moderate and sober a Third-Estate deputy as Adrien Duquesnoy admitted by November that the report of the Assembly's *comité de recherches* on conspiratorial activity made it difficult to reject its authors' claim to have discovered 'the thread of a criminal, profoundly criminal project to take the King to Metz, and that the most August personages, the Queen, perhaps, were involved in this plot.'[38]

Even if it is true, as Tackett points out,[39] that the number of conspiracy accusations and the grip of conspiracy fears on elite political thinking increased in response to the royal family's abortive flight from Paris in June 1791, it is no less true that many conspiracy charges were ventilated before then. At the core of most of these charges lay the claim that the government was riddled with counterrevolutionary plotters, who were abetted by counterrevolutionaries from outside. In the words of the pamphlet *L'Orateur du Peuple*, published in early 1790, 'France is surrounded by Catilinas.'[40] The willingness of moderates to accredit reports of conspiracies may have been tempered by the fear of inciting further popular disorders, but the abolition of censorship made it impossible to silence the radical press, which fed the public a steady diet of conspiratorial charges that public authorities could not casually dismiss without arousing suspicions of their own complicity.[41]

What gave such charges plausibility and resonance was not only the well-advertised campaign of subversion by French aristocratic *émigrés*, but two other factors as well. First, there was the dismal state of the French alliance system, which left France virtually isolated after 1789. Having allowed the 1756 alliance with Austria to deteriorate in the 1780s, having abandoned Turkey to its fate at the hands of Russia and Austria in 1787, having failed to back Spain effectively against Britain in the Nootka Sound incident in 1790, France could rely on none of its former friends and allies for diplomatic and military support.[42] Well might propagandists like Jean-Louis Carra draw a connection between France's 'interior corruption' and 'the corruption of its foreign policy,' for the nation, having become 'entirely negligible in the political system of Europe,' was now 'publicly disdained by its allies and insulted with impunity by its enemies.'[43]

Second, in the spring of 1790 rumors began to spread that a so-called Austrian Committee under the direction of Marie-Antoinette was corrupting the government and eroding national security. The notion that Austria, too weak to rely on force of arms, was plotting to achieve European hegemony through barely palpable deception had enjoyed a long history, dating back to the sixteenth century.[44] Reenforced when the Franco-Austrian alliance of 1756 resulted in France's humiliation during the Seven Years' War, fears of an 'Austrian Plot' were further intensified upon Marie-Antoinette's marriage to the future Louis XVI in 1770. Now, it appeared, there was an alleged Austrian operative working against French interests at the heart of the French monarchy. By 1789, the Austrophobia diffused by radical propagandists like Carra had turned public opinion decisively against the Queen, whose impolitic personal activities made her a lightning-rod of criticism for other reasons as well. Broad and deep enough to taint a large cast of suspicious characters, Austrophobia acquired additional momentum in June 1791, when Austrian troops, repositioned on the French border, provided cover for the royal family's abortive flight from Paris, although they did not in the end intervene.[45] Henceforth, it was no longer the Queen alone whom patriots suspected of treason, but also the King, now charged in the popular press with having fostered 'a foreign and domestic war' by means of a 'cowardly and perfidious plot' of 'the coalesced houses of Bourbon and Austria.'[46] These and other alleged crimes earned Louis a reputation as 'another Catilina . . . a traitor [who] is not king of the French, but king of some conspirators.'[47]

If France had been weakened by internal subversion and 'surrounded by Catilinas,' it was hardly unthinkable or even unlikely that the entire Revolutionary project would fail and that the nation would slide back into 'despotism,' especially after France declared war on Austria in April 1792. Whatever the exact relationship between the war and the ensuing Terror, it is clear that armed conflict provided the ideal backdrop to scenarios in which a cast of once-trusted generals – Lafayette, Dumouriez, Custine – in fact or in appearance betrayed the Revolutionary cause with shattering effects on Revolutionary confidence; and the eruption of counterrevolution in the Vendée only amplified the anxiety such betrayals had engendered. Revolutionary leaders thus had good reason to fear for the future and publicly vent their worst nightmares. 'If it happens,' Saint-Just despaired, '. . . that the foreigner wins, that vice triumphs . . ., that our punishments do not pursue the hidden conspirators, let us flee into the void or the bosom of the divinity: on earth there will be no happiness or virtue for which to hope.'[48] Similarly, notwithstanding his confident assertion that 'the republic is invincible like reason . . . [and] immortal like truth,' Robespierre could well imagine the horror of despotism's triumph. 'All nature would be covered with a dark veil, and human reason would retreat to the depths of ignorance and barbarism . . . Like a sea without banks, despotism would cover the globe's surface . . . [and] the earth would be nothing but the patrimony of crime.'[49]

One way of cushioning the impact of such gloomy thoughts was to reinscribe the Revolution into the Enlightenment's scenario of inevitable historical progress. There was, patriots argued, a historical precedent for and predisposing cause of '*the* Revolution' that assured its ultimate victory, namely the 'revolutions' of *lumières*, which had instilled in the people an indelible appreciation of liberty. 'If the revolution acts with such vehemence and force,' contended the *Révolutions de Paris*, 'it is because the wise, the *philosophes* have long desired it, and because it occurred in all good minds and nearly all hearts before the conquest of the Bastille.'[50] Perhaps the most notable effort to provide assurance of the Revolution's inevitable triumph as a consequence of the Enlightenment was Condorcet's celebrated *Esquisse d'un tableau historique des progrès de l'esprit humain*. Heralding the ultimate victory of *lumières*, its final chapter undoubtedly provided some comfort not only to later readers but also to the author, who composed it while on the run from the Terror. According to Condorcet, progress was rooted in humankind's proclivity to distinguish truth from untruth, a procedure that had yielded a steady accumulation of knowledge and the liberation of humankind from 'despotism.' Even if history was littered with epistemological and political reverses, Condorcet affirmed, *lumières* could now reach all corners of the world, with the result that 'the arrogance of despotism' would no longer 'impede truth with insurmountable obstacles.'[51] In short, history guaranteed the success of the new political order because nature had preprogrammed this outcome into the human mind.

Another way of providing metaphysical reassurance of the Revolution's ultimate victory was to root it in the bedrock of nature by establishing temporal concordances between major Revolutionary *journées* and notable cosmic events, an effort most evident in the new Revolutionary calendar.[52] In his report to the Convention of 20 September 1793, Romme noted how the proposed calendar revealed certain unmistakable signs of a natural providence fostering the Revolution. For surely it was not by mere chance that the autumnal equinox had fallen on the same day the new republic had been proclaimed (21 September 1792) and at the very moment when the sun had reached the zodiacal sign representing equality – Libra, the scales. 'This concordance of circumstances' he concluded, 'lends a sacred character to this epoch . . . which will undoubtedly be one of the most highly celebrated in the festivals of future generations.'[53]

It hardly required the birth of 'future generations' for this sacrilizing 'concordance of circumstances' to be ceremonialized, for already it had infused many of the Revolutionary festivals staged for the edification of the young.[54] As symbolic reenactments of the Revolution's major events, these ceremonies were designed not merely to praise virtuous patriots and execrate their enemies, but also to reenforce belief in the inevitability of the Revolution's success at the end of a long, arduous process. Thus, on the first anniversary of 10 August 1792, David scripted a march that began at the site of the Bastille's ruins to commemorate its storming on 14 July 1789, proceeded to a second station to commemorate the return of the royal family to Paris on 6 October 1789, and concluded at the Place de la Révolution, site of the king's execution on 21 January 1793, where ninety-six torch-bearing *commissaires* competed for the honor of igniting an enormous wood pyre to extinguish memory of the tyrant.[55] Such ceremonies reflected a politically correct optimism that a people 'made for liberty' would surely 'be able to foil all the plots of the sedition-mongers and traitors, who have . . . resolved to devour us.'[56] By repeatedly displaying images of despotism, its satellites, and its associated perversities – the Bastille, egotism, ambition, vice, and discord – and disposing of them through restormings, burnings, and the like, the government sought to provide at least symbolic reassurance of the Revolution's eventual triumph.

The Terror

As sharply as patriots tried to distinguish 'Revolution' from 'conspiracy,' the difference was always in danger of eroding to the point where the two phenomena once again resembled each other. In part, this blending was promoted by counterrevolutionaries who forcefully assailed the Revolution as a criminal plot against religion, nature, and history by drawing upon the earlier crusading efforts of *dévots* against the *philosophes*.[57] But it was the dynamics of the Revolution itself that may have posed the greater threat to the notion of the Revolution as a distinctly nonconspiratorial movement.

This threat arose in part from the imperative to unmask conspirators who deceived the public into believing that counterrevolutionary activity was patriotic and patriotic activity was counterrevolutionary. How could the government, or any citizen for that matter, reliably distinguish between what Vergniaud called 'seditious insurrections' and the 'great insurrection of liberty' – in other words, the Revolution itself?[58] Early in the Revolution, as Barry Shapiro has shown, the new government showed considerable restraint and due regard for legal niceties in the prosecution of defendants suspected of counterrevolutionary subversion.[59] Thus, even when defendants had earned notorious reputations as running dogs of despotism as in the case of the prince de Lambesc, they were frequently acquitted by Revolutionary tribunals.[60] No less radical a journal as the *Révolutions de Paris* felt obliged to seek legal cover for the conspiracy charges it leveled by adducing 'legal presumptions' of guilt when it could not provide infallible 'proof,' and it proclaimed itself prepared to rescind accusations in the face of 'contrary facts.'[61] Likewise Robespierre, as late as March 1793, insisted upon the need for a rigorous litmus test of the 'conspirator' on grounds that, without one, the Revolutionary Tribunal would become an instrument of the Revolution's enemies.[62]

Yet in the end, neither Robespierre nor any of his associates could design such a test, for the guises of the enemy were many and constantly changing. Having insisted on a rigorous standard of proof for convicting plotters, Robespierre reversed course a year later. Penal law necessarily had to remain 'somewhat vague,' he contended, so that justice could deal expeditiously with dangerous conspirators, whose character typically exhibited 'dissimulation and hypocrisy.'[63] Because of popular demands for swift punishment of suspects and other developments, political imperatives came to override mere legalities; the republic, it appeared, had its own *raison d'état*, after all. Henceforth, the rights of defendants, among other political inconveniences, could be dispensed with on Robespierre's argument that all great convulsions of liberty since 14 July

1789 had been technically illegal and that it was absurd, as he famously put it, to 'want a Revolution without a revolution.'[64] When Brissot was hard pressed in July 1792 to prove the reality of the conspiracy he had repeatedly and opportunistically denounced – the infamous 'Austrian Committee' – he adopted much the same position. Brissot declared that he would accredit even those accusations lacking in coherence and containing unfounded charges against officials hitherto enjoying public confidence.[65]

The risk in adopting this position was that the same questionable procedures used to prosecute others could be and often were used to convict the accusers. As Desmoulins later argued, the Brissotins, having rejected the need for judicial-grade evidence in conspiracy cases, were hardly in a position to object when courts used equally flimsy standards of proof to convict them.[66] This was an argument that, needless to say, did not strengthen Desmoulins's own case when he in turn was tried as a Dantonist accomplice in the spring of 1794. Brissot, at the time of his own trial, insisted that prosecutors were obliged to produce the same kinds of moral and physical evidence as had been used by the Romans when prosecuting Catilina, evidence that Brissot claimed was lacking against him.[67] But unable to persuade the authorities, he lost his head quickly enough, Robespierre noting that it had been the ambitious Julius Caesar who, for self-serving reasons, had objected to Cicero's disregard of legal niceties before swiftly executing Catilina.[68] Soon after Brissot's conviction, Couthon, a former lawyer, dismissed the need for any material evidence whatsoever in conspiracy cases; so, too, did Billaud-Varenne, who pointed out that such proof was nearly always unavailable.[69] The bottom of this slippery slope was probably reached when Couthon, contending that facial expression alone proved conspiratorial culpability, urged his countrymen to become forensic physiognomists. Alluding to the telltale symptoms of guilt presented by the Catilinian accomplices, he affirmed before a loudly applauding Convention that conspirators could be identified by their wild eyes, fallen look, and dispirited gallows expression. 'Good citizens,' he demanded, 'seize these traitors and arrest them!'[70] It is difficult to determine the immediate public response to such injunctions, but they undoubtedly reenforced Thermidorean images of the Jacobins as unprincipled assassins.[71]

A second problem in maintaining the Revolution/conspiracy distinction arose when, despite repeated assertions of ultimate victory, the seemingly endless proliferation of plots against the Republic pressured the Jacobins to answer certain perturbing questions about their recurrence. If secret plots were really the last resort and 'infernal expedient' of the weak, why were there so many of them? What circumstances allowed counterrevolutionaries to stage, in Marat's words, 'their ever-reviving conspiracies – their ever renewed crimes'?[72] And why did the suppression of one conspiracy seem only to ignite the next one?

When replying to such questions, the Jacobins certainly pointed to and denounced the *émigrés* and foreign powers as immediate engines of subversion. Much was made of the counterrevolutionaries' malign cleverness in launching redundant operations, any one of which could sustain the counterrevolutionary momentum if the others were suppressed.[73] But deeper reflection on the matter led some republicans to the paradoxical conclusion that the ultimate source of conspiracy lay in the Revolution itself. For if the Revolution was a direct consequence of despotism, it seemed to follow that Revolutionary progress would generate an equal and opposite reaction in the form of counterrevolutionary conspiracy. 'When a country recovers its liberty, when that revolution is determined, but not finished,' Condorcet explained, 'there necessarily exist a great number of men who seek to produce a revolution in the opposite sense, a *counterrevolution*.'[74] In Robespierre's words, 'the ages that engender the greatest miracles of reason are also necessarily stained by the greatest excesses of human corruption. Crimes accelerate the progress of liberty, and the progress of liberty has multiplied the crimes of tyranny in redoubling its alarms and passions.'[75] According to this historical logic, the history of the Revolution would necessarily consist of an alternation between the advances of liberty and what one journal called the 'vengeance of force.'[76] If so, the proliferation of counterrevolutionary conspiracies could hardly be accidental to the Revolutionary process, but rather, as Brissot put it, 'in the very nature of things.'[77] Indeed, Saint-Just asserted, the process whereby tyranny and revolution engendered one another was governed by the iron laws of nature. We cannot expect the execution of the king to bring closure to the Revolution, he warned the Convention, for the 'moral order is like the physical order; abuses disappear for a moment, like dew evaporates from the earth; abuses soon reappear, as humidity falls again from the clouds.'[78]

By conceding that conspiracies were a necessary and possibly perpetual phenomenon, Revolutionaries effectively embraced a vision of the future distinctly different from that projected by the Revolutionary festivals, which dramatized the arduous struggles of a newly regenerated people successfully disposing of its enemies on its way to a more glorious age. Incorporation of conspiracies into the dynamics of the Revolution, by contrast, indicated that the suppression of one plot might well occasion others, each with a place in the genealogy of crimes against the nation. To be sure, this vision of the future was not so bleak as the victory of despotism imagined by Robespierre and Saint-Just. But it was bleak enough, for it suggested that conspiratorial assaults on the Republic would never cease, which in turn meant that the purgatory of 'revolutionary' government could never give way to the paradise of a truly 'constitutional' regime. However devoutly to be wished, the Revolution might never be 'over.'

Despite its grim implications, the notion of the Revolution as a struggle without closure against counterrevolutionary conspiracy did provide some political benefits. Most obviously it handed the Jacobins a convenient pretext to annihilate their enemies, for in denying the possibility of winding up the Revolution through peaceful compromise, it made perpetual terror appear as the only alternative to the victory of despotism. Thus in March 1794 Robespierre warned the Convention that if it did not immediately repress all the factions conspiring against the Jacobin government, 'our armies will be beaten, your women and children slaughtered, the republic torn to pieces by the blows of your enemies, and you will leave your posterity under the yoke of tyranny.'[79] A second benefit offered by the notion that conspiracies were inherent in 'the very nature of things' and arose according to a perceptible logic was the darker measure of time it provided to help make historical sense of an extraordinarily chaotic revolution. Each newly disclosed conspiracy could be explained as the response of despotism to the advance of liberty along a temporal continuum. In some cases, conspiracies – real and imagined – predating 1789 were grafted onto those rooted in the Revolution. A prime example was the long-standing 'Austrian Plot,' which resurfaced at Marie-Antoinette's trial when prosecutors and witnesses blended prerevolutionary accusations that she had participated in an Austrian conspiracy to recapture Lorraine with charges that she had consorted with 'traitors' to the Revolution, among them Lafayette.[80] Still later during the Terror, this history of criminal mischief was spliced with other allegations to produce the vast Foreign Plot, which Saint-Just explained as the product of multiple factions negotiating the twists and turns of the Revolution 'just as reptiles follow the course of streams.'[81] According to Saint-Just, the Foreign Plot originated in 1789 with the conspiracies of the duc d'Orléans and eventually fueled the subversions of prominent Revolutionaries such as Dumouriez, Brissot, Danton, and Hébert, each of whom had allegedly served a term as the central promoter of the counterrevolution.

However vast and elaborate, none of these conspiratorial narratives – even the Foreign Plot – achieved the canonical status enjoyed by the Revolutionary calendar and national festivals, and for good reason. As Mona Ozouf has shown,[82] celebrations of the great *journées* of the Revolution – the conquest of the Bastille, the fall of the monarchy, the execution of the king – were occasionally reshuffled in terms of relative importance. Yet the events they commemorated were so much a part of Revolutionary myth that the government could never officially represent them as counterrevolutionary plots; for if so sacred an event as the storming of the Bastille turned out to have been a counterrevolutionary intrigue after all – instead of a popular effort to thwart one – the entire Revolution risked desacrilization and dismissal as a tissue of counter-revolutionary plots. Nevertheless, what was true of the Revolution collectively was not necessarily true of its leaders individually, each of whom, according the Revolutionary doctrine of virtue, was potentially corruptible and therefore a potential traitor.[83] As the pace of accusation accelerated during the year II and the evidentiary requirements for convicting defendants of conspiracy became progressively less stringent, the history of Revolutionary leaders was reconfigured many times and at an ever faster pace. More and more false 'patriots' were 'exposed' in a network of treason extending both laterally and temporally, their accusers arguing that exposure of the filiations of some conspirators and their plots would make it easier to detect others. As Billaud-Varenne reassured his colleagues, the collusion of counterrevolutionaries could be proved by the 'conformity of their system and their plan with the principles and conduct of other counterrevolutionaries and of all those who have been declared head of some conspiracy.'[84]

The question looming over all these prosecutions, as Antoine de Baecque has suggested, was how far the process of rewriting the history of Revolutionary leadership could proceed without indicting the Revolution itself as one massive plot, an indictment that strangely echoed the claims made repeatedly by counterrevolutionaries.[85] In his last speech to the Convention, Robespierre denounced major elements of the Revolutionary government as parties to a 'conspiracy against public liberty,' charging that a 'criminal coalition' was operating inside the Convention with powerful accomplices in the Committees of General Security and Public Safety.[86] Little wonder that a celebrated contemporary print depicted the Incorruptible amidst a forest of guillotines, executing the executioner after guillotining all the French, for such was the logic of the Terror's remorseless witch-hunt that even the executioner was not sufficiently trustworthy to be left unexecuted. But if so, then at some point in the near future the fuel energizing the search for victims would be spent: if all citizens were suspects, who was fit to prosecute them? When so many self-professed patriots were serially exposed as traitors to the *patrie*, did not patriotism itself risk debasement as a guise of schemers plotting to subvert the new order? By the time the Terror collapsed during the summer of 1794, it had become entangled in a web of political contradictions largely of its own design.

From 9 Thermidor to 18 Brumaire

These contradictions hardly evaporated with the coup of 9 Thermidor, when the Committee of Public Safety imploded in a mass of mutual accusation. Traditionally viewed as a decisive turning point in the Revolution, the coup was in part an unintended consequence of the Foreign Plot and Grand Terror, which gave citizens reason to believe that treason had infected the Jacobin leadership, just as it had contaminated their enemies. Indeed, it took no time at all following 9 Thermidor for Robespierre – hitherto, the 'incorruptible' incarnation of the Revolution – to be branded, like so many others before him, the 'new Catilina,' who had participated with his confederates in some 'horrible conspiracy.'[87] The Thermidorean Louis-Félix Roux claimed that the 'new Catilina' and his accomplices had raised conspiratorial deception to a new level by inventing 'the art of speaking ceaselessly of conspiracy, so as to draw attention away [from the fact] that they were themselves the most villainous conspirators.'[88] In other words, denunciation of conspiracies – previously the duty and privilege of every good citizen – was now reconstrued as prima facie evidence of conspiratorial intent on the part of the denouncer. Whither *civisme* now? If Robespierre turned out to head the list of conspirators, François Furet has perceptively noted, how was it possible at this juncture to give meaning to the Revolution as a whole?[89]

From the perspective of the Thermidoreans, it was possible to restore historical 'meaning' to the Revolution only once, in the words of Bronislaw Baczko, 'the Terror was simultaneously condemned and eclipsed.'[90] At the heart of this process lay the task of driving a fresh conceptual wedge between 'conspiracy' and 'revolution' so that the Revolution could reemerge as a movement distinctly greater than the sum of betrayals against the nation, the latest instance of which was the recently discredited Terror. To provide ideological reinforcement to the shaky new regime of the Directory and achieve the elusive stability long sought by moderate republicans, the history of the Revolution would have to be rewritten once again.

Among the most penetrating analysts of where the Revolution stood after Thermidor was Benjamin Constant. In his *De la force du gouvernement actuel de la France et de la nécessité de s'y rallier* (1796), he not only renounced recourse to all popular insurgencies as vehicles of Revolutionary progress, but also condemned the conspiratorial mentality cultivated by popular leaders that had put virtually all citizens under suspicion.[91] Far from endorsing the well-worn, double-edged strategy of denouncing conspiracies in the name of the Revolution to achieve stability, Constant reversed direction with the telling argument that the very multiplicity of recklessly leveled conspiracy accusations had shredded the credibility of most of them. 'Who has not been denounced since 14 July [1789]?' he pointedly asked. 'After seeing Bailly and Pache, La Rochefoucauld and Marat, Condorcet and Saint-Just, Sieyès and Robespierre [become] the target of the same accusations, can one still believe in Revolutionary reputations? The [radical] factions have only one style . . . they randomly attach names to invectives.'[92] Reworking the theme that the Revolution had generated its own worst enemies, Constant departed from the standard view that counterrevolutionary conspiracies posed the most deadly threat to the Revolutionary cause; rather, he asserted, this threat derived from certain 'habits [of mind]' fostered by the Terror, 'which cause the collapse of all principles, the perversion of all opinions, and which weighs on all of society and each individual, at all hours and in all its forms.'[93] Indeed, he insisted, 'it is an infinitely more dangerous thing to revolutionize on behalf of virtue than to revolutionize on behalf of crime.'[94] Insuring the definitive termination of the Revolution required not the more intensive pursuit of suspected counterrevolutionary conspirators, a policy that had only generated the ideological contradictions of the Terror; rather, it required the cleansing of abused words like 'justice' and a renewed resistance to the nefarious, all-too-pervasive will of the 'factions' to 'present the truth in a way that offends reason [and] liberty . . . [and] inspires fear.'[95] Should the government not receive a more principled foundation, Constant warned, it would 'to return to tyranny by reascending the river of blood that . . . [has recently] flowed in the name of liberty.'[96]

If the reduction of radical revolutionary fever required the cleansing of political language, no word stood more in need of critical reassessment following the Terror than 'revolution' itself. As historians of this term have shown, the meaning of 'revolution' and 'revolutionary' had become so elastic by the onset of the Directory that they were applied to virtually every conceivable political party. Already under the Terror, Saint-Just had accused 'moderates' of misappropriating 'revolutionary' to disguise their own nefarious operations, an accusation that did not prevent St.-Just himself from exploiting the term when he assailed participants in the Foreign Plot for being 'revolutionary in the sense of crime.'[97] Inversely, Babeuf denounced the Terror as a 'counterrevolution' for violating freedom of the press, a term he also later applied to the régime of Thermidor; far from constituting the logical conclusion to the Revolution, this régime was in reality a product of a *'counterrevolution . . .* [which] is the unhappiness of the greatest number; it is this that we have achieved.[98]

Amid all this semantic indeterminacy, it is not surprising that the Thermidoreans and Directorials had difficulty articulating their own political mission. At a minimum, it was clear that the *dérapage* to the left, which in the view of the Thermidoreans had driven the Revolution far off the proper course since the Legislative Assembly, now had to be reversed. As early as 10 Thermidor year II, Barère put the Convention on notice that notwithstanding the enduring commitment to 'liberty,' a new, distinctly less inclusive phase of political engagement had begun, one in which power would be taken out of the hands of the people. 'On 31 May 1793,' he intoned, 'the people made their revolution; on 9 Thermidor the Convention made its own: liberty has applauded both equally.'[99] Did such language imply there had there been two 'revolutions,' not one? Few Thermidoreans or Directorials openly endorsed such a distinction, and in a solemn reaffirmation of its continuity with the politics of the Revolution before the Terror, the Convention voted to publish and distribute three thousand copies of Condorcet's *Esquisse d'un tableau historique des progrès de l'esprit humain*. Hailing it as a 'classic' made all the more estimable by the unmerited scorn heaped by Robespierre on its proscribed author, the sponsor of the resolution – Daunou – endorsed Condorcet's work as a foundational text for students, and by implication, all citizens. From it, he assured his audience, they would acquire a renewed sense of the Revolution as an irreversible historical advance. 'Your students, in studying the history of the sciences and arts, will learn from it above all to cherish liberty, to detest and conquer all tyrannies.'[100]

Well they might, but in the aftermath of the Terror how much political guidance could be provided by a text that exuded a now quaint confidence in the proclivity of the people to defer to the truly enlightened?[101] The immediate task no longer appeared to be the enlargement and engagement of popular sovereignty, but rather the 'condemnation' and 'eclipse' of an entire chapter of democracy. As Roederer put it simply, the principle of 'force' motivating the politics of the early Revolution now had to cede to the principle of 'order.'[102] Once again, it was Constant who perhaps best grasped the historical task facing those who would once and for all 'terminate' the Revolution without relapsing into the ancien régime. It was critical, Constant argued, to acknowledge that the Revolution had been only a 'road' not a 'goal,' and it was time, he urged, 'to turn our attention from that road, to see at last where we have arrived.'[103] A proper historical perspective, he contended, would illuminate three distinct stages of Revolutionary progress: on 14 July 1789 the people had demanded 'liberty'; on 10 August 1792 they had proclaimed the 'Republic'; on 9 Thermidor and 4 Prairial they had pronounced against 'anarchy,' whose suppression was now the principal item on the republican agenda.[104] Most critically, the suppression of 'anarchy' required the cessation of the very popular revolutionary activity that had engendered the Revolution – it was essential, in other words, 'for the French not to revolutionize against the Republic.'[105]

But could a republic born of popular insurgency maintain its authority after severing itself from the revolutionary roots that had nourished it since its inception? In the end, the Directory became hopelessly caught in much the same web of political contradictions as had entangled the Terror it sought to 'condemn and eclipse.' Failing to develop the solid, broad constituency based on Constant's 'principles,' the regime almost immediately ignored his advice to lower the political temperature and abandon the witch-hunts of the past. To be sure, opposition to the Directory on its left and right was not imaginary. From the outset, the régime was challenged by dissenters whose none-too-gentle political experience left them disinclined and poorly equipped ideologically and organizationally to act like a loyal opposition. But whether or not the second Directory could have generated a viable party system, there is no denying that the régime sought to strengthen its authority by noisily suppressing political activity that in some cases were of little or no serious threat to its existence.[106]

Although it was hardly an innocent undertaking, Babeuf's pitifully organized, ultimately abortive 'Conspiracy of Equals' of 1796 – analyzed by Laura Mason in Chapter 8 – provides a major case in point. In order to confect a 'red scare,' the Directory prosecuted a cast of sixty-four Jacobin alleged accomplices, many of whom had never in fact even known Babeuf, let alone conspired with him, while it proceeded to publish transcripts of the trial edited in such a way as to encourage the public to draw the politically appropriate lessons.[107] It is difficult to measure the impact of the government's efforts to discredit the left as a whole by means of this trial, but there are good reasons to believe that the government's campaign backfired. First, the veracity of the government's account of the proceedings was vigorously contested by the defense, which published its own version. Second, the defendants, who strenuously denied that there was any 'plot,' turned the tables on their accusers by charging that the government had abandoned the republican cause when it undertook to hunt down citizens who were true patriots. To prove their innocence, they ingeniously – and to apparent good effect – cited their all-too-evident incompetence. As Charles Germain pointed out, 'if all that has been proved so far is that the 'conspiracy' is a mere chimerical dream of those with an interest in sacrificing republicans, one would be convinced of this by one fact alone: [the absurdity of] an amateur like me [serving] as minister of war!'[108] Finally, none of the sixty-four defendants was convicted on the charge of conspiracy, and only a handful were found guilty on the secondary count of illegally advocating the constitution of

1793. If the Directory contributed to its own delegitimation through repeated violations of the letter and spirit of the Constitution of the Year III, then its patent abuse of forensic procedures in the Babeuf conspiracy could only clinch the argument that the régime had little respect for the rule of law. By the eve of 18 Brumaire, when challenges to the régime from the left escalated once again, the Directory had shown that it could neither strike effectively at the root causes of conspiracies, nor prosecute them without recourse to extra-legal force. Paradoxically, the Directory, like the Terror it had sought to 'condemn and eclipse,' fell victim to a conspiracy organized by some of its own leaders.

Despite the clouds of military glory trailing its eminent first citizen, the Bonapartist régime also had recourse to the politics of conspiracy accusation. Attracting a mere 1.5 million votes – 250,000 fewer than the constitution of 1793[109] – the Consulate was hardly an immediate runaway success. Indeed, the régime felt obliged to falsify results of the plebiscite on the new constitution by announcing that twice as many voters had supported it than in fact had been the case. It took more than two years, as Martin Lyons has put it, before Bonaparte succeeded 'in awakening the nation from its soporific indifference to the coup of Brumaire.'[110] Once again, conspiracies against the new régime provided the leavening agent.

As had been the case throughout the Revolution, not all these conspiracies were figments of the régime's imagination. On 24 December 1800 a bomb that was supposed to send the First Consul into an early retirement exploded on the rue Saint Nicaise in Paris. Its intended victim escaped unscathed, but the explosion killed an as yet undetermined number of other citizens and caused extensive property damage.[111] Although the loss of life and property was certainly real, the political significance of the assassination attempt lay in the opportunity to misrepresent and exploit it for purposes of consolidating the new, still shaky regime. Indeed, the cynical use of the affair by the government could hardly have been greater or more self-conscious, for although Fouché soon determined that the bomb had been planted by royalists, Bonaparte found it more politically expedient to blame the assassination attempt on a Jacobin conspiracy. Fouché's inconvenient evidence was quickly swept aside, and 129 Jacobins, whose names were drawn from a preestablished enemies list, were immediately exiled to penal colonies overseas without trial. Cambacérès summed up the procedure frankly enough when he observed that 'it would be misleading to speak of the crime [of the rue Saint Nicaise] as being the motive for this measure, which is [in fact] one of general utility.'[112] But it was Bonaparte himself who, in admitting that 'in the absence of legal proofs [the government] cannot proceed against these individuals,' rooted the whole judicial travesty most properly in its counterconspiratorial historical context. 'We transport them,' he declared, 'for their share in the September Massacres, the crime of 31 May, the Babeuf Conspiracy, and all that has happened since.'[113] A new genealogy of conspiratorial activity had now been traced, with the result that one by one – first the Tribunate, then the Council of State, then the Senate – the other institutions of state fell into line and formally approved Bonaparte's initiatives. Indeed, by passing the first *senatus-consultum* to authorize the anti-Jacobin repression, the Senate set a precedent for further manipulation of the constitution that would ultimately allow Bonaparte to emasculate the legislative branch and monopolize political power.[114] As Mme. de Staël sardonically observed, Bonaparte's repression of his opponents had insured that 'only he was permitted to be a Jacobin in France.'[115]

The legacy

Jacobin or anti-Jacobin? The notoriously ambiguous complexion of the Napoleonic régime was not simply a product of the *politique de bascule* Bonaparte practiced in his own meteoric career, nor merely of the contradictory Revolutionary and counterrevolutionary agendas he pursued once in office; it also derived from the complex interrelations between 'conspiracy' and 'Revolution' that attended the installation of his régime. Notwithstanding his mandate to rescue the Revolution from the revolutionizing that threatened to destroy it, Bonaparte was obliged to resort to conspiracy – a nearly botched one, at it turned out – to catapult himself into power. No sooner had he arrived there than he refashioned himself as an anticonspirator to consolidate his régime and create a consensus built on military glory earned abroad and a campaign of public works, including the restoration of law and order, at home. Little wonder that republicans and monarchists alike had difficulty assessing the complexion of his politics.

That Bonaparte's administrative genius enabled him to maintain his political grip longer than any previous Revolutionary government ought not obscure the fact that his *prise de pouvoir* entailed the reenactment of a script which in certain respects had been played out many times before. The Third Estate had capitalized on an 'aristo-ministerial' conspiracy to achieve its reorganization of government in 1789; the Brissotins had exploited the myth of the 'Austrian Committee' to stir up war hysteria and thereby consolidate its ministry in 1792; the Jacobins had used the specter of international counterrevolutionary conspiracy to execute the king, proscribe the Girondins, and establish the Terror in 1793; and

the Directory had publicized Jacobin and royalist plots over its four-year
life span to legitimate its own dubious policies. In resorting to conspiratorial 'crisis' to engender Revolutionary 'progress,' Bonaparte was not a
pioneer, but an imitator.

The implications of this phenomenon for French historical memory
were profound. As François Furet has magisterially demonstrated,
the Revolution of 1789 remained the touchstone of French political
debate well into the nineteenth century.[116] While the right portrayed the
Revolution as a transgression of the French national past, the left
represented it as a critical and necessary historical breach without closure,
a struggle that had to be won over and over again – most notably during
the Revolutions of 1830 and 1848, the Paris Commune, and the Dreyfus
Affair. These conflicting perceptions were undoubtedly the products of
sharp, persistent differences over political agendas and the definition
of the nation after 1815.[117] Yet they were also extensions of the
Revolutionary heritage, in particular the Revolution's historical vision of
itself. That vision had always been somewhat blurred because it had
embraced two competing conceptions of the future – one forecasting
inevitable triumph, the other an endless struggle against counterrevolutionary forces, for whose vitality some Revolutionaries claimed a
curious responsibility. The dominant Revolutionary discourse held that
conspiracy, marked by guile and ridden with vice, was uniquely the
weapon of the counterrevolutionaries, but in the end the Revolutionaries
had to admit that they, too, had engaged in conspiratorial activity, if only
for the sake of securing the Revolution. The result was a process of
historical auto-reflection which for at least a century seemed to push the
definitive triumph of the Revolution always beyond the horizon of
the present and into the ever more distant future. This outcome might
best be called Catilina's revenge.

Notes

1 See especially Keith Michael Baker, *Inventing the French Revolution:
   Essay on French Political Culture in the Eighteenth Century* (Cambridge,
   UK, 1990), chapter 9; and his 'Transformations of Classical Republicanism
   in Eighteenth-Century France,' *Journal of Modern History*, 73 (2001),
   pp. 32–53.

2 [Anon.], *Dénonciation à la France, à l'Europe, et à tous les peuples de la
   terre, de plus de cinquante mille brigands stipendiés à Paris, pour fomenter
   les troubles, la rebellion, & pour faire égorger impitoyablement les uns et les
   autres, & les principaux agens de cette horrible conspiration* (Paris,
   [1792–93?]), p. 4. Translation my own, as are all those that follow except
   where indicated.

3   As Jean-Claude Waquet observes, all the terms routinely employed to denote conspiratorial activity in the seventeenth century – *conspiration, conjuration, complot, cabale* – were in some sense *accusateur*. Jean-Claude Waquet, *La Conjuration des dictionnaires: Vérité des mots et vérités de la politique dans la France moderne* (Strasburg, 2000), p. 27.

4   Most notorious were the subversions of the Cardinal de Retz during the Fronde, which were immortalized in his memoirs. See J. H. M. Salmon, *Cardinal de Retz: The Anatomy of a Conspirator* (London, 1969).

5   Denis Diderot and Jean Le Rond d'Alembert, eds, *Encyclopédie: ou, Dictionnaire raisonné des sciences, des arts et des métiers*, 28 vols. (Reprint Paris, 1751–76), 4, p. 58; 3, p. 884; Pierre Richelet, *Dictionnaire françois*, 2 vols (Geneva, 1680), 1, p. 157. Waquet in *La Conjuration*, p. 35 shows that *cabale* – often used to refer to court plots – referred less commonly to conspiracies of the distant past and more commonly to conspiracies of the early modern period than *conspiration, complot*, or *conjuration*. But added together, the incidence of *conspiration, complot*, and *conjuration* was nearly that of *cabale* in accounts of early modern subversive movements. It would thus be incorrect to say that contemporaries conceived of conspiracies as obsolete forms of political action.

6   René de Vertot, *Histoire des révolutions de Portugal* (Paris, 1859), p. 1.

7   Thus, in its article on *conspiration*, the *Encyclopédie* mentioned the Catiline conspiracy before any other. *Encyclopédie*, 4, p. 58. For the eighteenth-century French appropriation of the classical past in general, see Chantal Grell, 'Le Dix-huitième siècle et l'antiquité en France, 1680–1789,' in *Studies on Voltaire and the Eighteenth Century* (Oxford, 1995), vols 330–331.

8   For modern English editions of the classical texts, see Cicero, 'Against Lucius Sergius Catilina,' in *Selected Political Speeches*, trans. Michael Grant (London, 1969), pp. 71–145; Sallust, *The Conspiracy of Catiline*, trans. S. A. Hanford (London, 1963).

9   Cited in Harold Parker, *The Cult of Antiquity and the French Revolution: A Study in the Development of the Revolutionary Spirit* (Chicago, 1937; reprint New York, 1965), p. 38. On the study of Cicero in the *collèges*, see pp. 32–33.

10 Cicero, 'Against Lucius Sergius Catilina,' 118–119; see also, Sallust, *The Conspiracy*, p. 174.

11 Marisa Linton, *The Politics of Virtue in Enlightenment France* (London and New York, 2001).

12 Cicero, 'Against Lucius Sergius Catilina,' p. 116.

13 Jean-Marie Goulemot, 'Le Mot *révolution* et la formation du concept de révolution politique (fin XVIIᵉ siècle),' *Annales historiques de la révolution française* 39 (1967), pp. 417–444; Mona Ozouf, 'De Thermidor à Brumaire: Les Discours de la Révolution sur elle-même,' *Revue historique* (493), pp. 31–66; Rolf Reichhardt and Hans-Jürgen Lüsebrink, 'Révolution à la fin du 18e siècle: Pour une relecture d'un concept-clé du siècle des Lumières,' *Mots*, 16 (1988), pp. 35–68; Alain Rey, '*Révolution*': Histoire d'un mot (n.p., 1989); Baker, *Inventing*, chap. 9.

14 Cited in Dale K. Van Kley, *The Religious Origins of the French Revolution: From Calvin to the Civil Constitution, 1560–1791* (New Haven, 1996), p. 250. Reichhardt and Lüsebrink, 'Révolution,' p. 37 cite a 1756 text of Didier-Pierre Chicaneau de Neuville in which the author speaks of 'revolutions caused by despotism.'

15 Charles-Louis de Secondat, baron de Montesquieu, *Considérations sur les causes de la grandeur des romains et de leur décadence* (Paris, 1967), pp. 122–123.

16 François-Joachim Duport de Tertre, *Histoire des conjurations, conspirations et révolutions célèbres, tant anciennes que modernes*, 10 vols (Paris, 1754–60).

17 Ibid., 1, p. 2.

18 Ibid., 5, p. 6; also his account of the Swiss secession from Austria, ibid., 1, pp. 368–411.

19 Cited in Daniel L. Wick, *A Conspiracy of Well-Intentioned Men: The Society of Thirty and the French Revolution* (New York and London, 1987), p. 43. On the benign meaning given by Diderot and Mercier to *conspiration*, see Waquet, *La Conjuration*, p. 234; for other examples, see Barry M. Shapiro, *Revolutionary Justice in Paris, 1789–1790* (Cambridge, UK, 1993), pp. 5–6.

20 Jean-Antoine-Nicolas de Caritat, marquis de Condorcet, 'Sur le sens du mot révolutionnaire,' in A. Condorcet-O'Connor and François Arago, eds, *Oeuvres de Condorcet*, 12 vols (Paris, 1847–49), 12, p. 615.

21 Rey, *'Révolution'*, p. 111; Reichhardt and Lüsebrink, 'Révolution,' pp. 43, 48–55, note that the term was still used by counterrevolutionaries in the plural to disparage these same events and that it had been used in the singular before 1789, usually in a positive sense, to refer to the Glorious Revolution of 1688 and the American Revolution.

22 *Révolutions de Paris*, n.n. (30 January 1790), p. 1.

23 Cited in Pierre Rétat, 'Forme et discours d'un journal révolutionnaire: Les *Révolutions de Paris* en 1789,' in Claude Labrosse *et al.*, eds, *L'Instrument périodique: La fonction de la presse au XVIIIe siècle* (Lyons, 1985), p. 160. The citation appeared in a sister publication of the *Révolutions de Paris* entitled the *Révolutions nationales*.

24 Rétat, 'Forme et discours,' pp. 160ff.; Baker, 'Transformations.'

25 Baker, 'Transformations,' p. 46.

26 Michael Fitzsimmons, *The Remaking of France: The National Assembly and the Constitution of 1791* (Cambridge, UK and New York, 1994); Timothy Tackett, *Becoming a Revolutionary: The Deputies of the French National Assembly and the Emergence of a Revolutionary Culture (1789–1790)* (Princeton, 1996).

27 Munro Price, *The Road from Versailles: Louis XVI, Marie Antoinette, and the Fall of the French Monarchy* (New York, 2002), chapter 4.

28 Thomas E. Kaiser, 'Nobles into Aristocrats, or How an Order Became a Conspiracy,' in Jay Smith, ed., *The Eighteenth-Century French Nobility: Reassessments and New Approaches* (University Park, PA, 2006), pp. 189–224.

29 Volney, *La Sentinelle du peuple*, 2 (20 November 1788), p. 7.

30 Dale Van Kley, 'From the Lessons of French History to Truths for All Times and All People: The Historical Origins of an Anti-Historical Declaration,' in Dale Van Kley, ed., *The French Idea of Freedom: The Old Regime and the Declaration of Rights of 1789* (Stanford, 1994), p. 91.

31 Kaiser, 'Nobles into Aristocrats.'

32 On the radical press, see Jack Richard Censer, *Prelude to Power: The Parisian Radical Press, 1789–1791* (Baltimore and London, 1976); on the press in general, see Hugh Gough, *The Newspaper Press in the French Revolution* (Chicago, 1988) and Jeremy D. Popkin, *Revolutionary News: The Press in France, 1789–1799* (Durham, NC and London, 1990).

33 Nicolas Ruault, *Gazette d'un parisien sous la Révolution* (Paris, 1976), p. 135.

34 Hans-Jürgen Lüsebrink and Rolf Reichhardt, *The Bastille: A History of a Symbol of Despotism and Freedom* trans. Norbert Schürer (Durham, NC and London, 1997).

35 *Moniteur*, 1(20) (17–20 July 1789), p. 169.

36 Ibid., 2 (29 Dec.1789), p. 500. This report was published in installments in *Moniteur* during the last week of December 1789, and *in toto* in Jean-Philippe Garran de Coulon, *Rapport fait au comité de recherches des représentants de la commune, par M. Garran de Coulon, sur la conspiration des mois de mai, juin & juillet derniers, imprimé par ordre du comité* (Paris, 1789). On its background, see Shapiro, *Revolutionary Justice*, pp. 45–48.

37 *Moniteur*, 2 (9 October 1789), p. 19.

38 Adrien Duquesnoy, *Journal d'Adrien Duquesnoy*, 2 vols (Paris, 1894), 1, p. 252; 2, p. 72.

39 Timothy Tackett, *When the King Took Flight* (Cambridge, MA, 2003).

40 *L'Orateur du Peuple*, 1(6) [1790], p. 43.

41 Indeed, Marat charged that government agencies authorized to investigate conspiracies had been penetrated by counterrevolutionaries and were covering them up. See Jean-Paul Marat, *Oeuvres politiques, 1789–1793*, ed. Jacques de Cock and Charlotte Goëtz, 10 vols (Brussels, 1989–95), 1, pp. 519–520.

42 This development has not been sufficiently stressed by historians. For recent overviews, see T. C. W. Blanning, *The Origins of the French Revolutionary Wars* (London and New York, 1986), and Bailey Stone, *The Genesis of the French Revolution: A Global-Historical Interpretation* (Cambridge, UK and New York, 1994).

43 [Jean-Louis Carra], *L'Orateur des États-Généraux pour 1789* (n.p., [1789]), p. 21.

44 Thomas E. Kaiser, 'Who's Afraid of Marie-Antoinette? Diplomacy, Austrophobia, and the Queen,' *French History*, 14 (2000), pp. 241–271; and Kaiser, 'From the Austrian Committee to the Foreign Plot: Marie-Antoinette, Austrophobia, and the Terror,' *French Historical Studies*, 26 (2003), pp. 579–617.

45 Tackett, *When the King Took Flight*.
46 *Révolutions de Paris* 102 (18–25 June 1791), p. 526.
47 Louis-Antoine Saint-Just, *Oeuvres complètes*, ed. Michèle Duval (Paris, 1984), p. 381.
48 Cited in Rey, '*Révolution*', p. 123.
49 *Moniteur*, 18 (20 November 1793), p. 462.
50 Cited in Rétat, 'Forme,' p. 160.
51 Jean-Antoine-Nicolas Caritat, marquis de Condorcet, *Esquisse d'un tableau historique des progrès de l'esprit humain* (Paris, 1971), p. 259.
52 For an illuminating discussion of the politics behind the Revolutionary calendar, see Yann Fauchois, 'La Révolution française, ou la volonté de prendre date,' *Revue de la Bibliothèque nationale de France*, 4 (2000), pp. 43–49.
53 G. Romme, 'Rapport sur l'ère de la république, par G. Romme [20 septembre 1793],' *Archives parlementaires de 1787 à 1860*, 87 vols (Paris, 1867–), 74, p. 551. Interestingly, Joseph de Maistre denounced the new calendar itself as a conspiracy. Cited in Mona Ozouf, *La Fête révolutionnaire, 1789–1799* (n.p., 1976), p. 262.
54 Ozouf, *La Fête*, pp. 262, 275.
55 Jacques-Louis David, *Rapport et décret sur la fête de la Réunion républicaine du 10 août, présentés au nom du Comité d'Instruction publique par David* (Paris, [1793]), pp. 2–6.
56 [Anon.], *Dénonciation à la France*, p. 8.
57 See Darrin M. MacMahon, *Enemies of the Enlightenment: The French Counter-Enlightenment and the Making of Modernity* (Oxford and New York, 2001), chapters 2 and 3.
58 *Moniteur* 15 (15 March 1793), p. 701. On the issue of transparency, see Lynn Hunt, *Politics, Culture, and Class in the French Revolution* (Berkeley, CA, 1984), pp. 44–46.
59 Shapiro, *Revolutionary Justice*.
60 On Lambesc, see Thomas E. Kaiser, 'Ambiguous Identities: Marie-Antoinette and the House of Lorraine from the Affair of the Minuet to Lambesc's Charge,' in Dena Goodman, ed., *Marie-Antoinette: Writings on the Body of a Queen* (New York and London, 2003), pp. 171–198.
61 *Révolutions de Paris* 14 (19 October 1789), p. 6.
62 *Moniteur* 15 (14 March 1793), p. 688.
63 Maximilien-François-Isidore de Robespierre, *Robespierre: Discours et Rapports à la Convention* (Paris, 1965), p. 295.
64 *Moniteur*, 14 (6 November 1792), p. 392.
65 Ibid., 13 (27 June 1792), p. 241.
66 Camille Desmoulins, *Histoire des Brissotins, ou Fragment de l'histoire secrète de la Révolution et des six premiers mois de la Révolution française*, in P.-J.-B. Buchez et P.-C. Roux, *Histoire parlementaire de la Révolution française*, 40 vols (Paris, 1834–38), 26, p. 268.
67 Gérard Walter, ed., *Actes du tribunal révolutionnaire* (Paris, 1968), p. 207.

68 Robespierre, *Discours*, pp. 225–226.
69 J.-N. Billaud-Varenne, *Discours du citoyen Billaud-Varenne, sur les Députés de la Convention mis en état d'arrestation par son décret du 2 juin, prononcé dans la séance du 15 juillet* ([Paris], 1793) p. 2.
70 *Moniteur*, 19 (16 March 1794), p. 707. On transparency and physiognomy, see Antoine de Baecque, *Le Corps de l'histoire: Métaphores et politique (1770–1800)* (n.p., 1993), pt. III, chapter 1.
71 On Thermidorean views of the Jacobins, see Bronislaw Baczko, *Ending the Terror: The French Revolution after Robespierre*, trans. Michel Petheram (Cambridge, UK, 1994).
72 Marat, *Oeuvres politiques*, 1, p. 490.
73 See Robespierre's comments on the bicephalous Foreign Plot, in *Moniteur*, 20 (25 March 1794), p. 34.
74 Condorcet, 'Sur le sens,' p. 619.
75 *Moniteur* 18 (20 November 1793), p. 457.
76 *Révolutions de Paris* [unnumbered] (30 January 1790), p. 1.
77 *Moniteur*, 13 (2 July 1792), p. 241.
78 Saint-Just, *Oeuvres*, p. 400.
79 *Moniteur*, 20 (25 March 1794), p. 34. Similarly, the Republican society of Chambray blamed the corruption of the military on the government's delay in prosecuting Marie-Antoinette (Archives Nationales C275 C11 712).
80 Walter, *Actes*, pp. 96, 128.
81 Saint-Just, *Oeuvres*, p. 761.
82 Ozouf, *La Fête*, chapter 7.
83 Linton, *The Politics of Virtue*.
84 Billaud-Varenne, *Discours*, p. 2.
85 De Baecque, *Le Corps de l'histoire*, p. 277.
86 Robespierre, *Discours*, pp. 307–308.
87 Louis-Félix Roux, *Relation de l'événement des 8, 9 et 10 thermidor, sur la conspiration des triumvirs, Robespierre, Couthon et St.-Just* (Paris, year II), pp. 10, 2.
88 Ibid., p. 2.
89 François Furet, *La Révolution de Turgot à Jules Ferry, 1770–1890* (n.p., 1988), p. 161.
90 Baczko, *Ending the Terror*, p. 48.
91 Benjamin Constant, *De la force du gouvernement actuel de la France et de la nécessité de s'y rallier* (n.p., 1796).
92 Ibid., p. 64.
93 Ibid., p. 99.
94 Ibid., pp. 99–100.
95 Ibid., pp. 101, 107 108.
96 Ibid., p. 109.
97 Cited in Rey, '*Révolution*', pp. 124, 123.
98 Cited ibid., pp. 148–149, 151.
99 Cited in Furet, *La Révolution*, p. 161.

100 M. J. Guillaume, *Procès-verbaux du Comité d'instruction publique de la Convention nationale*, 8 vols (Paris, 1891–1958), 6, p. 11.
101 On the deference of the people toward the elite, see Condorcet, *Esquisse*, p. 264.
102 P. L Roederer, *Journal d'économie publique, de morale, et de politique*, 1 (10 Fructidor year IV), p. 2.
103 Constant, *De la force*, p. 38.
104 Ibid., p. 29.
105 Ibid., p. 98.
106 Isser Woloch, *Jacobin Legacy: The Democratic Movement under the Directory* (Princeton, 1970); for a critique, see Martyn Lyons, *France under the Directory* (Cambridge, UK, 1975), p. 224. On state repression, see Howard G. Brown, *War, Revolution, and the Bureaucratic State: Politics and Army Administration in France, 1791–1799* (Oxford and New York, 1995).
107 Lyons, *France*, p. 34; Laura Mason, 'The "Bosom of Proof": Criminal Justice and the Renewal of Oral Culture during the French Revolution,' *Journal of Modern History*, 76 (2004), pp. 29–61.
108 Lyons, *France*, p. 35.
109 See table in Martyn Lyons, *Napoleon Bonaparte and the Legacy of the French Revolution* (New York, 1994), p. 72.
110 Lyons, *France*, p. 234.
111 Estimates of the number of victims killed vary considerably: D. M. G. Sutherland, *The French Revolution and Empire: The Quest for a Civic Order* (Oxford, 2003), p. 314 estimates the number to be between 39 and 78.
112 Cited in ibid., p. 315.
113 Ibid.
114 Georges Lefebvre, *Napoleon*, trans. Henry F. Stockhold, 2 vols (New York, 1969), 1, p. 127.
115 Germaine de Staël, *Considérations sur la Révolution française* (Paris, 1983), p. 369.
116 Most notably in Furet, *La Révolution*.
117 See Pierre Birnbaum, *The Idea of France*, trans. M. B. DeBevoise (New York, 2001).

Index

.